# THE
# JAPAN
# EXPERIENCE

# The
# Japan
# Experience

*edited, with an introduction, by*
RONALD BELL

WEATHERHILL
New York • Tokyo

*for Kyoko*

The characters appearing above the sequence number
of each interview read *taiken* (personal experience).

FIRST EDITION, 1973

Published by John Weatherhill, Inc., 149 Madison Avenue,
New York, N.Y. 10016, with editorial offices at 7-6-13
Roppongi, Minato-ku, Tokyo 106. Protected by copyright
under terms of the International Copyright Union; all rights
reserved. Printed in Korea and first published in Japan.

*Library of Congress Cataloging in Publication Data:* Bell, Ronald,
1931—/The Japan experience./1. Japan—Foreign opinion./I.
Title./DS822.5.B44/301.15′43′9152034/73-9657/ISBN  0-8348-
0084-5

# CONTENTS

# INTRODUCTION

NEVER BEFORE IN HISTORY have so many Japanese been exposed directly to foreign influences and so many people had so much firsthand experience of the Japanese. The Japanese sell watches and cameras in Germany, rotary-engine automobiles in the United States, color television in Brazil and Egypt, the world's largest ships to a dozen nations; they buy fertilizer from China and lumber from Alaska, build hydroelectric dams in Thailand, and operate luxury hotels in Indonesia. So astonishing has their economic growth been in the last twenty years that the leaders of developing countries point them out as models for their countrymen to emulate, while the leaders of developed countries meet to discuss how to blunt the thrust of their economic drive.

As Japan's economic growth expands, so does her international influence in a number of other areas. Housewives in Vancouver arrange flowers according to ikebana principles, meditators in San Francisco and Paris concentrate on achieving Zen enlightenment, a Dutchman has won a world championship in judo and an American has won a sumo tournament, Australians study brush calligraphy, and architects in America and Europe ponder the "ultramodern" concepts of Japanese architecture. The twenty-first century may or may not be the

Japanese century, but failure to achieve that goal will not result from any lack in the Japanese of ambition, energy, or pride. Make it or not, the Japanese—those "debtors to the ages" —will no doubt provide the world with a lesson to remember before their day in the sun is over.

Who are these people who have launched themselves so vigorously and, for an insular people, so daringly into the international sphere? Fifteen or even ten years ago, who could have predicted their astonishing successes? And today, in spite of all their international contacts and a continuing flow of books and articles about them, they remain little known in the rest of the world. Are they the unique people their scholars insist they are, or merely pushy imitators, first of China's ancient culture and then of the technology of the West? Is their well-known politeness motivated by the desire to create harmony, or is it a mask that conceals a sealed provincial heart, clannish and secretive? Are they the world's most sophisticated aesthetes, or naive primitives with only a veneer of civilization between self-control and fanaticism?

The assumptions implied in these questions point to the complexity of the Japanese, a complexity that has evoked (and continues to evoke) descriptions replete with paradox and contradiction. Ruth Benedict, for example, in her still very valuable *The Chrysanthemum and the Sword*,[1] lists ten traits and their opposites and states that these contradictions are the essence of books on Japan and are all true.

Several years ago the American sociologist David Riesman reported that a Japanese acquaintance told him that because the Japanese have trouble understanding their own culture, they don't see how foreigners can understand it.[2] The implication that the Japanese cannot be understood by foreigners is bound to irritate. It sounds suspiciously like the opening line

1. Ruth Benedict, *The Chrysanthemum and the Sword: Patterns of Japanese Culture* (Boston: Houghton Mifflin Co., 1946).
2. David Riesman and Evelyn T. Riesman, *Conversations in Japan: Modernization, Politics, and Culture* (New York: Basic Books, 1967).

of the "inscrutable Japanese" argument: "We Japanese can understand the West, but Westerners cannot understand us." This viewpoint rests heavily on the presumed uniqueness of Japanese culture: no Western analogs, therefore no understanding of Japan. Coming from the non-Japanese side, the argument usually maintains that the Japanese are so different ("They do everything backwards") that it is all but useless to try to understand them. By implication it usually means, Why bother? By and large the people interviewed in this book agree that there are truly unique aspects of Japanese culture, and yet I doubt that a single one of them would admit to finding it incomprehensible. Difficult, yes; impenetrable, no.

The Japanese do indeed have some difficulty understanding their own culture, at least in terms of the kinds of concepts the West is used to. This difficulty arises in part from a penchant for ambiguity together with a general dislike for abstract, logical thinking, which is thought to be cold and *ningen rashi-kunai,* or "nonhuman." These traits naturally make it difficult for Japanese to convey their experience of reality to non-Japanese.

Nevertheless, as Japanese contacts with non-Japanese peoples increase in number and intensity, interest in and understanding of the Japanese grow. In order to succeed in becoming *sekai dai ichi* (best in the world), the Japanese are being forced to gaze long and hard in the mirror the eyes of the world offer—to see themselves as others see them. It has become necessary to explain themselves in concepts the rest of the world can understand, and in the process they are feeling the need to better understand themselves.

For outsiders, Japan presents many genuine difficulties to understanding. Not the least of these, as Fosco Maraini (Interview 1) says, is the problem of language. The formidable nature of the Japanese language is compounded by the way in which it is used: politeness, for example, can force speakers into such circumlocutions that comprehension of all but the vaguest of meanings is impossible. And so much can be, and often is, left

to the listener's or reader's imagination that it may be difficult
for two Japanese to agree on a precise meaning. Some of this
difficulty is due to the ambiguity inherent in the language, and
some, because little genuine criticism has developed in Japan,
is due to the cavalier attitude toward exposition and clear
thinking referred to by John Nathan (Interview 8). The increasing number of translations from the Japanese, particularly
of scientific and technological works, however, suggests that
difficult though the language and way of thinking may be,
full understanding is by no means impossible.

As one means of overcoming misunderstanding, Maraini
suggests reliving from the inside the mental universe peculiar
to the Japanese and points to the need for humbleness if this
way is to succeed. Donn Draeger (Interview 7), speaking of
the Japanese martial arts world, points to the need for the
foreigner to "learn to control his ego, his striving to make his
identity highly distinct." He goes on to say that the stumbling
block for the foreigner is individualism. The need is the same,
I believe, in any area of Japanese life.

In discussing his own difficulties of assimilation, Iwao Hoshii
(Interview 4) points to the necessity of a deep and very broad
understanding of Japanese culture for intimate communication.
Charles Gallagher (Interview 12) mentions the exclusivity, or
"inner recess" aspect of the Japanese character that keeps
foreigners at a distance. This proves to be a sometimes impenetrable barrier to the foreigner's hoped-for degree of
intimacy. Angela Carter (Interview 2) points to a further di-
mension of achieving understanding when she mentions the
difficulty that faces the foreigner in creating believable Japanese
characters in a work of fiction. Few people would deny that this
is a task of imposing dimensions, and yet Donald Richie (Interview 3), who has lived in Japan for more than twenty-five years,
has succeeded, in my opinion, in his novel *Companions of the
Holiday*.[3] Of a different order but perhaps as rare an achieve-

3. Donald Richie, *Companions of the Holiday* (New York and Tokyo: Walker/
Weatherhill, 1968).

ment is Jesse Kuhaulua's (Interview 16) endurance and success in sumo, not only in the ring but even more in that sport's
rigorous traditional life.

These accomplishments, and doubtless there are many
others in many walks of life, show that no matter how formidable getting to know the Japanese appears to be, it can be
done. And even if complete understanding is truly impossible,
there is, to be sure, a great deal to be learned through close
experience with the Japanese and from the people who have
taken part in what I call the Japan experience.

This book, consisting of seventeen interviews, is intended
as a documentary of present-day Japan as it has been experienced by foreign residents. As such it probes not only
today's Japanese but also the attitudes and emotions of the
foreigners who live in Japan. While the book focuses chiefly on
the Japanese, the interaction between them and their foreigner
community is a theme that has been of continuing interest to
me. Consequently, the degree to which foreigners feel themselves to be integrated in Japanese society is a matter that
comes up for discussion often in these pages.

For years I have heard it said that no foreigner, no matter
how long he has lived in Japan or how well he speaks the
language and observes the intricate proprieties, has ever been
truly accepted in Japanese society. He is alway a *gaijin*, literally,
an "outside person." The problem has never been a strictly
personal one, since I have from the first relished the freedom
from many proprieties that a *gaijin* enjoys, while having learned
to live with the annoyances he must put up with. But over the
years, I have unhappily watched more than a few friends
become embittered because they believed they were being
closed out of areas of Japanese society to which they felt they
should have had free access. Too often they could not come to
terms with their unending "foreignness," their inability to get
themselves accepted as individuals and not simply as *gaijin*,
and they ended by leaving Japan. The responses to my questions about the matter, although they vary widely, indicate

that this is or has been a pressing problem for many foreigners in Japan.

With the exception of Brian Victoria (Interview 6), the interviewees who responded to questions about militarism in present-day Japan did not see any danger from that quarter in the near future. Nevertheless, the prospect of a powerful Japanese military force is a real and frightening possibility in the minds of a rapidly growing number of people around the world, particularly in Southeast Asia. Ten years ago most foreign residents of Japan, including myself, if asked whether or not Japan's leaders aspire to lead her into the first rank of military strength, would have answered with an emphatic no. My own certainty was founded on the conviction that without exception all the Japanese I was acquainted with were ardent pacifists. World War II, they passionately believed, had been a stupid blunder, a humiliating mistake, and the lesson it had taught had seared their hearts. Never again would the nation's leaders be able to take the Japanese people down that fiery path of needless pain and suffering. The Japanese constitution emphatically and clearly renounces war forever, and no Japanese prime minister since its promulgation has dared insist that the "peace article" be revised. No more Hiroshimas!

It *is* premature to speak of "resurgent Japanese militarism," as though Japan were testing nuclear weapons and recruiting fledgling kamikaze pilots. She is doing nothing of the sort. Disturbing signs do exist, however. Chief among these is the fact that few Japanese seem to care deeply enough about peace anymore to protest the dying of the peace ideal. By ignoring the constitution's injunctions against rearming, the ruling oligarchy has given this ideal the kiss of death. And by accepting this situation with apathy, the Japanese people have insured its death. Now that the peace clause is essentially meaningless, the military buildup can continue and the constitution's "peace article" can be put away in a museum at Hiroshima where, like that city's memorials, it can be viewed as a relic of a bygone era.

The ghost of Yukio Mishima haunts this book. To me it is curious that this should be so, for when I conceived the book plan, the thought of asking questions about Mishima had not crossed my mind. I have never been an admirer of Mishima, either his personality or his work, finding little pleasure in his, to me, cold narcissism and humorless, contrived plots.

Why then bother with the man? I am not sure yet, but I suspect that he haunts me because he personifies (even in death, especially in death) a frightening element in the Japanese character. This fear deserves some explanation. Japan is as peaceful a country as one could hope for, or at least reasonably expect. Tokyo is safer by far than most big cities elsewhere. The Japanese countryside is even safer. The Japanese have a well-deserved reputation for maintaining an ordered existence, and a deeply rooted abhorrence of violence is everywhere apparent in their everyday life. The reason at the root of the fear is that Mishima consciously chose, finally, his nonrational (perhaps antirational) impulses over his rational powers and publicized that choice in such a vivid manner that the youth of Japan could hardly ignore it. By the manner of his death, Mishima forged a link between past and present and loosed upon the affluent land the neglected spirits of the brave (if foolhardy), pure-hearted (if naive) warriors of the near and distant past.

So the ideals of the past (loyalty, duty, courage, obedience in the face of death—ideals, by Western standards, often unreasonably, hideously demanding), hopefully thought by many to have been buried with the ashes of the dead of the Pacific War, for good or for ill, will have to be reexamined. As will today's values, which are undeniably materialistic. Twenty years ago Japan's young people looked with admiring eyes at America as the land of the free and the home of the brave, as well as the land of plenty. But Vietnam has destroyed that vision, wasted it as surely as napalm does a grass-roofed hut.

For the time being, the Japanese appear to be without an image of greatness to look up to. And the times are easy, as a trickle of the great affluence at the top reaches even the bottom of the social heap. But let the phenomenal growth come to a halt or even seem to be reversing itself, then who knows what roots of daring or violence will be touched?

Experiencing Japan is by its very nature an unending pursuit. No group of outsiders (or "insider-outsiders"), however large or however gargantuan its appetite, could ever hope to take in more than a bit of a phenomenon as complex as Japan. Even if they could, no book could ever hold the sum of their observations, reflections, and opinions. The aim of this book is far more modest: to present a slice of that vast experience, a slice of history. If it succeeds in that, it has been worth the effort that brought it to birth.

MORE THAN MOST BOOKS, a book of interviews is a collaborative effort, and this one is no exception. For their help in preparing this volume I am especially grateful to the following people. To the seventeen interviewees, who gave so graciously of their time and wisdom, I am indebted most of all. For suggesting interviewees or interview questions, I would like to offer my thanks to Albert Brewster, Emile Dubrule, Anita Feldman, Peter Grilli, Charles R. Temple, and Suzanne Trumbull. Further thanks are due Suzanne Trumbull for expert editorial advice and assistance. And to Nancy Brewster and Misako Nemoto go my thanks for their typing services.

# THE
# JAPAN
# EXPERIENCE

# 体験

# 1

## FOSCO MARAINI
### Italian
### Cultural Anthropologist

A native of Florence, he is well known as the author of the best-selling *Meeting with Japan*. His first visit to Japan was in 1938, when he did field work on the aboriginal Ainus. His many years in Japan spanned the World War II period, when he was interned as an enemy alien. In 1971 his *Japan: Patterns of Culture* was published. He now teaches Japanese cultural history at the University of Florence.

RB: In *Meeting with Japan*[1] you gave an account of a friend of yours, an idealistic young Japanese man, who became almost overnight a xenophobic supporter of the military government of Japan. In the same book you noted the rapid change in the Japanese people in 1945 from ardent patriots to docile wards of the Allies. Do you think this propensity for making sudden shifts of allegiance is a fixed trait of the Japanese?

FM: I must say that I don't like the phrase "sudden shifts of allegiance." It only *seems* that there are sudden shifts of allegiance, and, of course, in practice there are, but I should say that these changes are due to the extraordinary sensitivity of the Japanese to surroundings, to environment, be it social or physical. And while there is always the possibility of sudden

1. Fosco Maraini, *Meeting with Japan* (New York: Viking Press, 1960).

changes by the Japanese, I would not describe them as sudden shifts of allegiance. The Japanese have a very deep instinctive feeling for what is happening around them. They face facts, face reality, and if they change drastically, as they did after World War II, when they accepted the Americans as their leaders, that is an example of their realizing that the Americans had indeed won, had a better military system—the Americans had been right, had won, and so one did not waste time nourishing bitterness but instead accepted the loss and the new leadership.

In this spirit, MacArthur was lionized, even idolized as the "blue-eyed shogun" when he took over. I remember quite well how I was astonished each time I observed Japanese behavior when MacArthur would go in or out of his head-quarters in Tokyo. There was always a crowd of Japanese who came to see him, very often hundreds of them, and they clapped for him. Now, this would seem to be a betrayal of allegiance. And it is—when you look at it from the outside, from a non-Japanese frame of reference. But from a viewpoint based on a completely instinctive approach to life this behavior shows recognition of the facts of the situation. And in fact this ability to face up to reality is a great strength of the Japanese. They recognized very quickly how the situation had changed and adapted themselves to it with a minimum of social disruption.

RB: Have you taken note of any permanent changes in the Japanese character since the end of World War II?

FM: Your question takes me to something very fundamental —namely, we have to ask whether people change or not. The longer I live, the stronger my impression grows that they do not—not fundamentally, anyhow. Superficially they do, the culture takes a new face—or perhaps I should say mask—but if you explore below the surface you usually see the face.

It is always fascinating for me to read books on one people by another people. Even if you go back centuries, these descriptions will give you a picture that is plausible and understandable today. You take the Japanese as seen by the missionaries of the sixteenth century—they had very much the same characteristics that you can observe in the Japanese today. You take the Germans seen by Tacitus, the Indians seen by Megasthenes, or, later, the Americans by de Tocqueville, the Russians by Balzac, and you find that traits which have undergone superficial changes reveal themselves as fundamentally unchanged.

So I can't say that I've observed any permanent changes in the Japanese character.

RB: Then you agree with the view expressed by Richard Halloran in his *Japan: Images and Realities*[2] that Japanese culture has remained fundamentally unchanged?

FM: Yes, I do agree with him. Looking at the Japanese today you find that they are just as intense—almost fanatical—pacifists as they were fanatical colonists or fanatical warmongers not long ago.

Really, the changes we see have to be interpreted; they should not be taken at face value. In practice you have to accept them as great changes, of course. If a people are fanatical for peace and not fanatical for war, you must behave accordingly. Certainly you must do so in a political context. However, psychologically, that is, considering motivation and personality traits, I don't find that the Japanese have changed.

RB: Do you think that democracy, in the Western sense, will ever take root in Japan?

FM: First of all, I don't take democracy to be something universal or a category that exists in space, say. It's a way of dealing with human affairs that has been developed by the countries in the northern tradition of Europe, and in fact it works mainly in the countries in the Anglo-Saxon and Scandinavian traditions. It does not work very well, for instance, with either the Slavs or the Latins. Also, the minute you get away from Europe, to places with completely different tradi-

2. Richard Halloran, *Japan: Images and Realities* (New York: Alfred A. Knopf, Inc., 1969).

tions, democracy does not seem to function very well at all.

On the other hand, however, there are traditions that have features similar to those of democracy in Africa, in India, and in Japan which may possibly bring results just as good. I mean we should not take the ideas that were born in our civilization and try to apply them blindly to other civilizations. It may be, for instance, that a people will develop ways of harmonizing human relations that bring equivalent results to those achieved by democratic means, ideas that are not amenable to democracy. In the Western sense of the word, I don't see much relation between democracy and Japan.

Now, however, the Japanese way of managing their affairs has had since ancient times many democratic features. For instance, the idea of *wa,* or harmony, is certainly a democratic idea. In practice it takes into account the needs, the wishes of a great number of people.

Going back to your question, I must say I do not see democracy taking root in Japan.

RB: Here you mean Western-style democracy?

FM: Yes, but the only alternatives are not democracy and totalitarianism. The Japanese have a way of their own which is not democracy but which *amounts* to something quite similar to it. There have been periods in Japanese history in which the will of a great many people have been taken into account in the way in which affairs were managed. Of course, during the long periods of military control, most of the long period between Yoritomo's time [1147–99] and the end of World War II, the military leaders, as soldiers always will, tried to simplify government into a kind of authoritarian system. But in the long period before that, one sees a noticeable effort to govern in concert with the will of the people—that is, between the will of the *kami* and the will of the *shimo,* those above and those below. And if you look at Japan today, in a number of ways it is not democratic, but in other ways it is very democratic. It may not function in accordance with the rules of democracy as it has been developed in the Anglo-Saxon countries, but it has many features that are democratic, the primary one being an instinctive cultivation of the *wa* ideal.

The Japanese do not really care for Western democracy. They especially dislike the rule of the majority; you know they often speak disparagingly of the "tyranny of the majority." You hear this often in regard to the ruling political party's unwillingness to compromise with its opponents and its disregard for their ideas and wishes. This conduct brings about the disharmony the Japanese abhor. Democracy does not work well with them.

RB: Would you say, then, that they can get harmony without repression?

FM: Of course it takes time and it works in a different way, but in the best periods of their history there has been harmony or a least a striving for social harmony.

RB: Do you think that Japanese society has been growing more restrictive politically since the end of World War II?

FM: Since the end of World War II there has been a certain amount of repression, but this is because not long after the war there was a period of disruption, of slackness, and so there had to be a, so to speak, taking up of the reins. The country was like a boat adrift on the sea and without control.

RB: During your years of residence prior to and during World War II you had an opportunity for observing and experiencing Japanese militarism at first hand. At the present time we are beginning to hear increasing warnings about a rebirth of Japanese militarism. Do you think there is any basis to these alarms?

FM: When a boy who has been in the habit of breaking windows picks up a stone, everyone gives out shouts of alarm. They naturally become afraid. Japan in the past has been like the stone-throwing boy, and as she increases her strength and grows in influence on the international scene there are bound to be people who will become excited. After the terrible experiences of World War II, however, the great majority of Japanese do want peace. There may be a minority which looks back fondly on the old order of things and wants Japan to be more assertive in the world, but it would take them a long, long time to win over the majority of the people to their view.

I really believe the great majority of the Japanese have been inoculated against militarism by the experiences of World War II, and this guarantees the conduct of the nation for a long time.

Before the war the Japanese had not experienced a military reversal and, except for the intelligentsia and some people who had traveled outside Japan, most people really believed that they were a race apart, a unique nation favored in special ways by the gods, and therefore unbeatable. I can assure you they really believed it, incredible though it may seem now.

The confrontation with the fact of complete defeat changed this. Not that it changed the people psychologically—it did not eradicate the tendency to fanaticism, but this intensity of outlook is now directed toward peace, you could even call it "militant pacifism" because of the extent to which it is carried.

Of course there are small, highly vocal groups, and these though not dangerous now could become so, but at the present I don't see much danger of a revival of militarism here. Militarists could not get a following. Not for a long, long time.

RB: In recent years there has been a growing demand for reinstating the emperor as the symbol of the nation so as to provide a higher degree of national unity. What do you think about the demand?

FM: Once the magic has been dispelled I don't think it can be recalled again. Anyway, legally at least, the emperor is the symbol of the state, but I don't think he could be made a deity, a *kami*, again.

As with a child who has been told there is no Santa Claus, that it's been his father all the time who put the candy and toys in the Christmas sock, you cannot resuscitate the illusion. Prewar belief in the emperor's divinity was based on very special circumstances. These have entirely changed; the belief would have nothing to rest on now.

RB: Should Japan scrap the constitution imposed on her by the Occupation authorities and, as has been suggested, devise one based on the "realities" of her social system?

FM: I don't think so. When the Japanese realize fully their economic strength they will exert pressures to obtain whatever they want, within the frame of the present constitution.

RB: Will this follow from their hierarchically structured outlook—their custom of looking at other people as being superior to or inferior to them rather than existing on a level with them?

FM: Yes, as they grow stronger their viewpoint of themselves in relation to others will change. It all goes back to the absolute pragmatism, *genjitsu-shugi*, of the Japanese. This goes back to the Shinto idea that this world is the absolute. If this life is the absolute it should be confronted realistically. Most Japanese, I would say, are not conscious that they think along these lines, but this idea is the real basis of their outlook on life.

RB: In two recently published books,[3] foreign writers have said that most Japanese do not like foreigners. Do you think this is true? Do you think it is true of any group or class of Japanese?

FM: Any country you could name has people who do not like foreigners. Certainly there are Americans who don't, and let's not even speak of the French, Germans, Italians, and British who don't. And in few countries in the world will you be treated with the genuine friendlinesss and hospitality that you receive in Japan.

From time to time you do come across individuals who for one reason or another do not like foreigners. Also there are foreigners here who make themselves disliked.

I don't know of any class of people as such who typically

3. Richard Halloran's *Japan: Images and Realities* and Mitaro Satsuke's (pseudonym) *Views from Here* (Nagoya: privately printed, 1970).

dislike foreigners. I've met many many Japanese—in all classes—who sincerely like foreigners.

Before the war you could meet a number of policemen who were antiforeigner, but they were probably under orders to be so. In these last few months I've been traveling about a great deal and I've met two or three very disagreeable policemen and I've met three or four extremely helpful policemen. So you just can't say they are antiforeigner, even though this is the group which you might expect to be.

I do believe that xenophobia among the Japanese is an individual matter, not one of groups.

RB: What has given you the most difficulty in adjusting to Japanese society? Do you feel you are accepted as an individual among your Japanese friends and acquaintances or are you still an outsider, a foreigner?

FM: Someone has spoken of dividing the countries of the world into two types: clubs and missions. France and China, for example, are missions: if you conform, if you learn the language and adopt their customs, the people accept you entirely. Britain and Japan, on the other hand, are clubs: you can be accepted and belong to them as corresponding associates, but you are never really a standing member.

RB: You are an associate member, then, in Japan?

FM: Exactly. The Japanese never look at you as a Japanese no matter how long you stay or how well you adopt their customs.

In any case, I feel that as a foreigner it is better to remain a foreigner, to keep your identity as a foreigner well marked while taking part in all aspects of Japanese life and yet not trying to be Japanese.

RB: Are there certain social advantages to being a foreigner here, then?

FM: Not really. But I think the Japanese like one to maintain one's cultural and national individuality. And the cases I've seen of foreigners who have tried to become Japanese, who have taken Japanese nationality, have not been favorable.

The real difficulty is with language. That above all. And of course you must learn the social customs and you must strive to interact with the people on a basis of complete equality. I don't think Japanese society is any harder to get along in than Western societies. In fact, for foreigners it's more difficult socially in England than it is in Japan. The circumstances may be different in America because of a less consolidated set of traditions, but in Europe, and especially at certain levels, society is virtually impenetrable.

RB: How has living among the Japanese affected you, your personality, your outlook on life, your basic approach to living, and your relations with people?

FM: This is a terrific question! A barrage of questions! I must admit, of course, that they are all legitimate and pertinent. Any Westerner who is not deeply shaken by the experience of Japan must be quite impervious to influences from outside. Some people may admire such "inner sturdiness" and compare the unassailable soul to that traditional paragon, the Rock of Gibraltar. If you observe the matter more carefully, however, it is not really like that. "Inner sturdiness" only means that the said soul, after having received a first wave of impressions somewhere and somehow during his childhood and youth, locks himself in and refuses to accept any further education from experience.

I will say quite frankly that Japan has affected me deeply, in many different and important ways. Your question is so comprehensive that I must answer it starting from somewhere. Where? Well, the basic point of course concerns my "outlook on life," and this leads me directly to religion, the very core of all inner life, be it individual or social.

Here you compel me to become personal. Your fault! I grew up in a prevalently Catholic country. Italian Catholicism is curious: on the one hand very shallow, on the other as spectacular and formal as grand opera. There is also a hereditary awe of the priest as magician, the man who has been granted uncanny power over invisible forces, one who can absolve sin, unite people into indissoluble unions, or exorcise demons. I remember noticing striking similarities between Catholic Italy and Lamaist Tibet, when I visited the latter country some years ago. The average Italian enjoys to the hilt all pleasures of life, takes pride in some picturesque blasphemy (*bestemmia*), and says he detests priests, but when it comes down to the main *rites de passage,* birth, marriage, death—especially death— then the holy man is called upon to perform his solemn and mysterious rites; the epicurean cum bold rationalist falls immediately to pieces.

When I first visited Japan, I must admit, I had thought very little about such matters. Religion in Italy is part of the landscape, like cypresses and olive trees. The long and sweet slumber induced in Latin countries by the Counter-Reformation has subtly and meretriciously bound the very idea of religion to the presence of glorious churches, sublime music, great painting and sculpture—anything that will enchant the soul and keep the mind away from dangerous thoughts. It was also clearly understood that this must be Civilization—with a capital C—that in these happy lands the good, the true, and the beautiful met and gently imploded into a work of utter perfection. Beyond the pale, that is, beyond the holy-water curtain of the baptized faithful, there could only be unenlightened barbarians and unredeemed pagans. The message was generally conveyed through hints and symbols, but sometimes it appeared in so many words, for instance in the famous formula: *extra ecclesiam nulla salus,* there is no salvation outside the church.

Japan was a shock. It woke me up. Here was a highly civilized country which had reached maturity and splendor along other paths, owing practically nothing to the spiritual forces which had become such fetishes in the West: classical learning, Christianity, the Reformation (or the Counter-Reformation, according to longitudes and latitudes). Here were also, all around, examples of moral coherence, of righteousness, of spiritual maturity, often more numerous and more striking than anything I had seen before. I cannot deal in detail with what was a long spiritual process, but finally the question appeared simply and clearly: does Christianity include history, or does history include Christianity? The answer was obvious. Christianity, the West itself, are not absolutes, they are relative, historical steps in the story of man. Civilization may flourish on many stems. The gods may be called by many names. Only man and the mysteries surrounding him are something final. All religions, all philosophies are attempts to bridge the chasm between the world of conscience and the challenges of existence, time, death, evil. No one has the key. There is no chosen people. All men—from Neanderthalers chiseling their stones to Einstein distilling theories about the universe—are spiritually equal, all live through the same predicament.

Perhaps I might have reached a similar view through other contacts and experiences, but I wonder if the itinerary would have been so clear and direct without the impact of Japan. The very existence of Japan is a challenge to most familiar notions cherished as true. Its symbolic importance is far greater than its puny place in world history. If there were no Japan it would be expedient to invent one.

Looking at things in detail, I find many points in which Japan has influenced me deeply. Everybody knows that the Western outlook on the world is monumentally anthropocentric. God himself as creator, lawgiver, and judge is really a Superman endowed with infinite longevity (eternity), supreme knowledge (omniscience), tentacular sensitivity (omnipresence), and so on. The orthodox view that God created man in his own image may easily be reversed: man created God in the image of his own dreams. The entire cosmic drama, seen through Western eyes, takes place among persons: God, angels (good and bad), man, prophets, saints, sinners; nature fades away in the distance as a background, beautiful, yes, but often equivocally so.

Japanese thought, both Buddhist and Shinto, takes positions which are different, sometimes opposite. "Where the Christian theologian explains Nature in the light of the numinous, the Japanese reach the numinous through their experience of nature," writes Father Joseph Spae in one of his extraordinarily perceptive studies of the Japanese soul. Well, that is exactly how I have come to feel! The Bible? A great anthropological encyclopedia, something, however, not essentially different from the *Kalevala* or the *Tao Te Ching*. But a tree, snow in the sun, a stormy ocean at night under the moon—these are true revelations!

Such thoughts came to me occasionally as a youth in the West, but I was promptly rebuked as a freak. In Japan I was delighted to discover innumerable kindred souls, countless treasures of art, a great body of poetry, gardens, a cult of flowers, significant silences, a world of supreme refinement, sudden illuminations of truth—all inspired by the apprehension of "the numinous in nature."

You ask me about "relations with people," how they have been affected by life in Japan. I think the general outlook, of which I have briefly spoken, affects this point too. A firm belief in the total, complete, absolute spiritual equality of all men in their confrontation with everything that is mysterious around us necessarily makes contacts easier, richer, more rewarding. And I am particularly thinking of contacts between Westerners and Asians, between people belonging to different civilizations, nourished by different religions.

RB: Are you still convinced that we can overcome the profound differences of East and West by reliving from the inside the mental universes peculiar to these civilizations? If so, how do we go about getting others to attempt it?

FM: Yes, I'm still convinced that that is true. The only way to bridge the gap between East and West is to relive from the inside the civilization to which you do not belong. It's necessary, in this case, for us to try to enter the Japanese spirit. Of course it takes a long time and it also takes a large degree of humbleness. And a certain pride, too. Humbleness in the sense that you must really renounce that extremely strong ethnocentric feeling that Western culture fosters. If you don't lose that, there's no hope for understanding the East. On the other hand, you must have the, in a certain sense, courage to look at the planet Earth, say, from a point in outer space, observing all cultures of man in the same fashion that you'd observe the behavior of ants. This of course is pride. You are really trying to usurp the position of a minor god and secretly steal his supreme objectivity.

RB: It seems to me that an intense desire to learn and a passion to shuck off our traditional ways are also necessary.

FM: Yes, of course. And it is certainly worthwhile. Though one should add: there are no shortcuts.

RB: How do we get people to attempt something so difficult?

FM: It's much easier now than it was thirty years ago, for instance, and it was easier then than it was sixty years ago. I believe it will become easier still because of rapid, frequent communications, the variety and richness of personal contacts. Also, the stream of books, studies, journals, et cetera, that are continually appearing allow us to get at the essence, the spirit of the great civilizations.

Both the East and the West are, I believe, moving toward a third point in space and time which may be the seed of a future world civilization in which there will be Eastern and Western ingredients intermixed, somewhat as in Western civilization there are Greek and Roman ingredients that are fused with Jewish elements. Think of the world two thousand years ago: the Jewish and Babylonian civilizations were entirely separated from the Greek and Roman traditions. In fact, the peoples were mortal enemies. But somehow in time a synthesis of the traditions of the Middle East and the West occurred in Europe. And this is the Western civilization of the last millennium and a half. Our civilization. History advances, alternating disaster and synthesis.

I think that the civilization of the future will be a synthesis of the East and the West, and of the North and the South too! This will come about through the exchanges we see today, through the mixing of various peoples. A moment ago we spoke of the interest in Zen among Americans. This is very good, I feel. It does increase understanding of one of the fundamental elements of Japanese and Eastern culture.

RB: What do you think are the basic strengths and weaknesses of the Japanese people?

FM: Let me answer in a rather roundabout way. Traditionally, we in the West see the power *in* the world, the absolute ultimate explanation of things as residing outside the world— the ultimate motor is God; whereas in Japan the absolute and supreme explanation of things is embedded in nature. It is like a god diluted and blended into nature. We have here two absolutely different models of the universe: one with the motor incorporated, the other with an independent motor. Out of this prime difference flow innumerable consequences that reach down to the simplest happenings of everyday life.

The Western way of thinking tends because of this orientation to employ dualistic terms: matter and spirit, the world and God, man and nature, individual and society, body and soul, good and evil, et cetera. The Japanese way of thinking is much less dualistic. It is often quite difficult in the Japanese language to know who is doing what to whom: where is the subject, where is the object? This inherent difficulty is complicated by the lack of one proper word for the verb "to be," although there are many ways to express the idea "to be." This uncertainty in thought and language between subject and object, between, say, the world and man, gives the Japanese their strength and weakness.

Their strength—why? Because they instinctively feel what should be done. They are not philosophers, not theorizers; but they are great when they follow their instincts. That is why they are great doers, great makers of things. They have their hands deep in life.

Westerners tend to look at life, at the world, as though sitting in a helicopter above it, while the Japanese swim in the actual flow of events. This gives them great sharpness of intuition and the power to build things, to make things with their hands: everything from a ship to a picture, from a poem to a scientific instrument. The direct relationship between Japanese man and the world gives him his power. At the same time it's also a weakness in the sense that it does not encourage a philosophic view of life, one that requires a man to stand outside affairs and detach himself from things. In fact, Japanese philosophy impresses one much less than Japanese art, industry, sports—anything that requires doing. Whenever they make something—works of art, works of industry—they impress you, but the minute you see them engaged in intellectual speculation, in philosophizing, you feel completely let down. I can think of very few Japanese books of thought or criticism that have impressed me well at all. Brilliant flashes of thought, yes—from Dogen-zenji to Okakura Tenshin—but sustained systematic thought, no.

This immersion in the stream of life also means that the Japanese are very conscious of their own group, of their own nationality, that they are rarely able to lift themselves above their group and look at their own society in an international perspective. This weakness is often referred to as *shimaguni konjo,* an insular spirit. The Japanese will have to overcome this condition as they strive to take a greater part in international affairs.

RB: What elements of the Japanese experience could and should be transmitted to the West?

FM: There are many. First of all there is this immediacy, or *nakaima*, living in immediacy with life and with experience.

It is strange that the Japanese always speak of the materialism of the West, because I think it is truly the other way around.(I don't use "materialism" with disparagement here.) And I think that Western thought tends to be abstract—especially in its German incarnation—it lives on a plane that very easily detaches Western peoples from life.

Supremely, the Japanese, particularly the artists—from the painter to the potter, the film director to the poet—oh, all Japanese artists—are in direct contact with nature and life. This we'd do well to learn from them.

Another important thing is their enthusiasm for achievement, their positive outlook on the world.

RB: In what sense do you mean "positive"? I'm thinking of the negativism of Buddhism.

FM: The Buddhist influence is certainly strong, but I feel that the Shinto influence is stronger. The Shinto background is extremely positive, this-worldly. Of course, this influence is rarely consciously present. In fact, most Japanese would laugh to hear anyone say that Shinto exerts a strong influence on their lives. But down deep it is the guiding spirit in their lives, their entire society.

The West, which I feel is nowadays in many ways in a state of crisis, would do well to adopt this zest, this positive outlook on life.

RB: Just at the time when Japanese art is gaining high praise and serious study outside Japan, some Japanese and foreigners have been speaking out about a steady diminution of Japanese taste, pointing to such phenomena as the plethora of plastic home appliances in "baby" colors; garish "art" refrigerators; the growth of "adult" comics and weekly magazines given over entirely to scandals, sensationalism, and sex; the artificial-flower boom; and the despoliation of the countryside with garish signs, drive-ins, and the inescapable hysterical loudspeakers. What do you think of this situation?

FM: When we look at the art of the past we need to remember that what we see is the cream of what actually was produced. Mediocre and poor art was discarded or left uncared for. And of course in all ages the good art was produced in much, much smaller quantities than the poorer stuff. The situation is the same today—lots of junk and a slender output of first-rate art. The junk will be allowed to perish, while the finest products—most of them—will be preserved and passed on.

RB: What about the cries of alarm we often hear nowadays about the dying away of art traditions?

FM: We've always had this problem. New arts and techniques are created and old ones die out. The artistic tradition in Japan today seems to me strong, flourishing. You need only walk through one of the large department stores in Tokyo's Ginza to see the remarkable flourishing of the arts—industrial arts and crafts. I doubt that there has ever been a time when so many beautiful products were being turned out by so many talented people. Of course it's a pity that some of the old crafts are not being taken up by the young artists, but you cannot force people to continue these traditions when their interests lie elsewhere.

I'd like to point to the strong line of continuity in the arts here. Look, for instance, at the neon signs of Tokyo and look at the pennants and banners of the fishing fleets. You can't miss the new translation of form and color from the banners to the neon signs. And lighting in the homes: twenty years ago the lights in most homes and shops were composed of a white plate and a bare bulb. In many cases there was only the bare bulb hanging down from the wire and socket. But look around you now—in the shops, coffee shops, bars, and in the homes—and you'll see that they are making truly beautiful lighting devices. Perhaps these are the best in the world.

The Japanese respond admirably to the challenge of new techniques. They love to make beautiful things, and when a new technique comes their way they respond to it enthusiastically and pour their good sense and cultivated taste into it.

Instead of mourning the dying of the old art traditions, we should probably be rejoicing in the great variety and beauty of the new. And we should not lose sight of the fact that technology is making these things in great abundance so that they are enjoyed not only by the privileged few but by great numbers of people.

The Japanese are truly masters of good taste. And when you think that the Chinese were great producers of Oriental art for centuries, it's sad to see the wares they put on show these days. Yes, I see no cause to worry about the present state of Japanese art.

RB: Do you think the epithet "economic animals" as it has been applied to the Japanese in recent years has any descriptive validity?

FM: The Japanese are generally hurt when they hear the term "economic animal" applied to them. They forget that in the West philosophers have spoken of man as a "political animal" ever since the time of Aristotle. "Animal" in this sense is not the derogatory *chikusho,* beast; it means instead having a soul and being a living being. I think "economic animal," then, is a purely descriptive term. It's not offensive at all. It may be now in the process of acquiring an offensive meaning, but this is a new semantic development. Words never stay quiet. They are always moving, rolling, being transformed logically and semantically by use—just like pebbles in a river.

However this expression is meant or understood, the Japanese have surely taken to economics! And they have done so in the way they took to militarism before the war. Because of their enthusiasm for business, they often appear to other people to place too much emphasis on economics.

I myself do not find this passion for economic development at all strange in the Japanese. Not when I consider their highly practical nature.

RB: What impact do you think Yukio Mishima's dramatic suicide will have on the Japanese people?

FM: The immediate impact has been strong indeed. There are few Japanese who have not been touched by it in one way or another. However, I don't think it will have a strong influence on the behavior of the people now. Of course, in the long run Mishima's suicide may be like a time bomb, producing its greatest effect at some later time—in twenty or fifty years or more. However, that is a matter for our sons and grandsons to deal with!

RB: Do you think that Herman Kahn's prophecy[4] that the twenty-first century might well be the "Japanese century" is soundly based on the conditions of present-day Japan?

FM: Yes, it's soundly based on the conditions of today's Japan, but of course no one can really know if it's based on the conditions of the world. If we left Japan alone, in a sort of scientific experiment, it would most probably develop along the lines indicated by Kahn and, for that matter, Hakan Hedberg, the Swedish economic journalist.

The weakness of Kahn's position is, I believe, that it seems to be posited in just such a void. Taking the present curves of development and extrapolating them into the future is fraught with all kinds of dangers. The continuation of these curves depends more and more on Japan's international relations, and since the international situation may change drastically or dramatically, no one can really foresee what the future holds.

RB: Then you don't want to take a mental leap to the future to forecast what kind of century the next one will be—to project what a "Japanese century" might be?

FM: I'd really like to know what it would be myself!

RB: Well, what might one feature of it be? For instance, what feature of the Japanese culture of the future would other peoples want to imitate?

FM: Certainly if they became the most influential people, they would have their imitators, just as all the world imitates the Americans.

The interesting aspect here is the way the Japanese may develop spiritually. One eventuality might be a complete estrangement from Asia, together with a spiritual absorption into the West. This would be ideal for the West, by the way! Through the last three or four centuries the West, because of its enormous development and success, has become extremely ethnocentric. Therefore, the enrichment by a totally different culture—non-Christian and non-Aristotelian—might open to

4. Herman Kahn, *The Emerging Japanese Superstate: Challenge and Response* (Englewood Cliffs, N.J.: Prentice-Hall, Inc., 1971).

us completely new ways of thinking, unforeseen ways of an-
alyzing life. A different outlook on life would be a great
thing for the West.

In this view of the future, Japan would become a part of a
new Europe and America, a new member of the Western
community. This is not impossible at all. What, ultimately,
is the West? In a sense just a club, one which accepts new
members from time to time. It started with Greece and Rome,
then gradually took in the Germanic tribes and the Slavs;
later accessions were the Magyars and the Finns. Even now
it is on the point of accepting the Turks!

Some of these, the Finns and Magyars, for example, did not
have a very important culture of their own and were absorbed
completely, religiously and culturally, into the stream of
Europe. But now Europe and the West are opening themselves
up much more to the rest of the world. They have to, or they
will go under spiritually, and probably physically, as well.
So I feel that with a Japan integrated fully into the Western
community, both she and they would benefit immensely, both
would be enriched beyond all imagination.

Of course Japan would then be in a very awkward position
in respect to the rest of Asia, particularly to China. I see that
Japan now faces various openings, different paths to the future.
Which way she will take is impossible to predict, I believe.
There are, however, these two great possibilities. One is that
she will join the West, producing in the combination something
quite new, a steppingstone toward a total world culture. The
other is that she will develop her Asian roots and base her
future on them.

体験

2

# ANGELA CARTER
British
Novelist

Winner of the Somerset Maugham Award for fiction in 1969, she went to Japan on the travel grant that accompanied the award. During her two years' residence there she wrote several articles for the British magazine *New Society* on such varied topics as Japanese comic books, bar hostessing, and the capture of the Sekigun-ha (Red Army Faction) revolutionaries in 1972. Her most recent novel, *The Infernal Desire Machine of Dr. Hoffman,* was published in 1972 in Britain.

RB: What interests you most about the Japanese?

AC: It's a country of a different destiny. It's the only country outside the Western tradition, or outside the immediate experience of colonialism, that has all the familiar things, like newspapers, magazines, television, coffee shops, and people who identify with T. S. Eliot and Camus and so forth. And yet it's absolutely and completely different. Everything is the same and everything is different. And this goes for Tokyo—for the actual physical appearance of the city—and I think also for the psychological patterns. There is a great deal of common ground between us—and then they freeze into Japanese attitudes, and then they are lost to me.

RB: By a different destiny, do you mean that they have been or are now headed in different directions?

AC: It's a difficult question to answer because I know little about Japanese politics. I think that since they emerged they've always seen themselves as the saviors of the world, in a sense, a chosen race. This means that the analogies would be Israel and the Third Reich. Clearly they're not the saviors of the world, and clearly they're not, I think, going to rule the world. But this doesn't alter the fact that there does seem to be this sense, this conviction of superiority, that is bound to lead to a different destiny from, you know, a country like my own, which ruled the world and then sort of slumped back into a noisy decadence, and maybe now has no destiny at all.

RB: Why does this aspect of a different destiny interest you so much?

AC: Because of the difference. I'm not terribly bothered about their destiny—I'm not terribly bothered about anybody's destiny. It's the fact that everything's the same and everything's different to what I'm accustomed to.

RB: You don't find this sameness and difference unsettling?

AC: Sometimes I find it unsettling, but I don't find it as unsettling as many people I've talked to do, many foreigners here. I find it exhilarating. I find it especially exhilarating in situations where I'm not particularly close to the Japanese.

RB: Some foreigners seem to think that this is part of a mask the Japanese wear, that they are pretending to be something they are not, and this upsets them terribly, this feeling that the Japanese should seem to be so like Westerners and then should behave so very differently. These people feel this is deliberate falsification.

AC: The experience of a young Japanese of my age is very much like mine. I'm not talking about the fact that he may be a company man or a dropout or that he probably hasn't been able to establish the same equilibrium that I have due to the acute cynicism, the fortunate decadence, my country has given me. But they will have read the same books, they will have read *The Catcher in the Rye* at the same impressionable age, they will have seen James Dean when they were fifteen, they will have heard early Elvis Presley at the same time that I was listening to him, they will have read Camus at the same time, when it changes your life—though it might not have changed theirs to quite the same extent because Japan's is a less flexible society than my own. Their intellectual experience will have been very similar to mine. And then what you come up against is the jarring fact—for instance, I was standing somewhere once and I saw this young girl running down a flight of steps, and clear as anything, I thought, She never realized that Christ died for her sins.

RB: She probably doesn't care.

AC: Not only does she not know, she wouldn't care if you told her. Yes, because he never did. I mean, he didn't for mine either but for twenty years an awful lot of people told me he did. And though I think that in my heart I always thought there was something funny about this proposition, nevertheless it is part of the equipment I grew up with. What I mean is that the Judeo-Christian tradition was built into me at some point. I've consciously rejected it, but I've obviously retained some of it on an unconscious level. And it isn't in them! And I think this makes an immense difference. It makes them happier. And it gives them the potentiality for being very, very much nicer. And it *does* make a sense of a different destiny. Maybe that's it. But it means they don't have to work so hard, and I'm a great puritan and I think people should work very hard at making themselves.

RB: At making themselves?

AC: Yes, making themselves good.

RB: What has given you the most pleasure while living in Japan?

AC: I've got two answers. One would be that in spite of everything it can be very beautiful. And this upsets me.

RB: Certainly not Tokyo.

AC: Well, bits of Tokyo are. And the lifestyle is very beautiful. It really is.

RB: Not the company man's.

AC: The company man is very abhorrent. But even so, monsters though they are, occasionally even they are . . . graceful. Graceful not in the religious but the physical sense.

RB: How do the arts affect you?

AC: I don't know much about the modern arts—what I've seen of them seems derivative. But the traditional arts both take my breath away and leave me cold.

RB: Why the coldness?

AC: Because they are abstract. Take calligraphy, a means of communication that's been transformed into an abstract art form, and at this point it ceased to be a medium of communication. I mean, it's very, very beautiful and you can see in any sample of calligraphy, you can see the man at work. You see the man at work but you don't see the man.

RB: You think the work becomes more important than the man?

AC: Yes.

RB: Is there a loss of humanity—that is, does the art become more important than people, say?

AC: I think that in Japan art becomes far more important than life. Because they make life an art, and once you do that you forget how to live. One of the things Japan has done for me is to make me very aware that I am a European. I know that England was always a sort of island to the European tradition, but . . . how can I put it . . . every now and then I find myself thinking of Rembrandt's self-portrait with nostalgia.

RB: What was the second way you said you could answer this question?

AC: Well, Japanese men—fellows! And this is, really, the answer that came instantly to my mind.

RB: Japanese men have given you the most pleasure?

AC: They're very beautiful!

The young men, the Shinjuku people, have this very pure kind of dandyism that isn't a matter of clothes but has evolved into a method of presenting themselves to the world. When they grow their hair long they look like the best kind of Red Indian, and nature often blesses them with very impressive cheekbones and passionately sensitive mouths. And they move very beautifully. Yes, indeed. So a good deal of my pleasure has been aesthetic, really. I always like people to be beautiful. It seems the very least one can do.

Then, I lived with a Japanese national for a year. It is a great adventure to love a Japanese; much more so, maybe, than any of the other cross-cultural, cross-racial explorations, because of the peculiar severity of the Japanese idea of themselves. And one never knows where it will end because one becomes very much aware of the limitations of one's own culture as one—well, at any rate, I—learned more and more about the sheer horror of being Japanese, of being a Japanese man, of the Procrustean bed of the traditional mores. But I was very happy most of the time, though it was always a complicated, feverish kind of happiness, because it was the kind of savage excitement an explorer feels in virgin land. There was a dreadful confusion of expectations and I never knew what was going to happen next, because of the confusion. It was both an enriching and a devastating experience, and in many ways it was an affair with Japan itself. I went in the deep end and chose somebody who embodied much of the tensions of the country. And it *is* both enriching and devastating for a foreigner to live here, because of the confusion.

RB:   Well, then, what's been the least pleasant aspect of your stay?

AC:   Japanese men! Because they are very, very winning.

RB:   What do you think about Japanese men?

AC:   They come in so many gradations of male chauvinism that it's hard to give an honest answer. The structure of personal relations here is really a mystery to me. I don't really see what either party is getting out of it most of the time.

RB:   In male-female relationships?

AC:   Yes. Except on the one hand a minimum of physical

comfort and on the other a maximum of psychological discomfort.

RB: And affection?

AC: They seem to become affectionate with age. It seems to be a phenomenon of the aging process. Maybe I didn't stick around my own fellow long enough. They seem, after thirty or forty years—they probably are happier than married couples in the West. Because, I think, their expectations have been less, so much less, from the married state that after thirty of forty years of minimal companionship they suddenly find themselves thrown together in their old age and most of the people they know have gone away or died and they are, you know, really quite surprised and pleased with each other. Old couples often seem, you know, to get on very well.

RB: I wonder, now that you have more love marriages occurring—cutting down the number of arranged marriages— if this will continue to be the case. Because love marriages of course create more expectations.

AC: I'm sure the divorce rate will go shooting up, really.

RB: It's already on its way up.

AC: I'm sure it is; it's inevitable.

RB: In what ways have Japanese men been unpleasant?

AC: Well . . . my random sampling has been, you know, intensive.

Some younger men, a very limited number of Japanese men, appear to have reached emancipation at one great leap, without having gone through any of the halfway stations. They just seem to have jumped there and don't bother their heads at all about the outward appurtenances of masculinity, the butch, aggressive bit—with the result that they are sexually and emotionally very well adjusted indeed. But these people don't happen very often and usually, when they do, they are, for some reason, outside the everyday matrix of Japanese society.

No. In general, Japanese men seem to find women who cannot be easily categorized as either wives or mothers a great

threat. And wives, to a very large extent, become mothers—
mother substitutes. Boy babies seem to have an extraordinarily
intense relationship with their mothers and this does seem to
feminize them, somewhat. So Japanese men will have areas of
sensitivity denied to many European men. But you can't escape
the Oedipal situation just because you don't know who Oedipus
is. And Japanese mothers indoctrinate their sons so well with
the notion they are the lords of creation that they imbibe the
notion of absolute male supremacy with their mother's milk,
alas.

The horrid result of all these unacknowledged Oedipal
tensions is that Japanese men often treat women who can't
be classified as mother or surrogate mother as ambulant
sexual orifices and regard any manifestation of intellectual
activity or even proper female pride in a woman with open
amazement and ferocious derision, as if such a thing were a
threat to the very fabric of the world. So they want to relegate
women to two simple positions—on their backs, or at the sink—
so they can feel safe.

But the pictorial content of the comic books and the porno
magazines exhibits a very real fear and hatred of women, maybe
even of the feminine principle. The recurring themes of bondage
and mutilation . . . men must be very much afraid of women
if they want to load them up with so many chains and cut off
their breasts and I don't know what.

Lesbians, as well—there are lots of lesbians in Japanese
pornography. The Japanese seem to find the notion of female
homosexuality tremendously exciting, but I guess that, really,
sexually self-sufficient women are a terribly consoling idea.
Because I occasionally have the feeling that men here are disturbed by women's sexual and emotional demands and may
feel a generalized inadequacy. And they overcompensate with all
that butch, aggressive bit that bores the ass off me, personally.

All the same, I think the family structure, those poor,
overmothered boy babies who get all that female repression
and frustration worked out on them, and the inevitable am-

bivalences towards their fathers, well, I think all this has a bearing on the authoritarian personality. And that's the Japanese personality, isn't it? Maybe, to use a very crudely Freudian model, they love and venerate their father figures so much because they want to murder them. But this is a very rich field of speculation that I am, unfortunately, totally unqualified to explore. Though I think a society that systematically degrades and abuses women cripples men as well as women.

Yet people here are much less oppressed and inhibited about sex itself than in the West. Only when sexual activity involves emotional activity, well, then men often seem simply not to know what to do. And they just can't cope, if ever—horrid thought—they have to relate to women on equal terms.

RB: Traditionally, of course, Japanese men are not supposed to show much emotion, most especially romantic emotion, or much interest in "feminine" affairs.

AC: But they'll commit suicide for love at the drop of a hat. I think the whole culture is intensely romantic. It's one of the most rigorously, savagely romantic countries in the world. Obviously it's romantic; traditionally it places no value on reason at all. It works exclusively from the heart, doesn't it?

RB: Yes, it does.

AC: It's romantic in its art, it's romantic in its behavior, it's romantic in its attitudes to relationships; I mean relationships in general, not just man-woman relationships. The lord and his servant is one of the most romantic relationships in the world: my master right or wrong, my country right or wrong. Reason is derided here. And of course the very mention of reason in a love relationship here is treated as evidence of the absence of love.

RB: Yes, you often hear Japanese say Westerners are too cold, don't you? Too rational, too cerebral.

AC: Oh, yes! What it quite often boils down to is: If you don't want to jump into the crater at Mount Fuji with me hand in hand, how can you possibly love me?

RB: That boils it down, all right.

AC: A girlfriend of mine once had an affair with a Japanese man. They had a rather tormented first five months when he would do no more than occasionally touch her foot under the *kotatsu*[1] and then retreat, quivering. And then, finally, he told her he had dreamed of her, he had dreamed that they had gone to a beach at sunset, and they had made love, and then he had cut off her head and swum out to sea holding it and drowned himself.

She said to me, You know, that's the first time I realized he was interested in me.

RB: Japanese love! But, of course, he was probably subtly communicating to her all along. But she just wasn't getting the messages, just wasn't on his wavelength.

AC: I realize it's all done with nuance, and that the quiver of an eyelid can mean worlds of, literally, unspeakable emotion. And if that's what you want, that's what you want. However, I, personally, would never have the patience to undergo six months—or five months, or six years, or ten years, or whatever —of a, you know, subtle emotional siege. The thing that disturbs me is that this sensibility, this exquisite sensibility, is broken by extreme hysteria; in fact, often it seems to be repressed hysteria.

RB: As an outspoken feminist, you—

AC: Oh, yes!

RB: —what do you think are the chances of feminism as a significant political force in Japan?

AC: I think that if the ladies can get it together, they have the only genuine source of radical change in Japan.

RB: Yes, *if* they can get it together. Do you see any signs that they might possibly get it together?

AC: I've seen signs, usually amongst elite women. I think it's inevitable that only the most intelligent women—anyway, probably even the most beautiful Japanese women—are the ones who are most aware, most radically aware. I'm sure lots

1. A combination table and leg warmer usually covered with a blanket.

of Japanese women are aware in their skins. But there is a
kind of female chauvinism that you get amongst elite Japanese
women; they look at their menfolk with shudders of well-bred
disgust. Women's language can be quite different from men's
language in Japan. I once heard a very elite woman say, I
wouldn't want to talk like a man. Who would want to talk
like a man—vulgar, barking, crude language? Why, we want
all the men to talk like us!

RB: Yes. And the problem is they need to get it all together,
huh?

AC: Yes. I don't think they're going to get much chance.
I think that, however unconsciously, the masters are aware that
they cannot allow women to have too much freedom here or the
social structure will be disrupted. I think the masters have
always—well, Japan is the best man trap in the world, the
most efficiently designed man trap in the world. And the masters know how to rule.

RB: By "man trap" you mean "human-being trap"?

AC: Yes, human-being trap.

RB: And you think that the leaders of the country will not
allow women too much power, will hold them in check?

AC: Well, I think they'll segregate education, they'll have
the girls back to doing something like six hours' forced tea
ceremony a day, you know, and they'll tell them that they make
the very finest wives in the world, and that'll make them feel
very happy.

RB: Would you say that this awareness among women that
you spoke of is widespread?

AC: I haven't really known enough Japanese women to
say how widespread it is. My heart bleeds for some of the girls
I have known. Partly because some of them don't know what
is happening to them. They are having their brains excised
by this society and don't realize it at all.

Things have a tendency to happen very quickly in Japan.
The labor shortage is already putting many, more and more,
women into important work, like teaching. I have met some

perfectly splendid women in Japan, women of all kinds. Many women, however, are so happy with the present situation—in which they have unlimited power, within the home—and they can't see their position in the home as degrading. And they don't want to change it, not basically. Besides, I'd rather be a Japanese housewife than a company man. Anyone in their senses would.

RB: Oh, yes, I'd make the same choice.

AC: Yes, if you have the kind of power and responsibility of the Japanese housewife and the ability to organize your own time in the best way, the ability to run your own life as you please—you know, within the limitations of the profession of housewife—then obviously you're going to be loath to give it up for an ordinary job.

And this is why, when it comes, if it comes, the change will be so radical. Because women will want jobs that will give them as much power and responsibility as they now have. And they won't get this in the Japanese structure unless the structure is changed radically.

RB: You've said to me in conversation that you don't think you could write a novel about the Japanese. Is this because you find them "inscrutable"?

AC: I don't find them inscrutable; I'm afraid I find them terribly scrutable. I think it is a technical problem. If you're writing a naturalistic novel of people of a different culture and these people are going to be main characters, then there are whole areas of their experience that one can never touch. Like what I was saying about the girl running down the steps: I can't begin to put myself into the position of a Japanese. I've said their experience was rather like mine, and that is true, but I can't imagine always having slept on *futon*,[2] always having had green tea for breakfast—I know many of them haven't, of course. But, indeed, their kind of dislocation: that of the people I've known here who have never had green

2. A quilt used as a mattress.

tea, have never slept on *futon,* and yet they know that a hundred million people all around them are doing just that very thing. This kind of dislocation, the kind these outsiders are experiencing, I cannot imagine. Also, to have had a Japanese hamburger as the only kind you've ever known, oh! . . . to have read D. H. Lawrence in translation, for it to have taken one six years to have learned how to read, when I learned in three months.

And, you know, if I wrote a naturalistic novel about Japan, it would be about Europeans in Japan, you know, like Hemingway's novels about France: there are precious few Frenchmen in them.

RB: What do you think of Japan's novelists?

AC: So much is lost in translation that it's hard to say. But, anyway, I think Tanizaki is one of the world's great novelists. He is partly because he knew what he was writing about. I think that his work is all about the great confrontation—or the mini-confrontation, depending on which end of the telescope you're looking through—between East and West. But that was his thing, he was writing about a changing morality, I think. And part of his genius was that he wrote about this changing morality without ever telling you that he was: he didn't dot the i's and cross the t's, if you know what I mean.

There's a metaphor in one of his novels, the one called in English *Some Prefer Nettles,* it's about a man who goes back to Japanese culture. The metaphor is the *bunraku* puppets. I have the horrible feeling that this is how Tanizaki saw his countrymen, he saw them as very decorative puppets. I might be completely wrong, of course. I'd very much have liked to have met the old man, if the old man would ever have managed to, you know, say something civil to a foreign woman.

RB: Well, what about Mishima?

AC: What about him?

RB: Do you think he was any good?

AC: Well, reading his novels is like being on a train with someone very unpleasant, like being on a train with a compulsive madman, and he starts a conversation with you and he goes on and on and on, and he starts telling you about himself and he tells you how he first masturbated when he was eleven and he realized it was terribly wicked and how his grandmother used to hit on the ceiling with a stick and it used to frighten him very much because he used to think that the house was caving in because he masturbated and his voice gets, you know, more and more and more and more agitated and his hands, he starts pawing you with his hot hands and his hot breath is blasting in your face and . . . well, he's forcing you to listen to this very, well, really rather adolescent . . . well, *Angst*. I don't know, but I think he's really trying to write about evil, but he really doesn't know what evil is. He thinks it might have something to do with . . . well, you know, very beautiful young boys, but he's not sure.

RB: How did his death affect you?

AC: I'm afraid I had the standard European, and indeed, sophisticated Japanese reaction that he was a . . . buffoon! There's much more to it than that, obviously. Sometimes when one looks around one can understand why he did what he did.

RB: Looks around in Japan?

AC: Well, yes. One doesn't have to be a right-wing fanatic like Mishima to realize that the Japanese have sold their souls for a mess of . . . color television sets.

RB: You were saying something about people making themselves. And Mishima did in a way make himself, physically at least and perhaps psychologically, and he did it out of rather unpromising material, they say. He built himself into a new person. But you meant making yourself in a moral sense, while Mishima made himself, well, artistically, didn't he?

AC: As though he were a work of art.

RB: Yes, made a work of art and then destroyed it.

AC: The Japanese, I think, have always wished to make themselves works of art. They have an urge towards self-destruction. They make themselves perfect—perfect on their own terms. The thing is, once you have a perfect work of art

what do you do with it? You see, that is a moral problem. And
I sometimes think the Japanese aren't very good at morality.

RB: Or very interested in it.

AC: I've used the word "morality" in the widest sense.
I mean by morality what kind of things are we alive for? What
should human beings *do* with themselves? And simple ethical
concepts like "right," "wrong," "truth," and "justice." And
I don't see much evidence of a passion for ethics here. Not
much.

体験
3

## DONALD RICHIE
### American
### Writer

Mr. Richie has lived and worked in Japan for many years since
1945, when he first arrived there as a member of the U.S.
Occupation forces. His books on Japan include *The Japanese
Film* (with Joseph Anderson), *The Land and People of Japan,
The Films of Akira Kurosawa, Ozu, The Inland Sea,* and
the novels *Companions of the Holiday* and *This Scorching
Earth.* Until recently he was Curator of Film at The Museum
of Modern Art in New York. At present he works and resides
in Tokyo.

RB: What do you think is behind the intense desire of so
many foreigners to be constantly trying to get at the heart of
Japan, to find the real Japan?

DR: As one of them, I could say that I think one of the reasons that people like Japan so much—the kind of foreigners who come here and the kind who stay—they are often the kind of people who don't find much reality where they've been before. They come to Japan and they find a reality which by its strangeness makes it stand out, makes it more real than wherever they came from. The more that they would get to know the country, the more they would become convinced that there was something more and more real that they could find out about.

I think what I am doing is defining the romantic temperament. And I think that perhaps, though not the majority, certainly a great many of the foreigners here do betray romantic tendencies.

I am reminded of the words of a very well-known literary scholar, a foreigner, who said that trying to find the real Japan, the heart of Japan, was like peeling an onion. You very painfully peel the first layer of skin, then the second, and down and down, until you finally get to the core of the onion, which, of course, is empty. Now, this I think you can say of all countries. But it is only in peculiar countries, like Japan, that one strives to reach this real, this unattainable. It's a romantic ideal, I think. After all, the romantic ideal is just what it is— it's an ideal. And a person who feels this way about life is one who always feels that somehow or other the life that he is leading, or the life that he knows about, is not sufficient. That somewhere, someplace, there is this sort of ideal country, this pure, this distilled state, this essence. You never find this in a person who is well accommodated where he is. This tendency leads to great explorers, great artists; it leads to a lot of things, but it doesn't lead to the kind of person who is satisfied with his surroundings. Consequently you'll always find this kind of person trying to find the heart of something, simply because he does not, indeed, cannot realize that either there isn't any heart or else the heart is where he is, wherever that happens to be.

RB: And Japan, you think, has a particular appeal for this kind of person?

DR: I think it does, yes. For foreigners who come here Japan represents a kind of clean slate. Things are very strange for him. Nineteenth-century travelers used to call it the little land of topsy-turvy, and phrases like that. Of course these descriptions are wrong to the extent that they are condescending, but they are right so far as observation goes because things are, from our point of view, upside down. And so if you take a country where little is understood it is very easy to read an ideal into it. People who come to these shores for two weeks go around raving about the country. In fact, one may speak about the sort of three classical stages of the foreigner's attitude toward Japan. The first one is usually infatuation—if they are going to like it at all—where everything Japanese is splendid. The second stage is where everything Japanese is horrid. The third stage, which is where most of us are who have been here as long as I have, is not a romance and it's not an argument, it's more like a marriage. And you know that it is what it is, but nonetheless you go off looking for the real thing, as I do from time to time.

RB: Very often I hear long-time foreign residents complain that Japan is changing rapidly for the worse. Do you think this is a case of nostalgia for the good old days, or are modernization and increasing material wealth really destroying the best in the Japanese and their culture?

DR: Well, if what I say about the romantic disposition of many of the residents who have stayed in Japan for a long time is true, then it would follow that they wouldn't like any change at all. Because what they have really escaped from, rather than come toward, is a kind of security for them: they can always go off chasing after the real and the ideal. But I think they would resent change. I know it is wrong of me, unreal of me in a way, to resent the changes that are going on, yet I find that emotionally I do resent them.

But, of course, the romantic attitude tells everything about those suffering from it but doesn't show anything much about Japan itself. Objectively, Japan has been changing so rapidly in these past five to ten years that I think it has probably transformed itself more than any country I know anything about. The amount of tearing down, the amount of building up, the number of attitudes you can catch in the process of changing make me think that it really is changing indeed. And I suppose it is a question of age. If you are of a certain age, then any change is a good thing; if you are my age, then you tend not to like change. I feel that the best in Japan and in Japanese culture is indeed being destroyed. The best? I don't know—but anyway the unique in the culture and in the people is being destroyed simply because it is no longer economically feasible to have many of the cultural virtues they had before. Also, I think the strongest aesthetic virtue of the Japanese was always based upon *wabi,* on a frugal spirit. You purposely work within very small confines, you purposely choose the common, the ordinary. The product may be an object that costs fifteen times more, actually, than the more showy things, but nonetheless, you prove a kind of integrity by displaying a kind of poverty. Now, this kind of simplicity, this kind of directness, is probably responsible for more great art, I suppose, than anything else.

The Japanese have long believed that if you are materially poor you are undoubtedly spiritually rich. Now, this, of course, is not true. It is like George Bernard Shaw's remembering that when he first started writing anybody who was poor was automatically good. This is cant. But cant is also responsible for great art, I believe, sort of despite itself. And in Japan I find this attitude going, changing so swiftly in this new age of affluence. Changing so much that to young people I know, a great deal of their culture is no longer understandable to them. A great many of the words have changed, the language itself is changing so rapidly. Attitudes—ones I am quite familiar with, having been here twenty-five years—I find myself using and I am met with incomprehension.

RB: What elements of Japanese culture could be transmitted to the West?

DR: I sometimes wonder if any of them can. Certainly the outward appearance, the form, can be more or less transmitted. When I think of the Western cultural things that have been transplanted here and what they have turned into, it makes me wonder if anything that one knows here in its pristine state can truly be successfully transplanted. People try with haiku and other things; I think it is impossible. People take over *kabuki* and take over *kyogen, noh,* and other arts, and that is sort of a *nisemono,* an imitation, which is sort of nice but has no effect.

I think what can be transmitted and what is being transmitted, although I don't think it is being taken wholly from Japan, is a kind of attitude toward life which one sees in young people in the West. This is evident in the interest, however half-cocked it may be, in Zen Buddhism and so on. It is a kind of Asian attitude toward things, which the Japanese refined, probably more than the Indians, Southeast Asians, or even the Tibetans. It's the kind of attitude which historically and classically doesn't feel it necessary to use logic, for example. The Japanese mind, in writings certainly and in conversation also, is one which is ordered, very strictly ordered sometimes, but is not rational in our sense of the word. The way that we write and think is hopefully—this being the Western classical ideal—that A is followed by B and B is followed by C and so on, which is a nice way of ordering but is only one of the possible ways. It's used mainly to show how you arrived at a conclusion, but it tells nothing about the conclusion itself, nor does it say anything about the kind of brain that is making these assumptions. Our assumption of rationality, I think, is mainly that— just an assumption. And there are other ways of thinking about things where it is possible, for example, to entertain at the same time two ideas which the West would commonly find antithetical. The Japanese do this all the time; people who know the Japanese are all familiar with examples of it. The one that everybody remarks about is the man who can be a good

Buddhist, a good Shintoist, and maybe a Christian on top of that, all at the same time, and suffer no inconvenience at all.

This attitude is something which does not come naturally to people within the Western tradition, which from the Greeks on has been going in the opposite direction. But we've seen where that leads: it leads to bankruptcy, and moral and spiritual bankruptcy is what the West is in at present. This Asian attitude you can find in some Western things; for example, the popularity of the books of Herman Hesse right now. A book like *Steppenwolf* would never have been popular except in a time when all traditions that one has known in the West are dissolving and are proving to have been nothing at all. So you turn to something else. And what people are turning to, perforce—whether they ever heard the name Japan or not— is another way of thinking about things, one which is shared by a number of Asian nations, shared by a number of Asian religions, particularly Buddhism, more particularly Zen Buddhism. And this has proved appealing. I think it is also ironic that this attitude should be growing in the West at the very time it is losing all force here in Japan.

About the other elements of culture, I think it is not so clear. I don't think *ikebana* means the same thing in the West that it means here. The tea ceremony doesn't mean the same thing. They are artificial graftings. They may grow into something else. The fact that Japan has taken so well from the West says more about its digestive powers than it does about its selectivity. The Japanese national stomach, if you want to call it that, has the strongest gastric acids in the world. And they can turn anything they consume into something which is ineluctably Japanese after a time. The West has never been very good at that. We still have the word "chauffeur" in the English language and we mean it as the French do. When we take things over we tend to keep them separate.

RB: What has given you the most difficulty in adjusting to Japanese society?

DR: I suppose the answer to that no matter what country

is involved is always the same and the answer is: the people. When one lives as an expatriate, and lives among people who don't share one's unspoken assumptions, which I think are the only true basis of communication, then you always have a communication problem. You learn the language in hopes that this will go away, but it doesn't—not in any country. And then you come to the realization that after all you had an equally great communication problem in your own country, which is probably one of the reasons you left. There are, of course, dramatic differences, that is, between the way foreigners are treated here and the way Japanese are treated—being stared at, things like that. But I don't think that adjusting to Japanese society is really that difficult. I think the difficulty is with anybody being unable to adjust to any kind of society including his own. And those who came here openly admit this. Those who stay and try to make the best of it don't admit this usually. But after all the whole concept of society is antihuman. That's one of its functions, as Freud pointed out.

One of the joys of expatriation in Japan is that the Japanese do not regard you as Japanese, they regard you as an outsider, and so you, escaping from your own society's rules, are not really subjected too much to Japanese rules—which are really no different than the rules are, say, in America, where I come from. They are the same kinds of rules, although they tend to be different in some respects—they are applicable to different areas of life, and are regarded with different intensities. The foreigner finds himself mainly exempt from these because the Japanese don't expect him to know about them. And if he does know about them they don't really expect him to go along with them. In other words, he is not forced into society in this sense. So the problem that is presented to anybody who comes here is how to be a one-man society, because that's what you end up being. You find, to be sure, a little America here, and a little Belgium, and a little France, and whatever else among some people, particularly those attached to the embassies. But among the people who have come over here to do work, or to observe, or just to live, you find them turning into one-man societies—quite happily, I might say. That's an amazing thing to happen, an amazing thing to be able to do.

RB: Do you feel that you are accepted as an individual among your Japanese friends and acquaintances, or are you still an outsider, a foreigner?

DR: Both, naturally. We were talking earlier about antithetical statements being held in the same mind. It's probably wrong to stress this, because come to think about it, this is what everybody does, you know—I do it, I hold antithetical assumptions and use one at one time and the other the next. But I don't think anybody does it more graphically, perhaps, or more openly or innocently or more plainly than the Japanese.

So to some Japanese sometimes I am a friend, and the next time perhaps I am a foreigner. I think it works this way: to a Japanese, when I first meet him, I am a *gaijin;* then after he gets to know me for a little while I am an *Amerikajin;* then after he gets to know me pretty well I become a bundle of contradictions, which is human, and which goes under my name. This doesn't mean that he won't slide back, or that I won't slide back, from time to time, because I think of him as being a Japanese, too, instead of Taro Suzuki, or whoever. But between the two of us, there are times when we really think of each other as being people.

On the whole, however, I would say that the Japanese tend to think of foreigners as being less individuals, they think of them in a group sense. You don't find this grouping tendency so strongly in Americans. But then Americans don't think much about people, I think. And an American national attitude is simply that we are all foreigners together in our country. In Japan you hear little boys playing on the street telling their father furtively, *Gaijin, gaijin da* [Foreigner, it's a foreigner]. I don't think we would find little boys in America pointing to a Japanese and saying, Foreigner, foreigner. This is partly due to the fact that we look so utterly different to the Japanese, and the fact that they are a fairly homogeneous race. But it has a lot to do with other things, too, I think. It has to do with their being an island people. The British, for example, don't point and say, Foreigner, but they look the word at foreigners. The Sicilians, of course, behave just like the Japanese do—they are quick to point out the foreigner and word goes from house to house and all the housewives lean out of their windows and things like that.

As an individual here the temptation is to fall into a sort of morose, self-pitying state where nobody understands you, and worse yet, nobody thinks you are authentic. But in no place else do they think you are authentic; you always have to prove your authenticity to people, you know; you can't expect to get it like a piece of cake. And in Japan I think that this is what the well-adjusted foreigner is doing—every day he is proving his authenticity. You have to teach people, in a way, that you are real—you have to have some meaning for them. And Japanese are very often extremely adept at seeing only the outside view of things, taking the package for the reality.

In this, I think, the Japanese are absolutely right. That is, along with other Asians they agree that the visible, outward reality is the only reality. I think one of the basic errors that Western civilization has made is an unwarranted assumption that there is indeed a heart to something, or that there is indeed a reality beyond the appearance of things. This is an assumption that has never been proved and out of it has come such misapprehensions as Western religion, for example, and the concept of the soul, for another. It is very babyish for Western man to insist upon having a soul. This is a kind of pabulum, which I must say Asia has gotten along very well without and now finds itself all the stronger for.

RB: You wouldn't equate the soul with the Japanese idea of spirit?

DR: No, because the Asian idea of a spirit is a large collective thing. We don't have any collective souls, we are supposed to have individual ones. The reason we were attributed a soul in the first place was because it was so personal. And it's our little rattle, our teething ring, which we carry around with us still. I think the Japanese are right.

When you look at life dispassionately you realize there is no such thing as personality. You have people saying, I don't like tomatoes, or I don't like fried eggs, or I am the kind of person who does this or that. When you hear this you always know the person is striving to identify himself, not to you, but to himself.

And while the Japanese do have likes and dislikes, of course, often you'll ask a person various questions about his likes, et cetera, and it turns out he likes everything or else he doesn't like anything. What are his hobbies? Well, he doesn't have any. The tepidity of these answers! That is, compared to the more lurid variations of foreigners. Can you imagine an American not telling you his hobby? Often the Japanese can't. And I think it's because until recently they felt no need for this kind of distinction-making. They don't have any fictitious soul or personality to support. On the other hand, they have something which is just as pernicious, just as mythical. This is their social sense. I think the Japanese in this are like certain kinds of crustaceans that have their bones on the outside rather than the inside. And the outside structure of the Japanese is what holds it together, to keep it from being jelly. This shell is the social self of the Japanese. We have all noticed our Japanese friends turning into anonymous beings when they take part in demonstrations or even on a picnic or a hike up the hill—they become many-handed, many-footed, many-headed social monsters in our eyes. Because we only have bad words for this— "lynch mobs," and other such terms—we equate this sort of mob or group action with bad things. But the Japanese don't do this. They use this groupism for bad things as much as anybody does, but they equate it with very good things.

RB: Sort of losing yourself in a group?

DR: Yes, presuming there is a self to lose. Because if we don't have a soul we still have a very strong sense of personal entity, and it is this, of course, which has given an enormous amount of trouble to the West in the last fifty years—it's given rise to a whole new school of philosophy, the existential school.

RB: There is, then, a terrible need for the Westerner to identify himself as a unique individual?

DR: Yes. This is the Western tradition and where it has led us. The Japanese simply do not have the problem, and they have no massive identity crises. When psychiatrists come over to study the Japanese, they are sometimes baffled. Freud's psychology, which recognizes a soul, a conscience, doesn't work in this country. Jung's works a bit, because it concerns itself with power, and money, and a collective conscience, et cetera, but not Freud's.

RB: Is there a way into Japanese society?

DR: Oh, of course, there is. It is a very well paved, brilliantly lighted boulevard with big welcome signs on either side; you can't miss it. It's the place in which the Japanese have put us. They have made a place in their society for us. And they let us in, and we can wander at will, if only within those confines. It is a quite elegant, extremely interesting ghetto, and people can live there forever very happily.

The problem, of course, and I think this is what your question implies, is: Is there any way into the real Japanese society? Well, then, of course, we can go back and talk about the "real" some more. But to short-circuit that, I think one might just say right off the bat that there are many places where the foreigner is not welcome. And if he does enter, the Japanese don't know what to do with him. If he gets there, and a surprising number of people do, then they put up with him. Well, once he's in, there is nothing one can do about it—he's there; that's reality and we'll do what we can, is the feeling. So pretty soon people forget that he's there and go on behaving as they ordinarily would. But he is certainly discouraged from doing things.

I remember once I was working some years ago for a sort of governmental agency that had films as its province, and they handled foreign propaganda, Japanese films, films that went

to festivals, and things like this. I was an adviser. I was interested in the structure of this company and how it could be
made more loose—it was very bureaucratic and tightly bound—
and how it could be made more useful, and how it could be
made more real in my sense of the word. Well, there came the
day of the big board meeting, and my position was high enough
that I should have been invited—given my job title. And on
the day that it was going to occur I had all sorts of suggestions,
notes and things I had made. And I was approached by
people who said, Oh, we have a great honor for you, because
today you are to be allowed to choose the film for the coming
festival, which is a very great honor indeed. I said, So it is.
I will do it first thing tomorrow, but now we have the board
meeting. And they said, Oh, no, you don't understand, we
need this decision right away. I said, But the film festival is
two months off, twelve hours isn't going to make much difference. They said, Well, we're very sorry, but you have been
selected to do this and this is your duty today, and unfortunately
this does happen to coincide with the board meeting, and we
are very sorry we can't have your interesting opinions on this
matter, but the fact is you can help us more by doing this
very difficult thing, of really thinking about it and selecting
the film for this festival.

I don't want to suggest through this anecdote that any
duplicity was involved. Everything was done innocently;
for if there is one thing the Japanese try to relax it is the kind
of cynicism which we would read into such a story in the West.

I doubt that anybody had a confab with anybody else. I doubt
that it was thought: We must at all costs keep the foreigner
out. I don't feel that anything of this sort happened. This is
the way one naturally does things here; that the person who
did this naturally realized that this was what was going to
happen; that it was natural that the man who gave me the
news, that his boss should tell him that Mr. Richie should do
this because he knows a lot about foreign films. No cynicism
was involved; but the end result is the same as if it were—I

was kept out of the board meeting. I was not allowed to have my say on something that was uniquely and purely Japanese.

This attitude is changing, incidentally. I am now much more taken into the middle of things than I was before. The Japanese bamboo curtains of various kinds are parting, there is no doubt about it. Of course I wanted this to happen all these years, and now I am in the paradoxical and ironic position of being sorry that it is happening. Because the more the Japanese let us in, the less they keep what they have.

RB: Who of your Japanese contemporaries, individuals or groups, do you respect most?

DR: I tend to respect the kind of Japanese who incorporates in his work, no matter what it is, many of the characteristics which make him Japanese. I admire Toru Takemitsu, the composer, very much. He writes in a completely contemporary idiom, but one measure of his work lets you know that he is Japanese. He does this not by the obvious ways another composer, Toshiro Mayuzumi, does—of using folk songs, Buddhist chants, and things. Rather he displays in music—and this is what I think a composer is supposed to do in a way—the kinds of patterns of emotions he discovers in himself, which, being authentic, are also Japanese. He is a great composer in that he has the necessary technical facility on one hand, long training in Japanese and Western music on the other, and the genius to put them together.

I admire Masayuki Nagare, the sculptor, for almost the same reasons. He has taken Japanese forms and made them internal to himself, and because he is contemporary they have emerged as contemporary art in the contemporary medium. But they are well based in continuations of Japanese craft. I was a friend of and admired—with some reservations—Yukio Mishima, who again did very much the same thing, writing psychological novels. But writing such novels he managed somehow to imply long-standing Japanese attitudes. And, of course, his final creation was a very definite commitment to a Japanese ideal. I also admire Yasujiro Ozu. Again, a man who used film, a twentieth-century medium, to show a continuum of Japanese ideas. Film being film, he was able to be more explicit than any of the other people I've mentioned so far. Through the world of *wabi,* which is what the Japanese world used to be, he was able to show attitudes, to show things that were absolutely true, absolutely basic about the Japanese, and by so doing, of course, make them universal. All these people I am talking about now that I admire are so Japanese that they've become universal. I don't like partial people very much. Another man I admire very, very much is one of my oldest friends, whom I met as a student many, many years ago, who has now through skill—in his case almost genius—and through completely Japanese ways of doing things, which he never learned but which were ingrained in him, become one of the richest men in Osaka.

All these men share a great deal in common, and what I find admirable in these Japanese is their continuation of their Japaneseness. It is ironic, perhaps, on one hand, telling on the other, that I, a man who has cut most of my roots with my own country, should feel this way; but, nonetheless, I do.

RB: Some years ago when you wrote about the films *Tsubaki Sanjuro* and *Harakiri,* you said that the mentality created by the Japanese police state continues into the present. In what way does it continue?

DR: By that I meant the whole legacy of the Tokugawa period, which was, of course, among other things the longest police state in history. And it would be surprising indeed if that attitude did not linger in Japan, seeing how it is such a a living part of Japanese history.

As you remember, the Tokugawa rulers were successful because they could take advantage of, on one hand, and partially create, on the other, this social aptitude on the part of the Japanese to weld themselves into large social units, all of which have had identical ideas—if they have had any ideas at all. They used this quite practically, not to say cynically, and they were able to balance politically all of the various forces in the

country, and so were able to maintain their system for almost
three hundred years. They did this, however, by rather rigorously repressing any sort of individuality, particularly political.
We all know of famous cases of martyrs who died, or worse,
at the hands of the authorities in Tokugawa times, because
the equilibrium was occasionally unstable.

The reason the Tokugawa regime collapsed was not because
of Perry and his warships, it was simply because it was going
to collapse anyway. Perry and the boats happened to arrive
at the right time, with an ultimatum, to be sure, which probably
hastened the end. Well, when you think about what the Tokugawa government based their precepts on, you find that in the
present these same precepts continue. For example, they had
very, very strong Confucian leanings: they followed the precepts of Confucius about the necessity for obedience to father,
the governor, one's feudal lord, and so on, up to the emperor.
Obedience was always a great thing in Confucian law and it
was a great thing in the Tokugawa period. It still goes on—we
have World War II to remind us of this, and we have things
in the newspaper every day to tell us that indeed so far as
superior-subordinate relations go, the sytem hasn't changed all
that much. The thing is that now in films like *Harakiri* and
*Tsubaki Sanjuro* we have men who have deliberately exposed
it. That's what Kobayashi and Kurosawa were doing. Kobayashi very earnestly, and Kurosawa with the lightest kind
of satire, were exposing these things as being inhuman, and
their work is part of the whole postwar trend for gaining freedom and, I suppose, individuality. Certainly both of these
directors are strong on the side of individuality, which, for the
Japanese, is a fairly new concept. People who exhibit individuality this strongly simply wouldn't have lasted in the
Tokugawa period. A picture like Kurosawa's *The Bad Sleep
Well*—which contains very strong implications of graft in high
business, and perhaps in government—simply could not have
been made in earlier times; no one would have dared to
produce it or, as happened during the war to other film critics

and film directors, Kurosawa would have been thrown into jail for it.

The pressures that created this situation still exist; but the thing is that right now the authorities tend to be somewhat powerless. In other words, if you run across censorship or repression, or if you're attacked, you have all sorts of places you can appeal to, like the Supreme Court, for redress. You don't have to put up with the punishment.

Yet I feel that the people who do make strong stands against this, and do get themselves into trouble from time to time, are so rare that I am forced to the conclusion that the majority of people are indifferent, and the majority of people, when it comes down to it, will submit. You see this submission in business all the time. The ordinary people will not stand for integrity; they will do what is expected of them simply to save themselves the trouble or the punishment. *Mendokusai* is a word that you hear in this regard, and it literally means it's too troublesome to do something. It's not trouble that's at the root of the problem: I suppose we'd have to call it a lack of integrity, but unfortunately English doesn't work too well in explaining this aspect of Japanese behavior.

We have a word we've long applied to Japanese behavior; it's hypocrisy. But we should watch our terminology because the word doesn't mean the same thing in Japan that it does in America. In Japan a man who plays both ends successfully against some sort of middle is not a hypocrite, any more than he is in America. In America it's called diplomacy, until it fails, and then it's called hypocrisy. In Japan nothing succeeds like success. I often feel that in Japan nothing really is a crime unless you get caught; if you're caught then it becomes a crime. This is what I meant when I spoke a moment ago about the two directors and their pictures. They succeeded, they got away with something. However, in the unlikely event that a great dictator would set himself up in Japan and want to return to Tokugawa methods, I think that he would have ninety percent of the population on his side, grumbling of course and hating every moment of it, perhaps, but, I still think, he could count on them.

RB: They wouldn't oppose him very strongly?

DR: I feel they would not oppose him. I could be wrong. I would rather hope to be wrong, but I don't think I am.

RB: You've also written that some Japanese directors have implied that theirs is a totalitarian state. Do you think Japanese groupism is too benign to be called totalitarianism or not?

DR: Well, it's a question of degree, of course. Yes, I do, and yes, I also think the Japanese directors who have said this are wrong. Because if you take one look around Japan, you will discover that in many ways it is one of the freest countries in the world. Certainly you can say political things in the press in Japan that you simply could not say in any other country including America.

RB: Even nowadays in America? Considering what the U.S. underground press says?

DR: Well, the Japanese don't only make antigovernment statements in the underground press; they say these things in the *Asahi,* and they say them in other big newspapers. But after all, what does one expect, I wonder. Naturally, any country which has a social entity such as Japan does is capable of being turned into something totalitarian, just as any country, such as America, that has an enormous investment in the individual has an equally great capacity for being turned into utter chaos, which is what's occurring.

I don't think Japanese society has any built-in safeguards as yet against the kind of totalitarianism these directors are talking about. But I think the fact that it isn't occurring now is, first, that it just did occur, as a matter of fact, during the thirties and forties, and second, that there is a definite change of attitude here, a sort of lip service to the idea of criticism and to the idea of individuality, which certainly exists in Japan now, and which did not exist before. One would think that a country in which a whole generation has enjoyed the fruits of this kind of freedom would be the first to rise in its defense if it were threatened. But as I have indicated, I don't think that the Japanese are capable of doing this, and indeed why should they be so? They don't have a deep tradition for the kind of individual action that we're talking about. For us, integrity is a very good word; I think it's probably one of the best words in the American language. The Japanese don't have a word for integrity, and they don't have any need for this. After all, integrity is based upon the idea that one is a sole, unique human being with one's own moral and ethical concepts. And the Japanese do not have this. They have, on the contrary, something which is certainly going to be better for them in the future, something as old-fashioned as an individual ethos. They're going to have this ability to be both personal people, that is, people who think they know who they are, which is all one can hope for, and at the same time they have a very, very strong social form, which is something other people simply don't have. If this form is misused, the system could turn into totalitarianism, and every day we see something in the newspaper that points up this kind of threat. So far nothing has occurred which would make totalitarianism probable. But as for the Japanese film directors who have said that their society is totalitarian, nothing has occurred, really, to make one think that.

One hears that the methods of big business, the so-called *zaikai,* in Japan are continuations of the feudal, totalitarian ethos. One is certainly inclined to agree if one only looks at their methods, which are very much like those of the feudal lords: instant obedience; instant sort of holding up of the house flag, as though it were a clan war emblem; the intense pride in whatever brand of tape recorder, whatever brand of camera, whatever anything the company is producing. But similarities with the feudal era end there, I think, because if you look at what these things are about—the big companies are about making money, and the whole totalitarian system of the To-kugawas was about life. And nowadays, there is always an escape from the large company dormitories; there was no escape at all in the Tokugawa period. But the people who live in these dormitories, the curfew, the things they have to put up with, they want to put up with—this is why they are where they are. The people like to have their marriages arranged, they like to have their outings planned so they all go together, they like these things. If they didn't, they wouldn't be in the companies, they'd simply be someplace else.

The Japanese mentality could very well be taken over by something totalitarian, but I certainly do not think that the giants of Japanese industry, as one example, are even aware of this capability, and they wouldn't even want a totalitarian arrangement. After all, if you have slaves, then you don't get the kind of production that you get when you have willing people who innocently and trustingly put their whole lives in your factory and into your hands. We Americans would call this a kind of con game, and we would find the big companies culpable, but I simply don't think that our viewpoint applies to this situation. It is certainly pertinent in this regard that the majority of the people work happily in these places. By using this system the Japanese may lower themselves in our estimation, but it really ought to show us that there is another way of thinking about things, that there is another approach to life, that our approach to life—the fiercely individualistic, carefully guarded soul theory of the Westerners and, particularly, Americans—is not the only viable answer. We hate totalitarianism, and we are right to, given our background.

RB: Do you think that such epithets as "economic slaves," "economic animals," and "salesmen of death," as applied to the Japanese of today, have any validity?

DR: They have a certain validity to the people who are saying them. If you remember that "salesmen of death" was used as sort of a political slogan by leftist forces in Japan about Japan's affiliation with the Americans and what America was doing in Vietnam. The "economic animal" epithet was thought up by an ex-ambassador who used this to talk about the Japanese, and in effect, the context in which he said it was about Japan's international success in world trade. "Economic slaves"? I don't know who thought that up. But anybody who would think up something that melodramatic and lurid must have something else at stake. Certainly not slaves, because slaves don't have any volition of their own, and the Japanese have more volition than anybody else, at least more chance for volition. Not "economic animals" because we're all economic animals—we're all living on a certain amount of money; we all want more; we all try to get more. "Salesmen of death" I'll simply dismiss.

I don't think that these terms are accurate. They are accurate only if you consider who said them and if you consider them as only partly applicable.

RB: Ironically enough the "economic slaves" label was put on the Japanese by students brought to Japan by the Japanese government—Southeast Asian students particularly—and sent to school here, and they feel that the Japanese work too hard and spend too many hours working and trying to make money.

DR: The history of the world is based upon people observing other people and finding something the matter with them. In this regard the qualification "too" is interesting. By whose standards is one doing too much of anything? There is no point in judging any country from any other standards than those enjoyed by the natives of that country.

On the other hand, I feel that this enormous interest of the Japanese in making money is working toward the detriment of everything, eventually. The Osaka mentality for getting all you can in the way of money no matter how you get it has infected the entire country. Whether it came from Osaka or not I don't know, but it's all over Japan now—it's endemic. It is almost a parody of the thing Sinclair Lewis used to make fun of in America in the twenties. You get people who will happily, but literally, work themselves to skin and bone for one of the big companies, and be very pleased, happy, and proud to do this. One can understand this. We all know that nice, warm feeling that comes when we really associate ourselves with a large group. This is what we all really want to do; it's just that the Japanese can do it better than most people do. But, nonetheless, the aim of all these good, warm feelings is more money. And this has finally been openly acknowledged.

Up until ten, fifteen years ago the Japanese still wrapped money in white paper because it was thought to be dirty. They used to think about money the way we thought about sex. Money was always hidden, and when you paid anybody you had to have a special envelope to put it in. Well, this is gone now. The more you flaunt your money the better, and the more you have, naturally, the better. This is something new, and this affluence, as I've indicated before, is very, very bad, because it's destroying those other qualities. The reason I think this interest in moneymaking is bad is because it's lopsided, and I think anything lopsided is bad. America is in the midst of its chaos and finally gaining its equilibrium after decades of money grubbing. Things happening in America indicate that a majority of young people don't believe in a lopsided pursuit of money anymore. Ironically, again, just as we are coming out of it, Japan is going directly into it.

RB: Herman Kahn has written that the twenty-first century might well be Japan's century. If so, what kind of a century do you think it will be?

DR: If you believe in Spengler, it naturally will be Japan's. It's inevitable because, if you start in Babylon or someplace way back you can trace civilization right through America, and it would naturally come here for rather a short time before, I would think, it goes to China and back where it started from.

Materially, Japan is making what is called strides—it's making more ships than anybody else, for instance, and pretty soon will make more everything than anybody else. Certainly it will be one of the major material-producing countries in the twenty-first century. Consequently, it will have the highest standard of living. Yes, I suppose Kahn's right.

Now, whether I would like this kind of Japan or not—I don't think I would. After all, people who come here and intend to live here—people like me—tend to like the things they find here. But anyway I think Japan, in a way, is going to turn into a new America—with improvements, one trusts. The kind of smug America that existed in the forties and to an extent into the fifties seems to be in the cards for Japan if it continues its present course. Already an amount of smugness has been noticed by foreign residents, some of whom deplore it, others of whom, like myself, tend to favor it because it does mean that the Japanese are no longer *gaijin ni yowai,* giving in to foreigners, anymore for no good reason. The new confidence does indicate a sort of national pride, a pleasant thing in moderation. This pride is in evidence and it means a new kind of reality for the Japanese; it means less fear, for example.

But, no, I don't think I really like the developing situation at all. After all, it wasn't so much that I *came* to Japan, you realize, it was that I *left* America—there are other places I could have gone. It wasn't that I was coming toward something that was so wonderful, it was that I was fleeing from something that I really didn't like. It's ironic, but true, it always happens if you live long enough, that you will discover that the person that you loved or the place that you liked will turn into the very thing you hoped to escape from—this is the history of marriage, and the history of expatriation in all countries. Lafcadio Hearn talked about this during his last bedeviled years. And I think it's true.

Any country in the twenty-first century will be much, much more of a social-animal country than anything we've known before because simply by sheer force of the numbers of people on earth in the twenty-first century individualism will not be able to survive. Everybody will be group-thinking. And the Japanese know how to group-think better than anybody else. This is one of the reasons why they are fitted for world leadership—if they want it.

RB: One Japanese has recently been quoted as saying that while America has been the pattern for Japan to emulate in recent years, especially in the postwar years, it won't be long before Japan will be the pattern for America to emulate.

DR: Oh, it already is. You can see this in these little antennae of society which we call the minor arts. That's what they are, they are antennae—you can see it in fashion, interior decoration, and domestic architecture, and you'll be able to see it in more visible things before very long.

RB: In your opinion, is there any basis to the charges of rising Japanese militarism?

DR: None, and I've looked for signs, too. Ever since China started yammering about Japan's resurgent militarism, we've all been looking for it. But one can see what China is doing with such charges: finding the Mishima death replete with militarism, finding the poor old *Battle of Okinawa* film full of it, and so on. China is doing this quite cynically and quite purposely, and China doesn't believe it itself. No. And it's very, very strange. Right into this whole era of the Vietnam war, one still finds Japan, pathetically perhaps, trying to play little Switzerland, displaying attitudes like: We who learned the horrible lesson of war last and best will try to make world peace. One still sees Japanese people trying to do this. They do this because they have forgotten something all Asians know, and which everybody ought to, and this is that peace is unnatural—war is the natural state. No man is happier than when he is waging war. And the idea of getting rid of war, whether it's Eleanor Roosevelt's or Richard Nixon's, is fond imbecility. The Japanese used to know this, when they had their own wars, but one of the results of the police state, of course, was that there weren't any wars for two or three hundred years, and maybe they did come to think that peace was a natural state. Anyway, you still find Japan playing little Switzerland. And you find an antiwar attitude in this country that can only be described as virulent. This attitude may be mere lip service, I don't know, but certainly the Japanese have an enormous amount of aggressions of the kind which many countries use war to get rid of. But the Japanese have so many things built into their rather marvelously intricate social system that allow them to get rid of feelings of antagonism and things like this. So of all people, I think the Japanese would be the least inclined toward war of any I know of at present. The social system still functions, they can get rid of the aggressions legally, as it were.

There is a new feeling of national entity among Japanese, to be sure, and this very often in the history of the world has been used by unscrupulous or misguided or simply evangelical persons to build up, as in Germany and Italy, a concept of national unity which can then be used for whatever purposes the military clique wants. But in Japan there isn't any military clique. There is, however, a business clique which is made up largely of people who were affiliated with the old military clique. But then, of course, one must remember Japan has now succeeded in triumphantly doing everything that the Greater East Asia Co-Prosperity Sphere was ever intended to do. Japan has done it peacefully, and it's done it legally. It's gotten everything it ever wanted out of Southeast Asia and out of the rest of the world. And it did it all after the war. All the reasons for the war have now been satisfied, all the ostensible reasons.

However, there are going to be new reasons for further wars, of course, and the world is simply not going to sit by, I feel, and let Japan go on peacefully making money. The Nixon thing about Japan, for example, I would think is based upon nervousness on one hand and sheer envy on the other. His policies are unheard of—to have an embargo on another country's products simply because their country is doing so well with them. Trade wars are always based on the worst sort of envy. And here let me add that the term "economic animal" is used by people who are jealous of Japan economically. But militarism? No, not yet.

RB: In February, 1971, fifty foreign residents petitioned the Japanese government to provide them with the basic human rights guaranteed in the Universal Declaration of Human Rights when it considers its proposed new immigration bill. As a foreigner, how do you feel about this gesture?

DR: I suppose it depends on what kind of foreigner you are. As a Korean or a Chinese in this country I would feel very strongly and I would want to join the petitioners. As an American, I think it ludicrous. We don't suffer from being foreign in this country; on the contrary, we are given a status we would never dream of, could never hope for in our own country. I've often thought one of the reasons so many foreigners like it here and continue to live here is because for them this is the land of no competition. They can do things here, no matter how badly they do them, and receive an amount of money and recognition for them that would be absolutely unavailable to them in their own counties. I sometimes feel, in my lower moods, that this applies to a certain extent to me. I certainly know that I wouldn't have had the opportunity to start had I not come here. So the foreigners, if they are Americans, Englishmen, or Europeans, benefit very much for having been deprived of these so-called human rights. They are paid royally for this, and they only have to go home if they don't like it. The Koreans and the Chinese can't go home, and they have a very bad time. Because no one is more indifferent in these regards than the Japanese, and no minority in the world (no minority I know anything about) is treated more badly by a majority than the Koreans and the Chinese are by the Japanese. And it makes the black-white thing in America look like kindergarten in some ways because it is so pervasive and so insidious and it's an absolute blanket condemnation.

So, as far as this petition goes, if I were a Korean I would think very strongly about it. He even needs his legal rights protected, a thing white people here don't have to worry about.

On the other hand, I suppose, one of the things one has always known that one has to watch out for, as a foreigner here in Japan, is that government still follows the ancient Chinese model of bureaucracy. It's the bureaucracy which does the official work, to the extent that it does it at all. If this new bill were to mean that the bureaucracy would be given even more power, as it most certainly would seem to, and would be given judicial powers, and would be given powers of judgment by which foreigners would be kicked out and for what reason, then I think there is very good reason for anybody here to try to do something so the bureaucrats don't get that much power.

Indubitably there is a movement, a very natural, spontaneous trend in Japan toward just this kind of thing now. It goes along with the national entity, the feeling of pride in being Japanese; in fact you see more kimono on the streets than you used to. At the very time so much that's Japanese is being torn down it is perfectly fitting that a great many things should be coming back. Since bureaucracy, by its very nature, satisfies such a deep Japanese need—that need mainly being not to take responsibility for anything—I suppose that the bureaucracy will get larger yet.

I often marvel at the intricacies of the system that can arrange to make decisions for which nobody takes any responsibility at all. A consensus—that's what everybody here likes best. If you make a consensus, and then that becomes a law, or that becomes whatever you do, then nobody is responsible for it if it goes wrong, which I think must be one of the reasons they agree to agree in this fashion. It's like when somebody who works computers says the fault is the computer's, because the computer can take the blame for everything. You can always blame the computer. Computers don't make mistakes, but who knows who puts what information into it? And, therefore, the computer—more so in Japan than in most countries—can easily become regarded as a kind of deity; fallible, perhaps, but nonetheless something that will take the responsibility. It will never replace the bureaucracy in this country, which is of Chinese monumentality and of Soviet dimensions.

RB: What is your opinion of the Japanese students' anti-government movement?

DR: I am of two minds about this. I just don't know. This tells something about me and not much about the movement. I think if the students have an antigovernment campaign the situation is exactly as it should be, because there always ought to be one. I don't think any country is healthy unless it has countercurrents going on, even equally strong ones at the same time. The thing I don't like about Japanese student organizations and Japanese antigovernment movements is that they are never pure enough, at least never pure enough to satisfy me. At Narita, where three policemen were killed in riots directed against the new airport, the farmers had a terribly good point: they didn't want the planes there. The students came in to help them and the students came in to help themselves and the whole thing got very, very muddied up with political issues that don't really have much to do with the farmers. The farmers lose, and indeed they probably would, but one applauds their standing up. But in the meantime the students have muddied everything—what began as a very simple and human thing to do, based upon dignity and rights, has been turned into a political melee. This occurs all the time in Japan. Everything is turned into political hay for one side or for the other. I realize I am being naive in saying that this is not a desirable thing, but desirable or not, this is what invariably happens in all countries. But it happens in Japan with a clarity, a visibility, which other countries would try to cloak and hide, but which the Japanese don't feel any necessity to. You get all the muck and mud right out in the open. I am very much pro the farmers of Narita and I am rather anti the students of Narita who took advantage of and used the farmers' cause. If they had saved the day, I probably would think differently, but they did lose.

RB: How did Yukio Mishima's death affect you?

DR: I am really not in the position to say very much. My answer cannot have very much relevance to anything because I knew him so well and because he was a friend. And so I didn't judge Yukio as a major figure—I didn't see him as anything other than the person I knew, really, who had all these books that I read and who did all these things that I sometimes went and saw. I'd known him for well over twenty years; we saw each other a great deal.

I remember one conversation we had the summer before his death, though, that was, in retrospect—one always has lots of *déjà vu* after somebody has died—in retrospect it was sort of meaningful. I was finishing writing *The Inland Sea* and was having trouble with it, and I thought I'd just go off on another romantic quest someplace and renew my impetus. I told Yukio I was going to do this, and he asked why, and I said, Because I want to find the real Japan, or what's left of it, by which I meant the old Japan. He said, Well the old Japan is gone, absolutely gone. I said, That's impossible, surely in the country, somewhere—I am going to Tohoku, around there I can still find something of the mentality that I have kept in mind these many years. He said, No, you'll find a number of things have expired and the country places are the worst of all. Whatever it is that you and I once admired so much in Japan is absolutely gone, gone beyond the control to bring it back, gone beyond anything, and I am the only person who knows that. And so he was.

This was one of the things that he was hoping to do with this strange act of his, which was I think maybe to shock— he loved to shock people; flabbergasting the bourgeoisie was one of the things he did when he wasn't working. This kind of shock he thought would bring Japan back to what I know he thought of as being the straight and narrow. He was very much the puritan, and he realized that the Japanese ethos, the pure one that he was talking about—the Tokugawa one—is puritan. The Japanese puritan is not often recognized by us as being a cousin to our own, but he is. They have a social puritanism which is equally as strong as our Cotton Mather hell-and-damnation one. And he knew this very well and he approved of Japan's and he liked it, which is what he meant by his last words; he didn't mean Emperor Hirohito, he meant the emperor system, and he hoped to reaffirm everything by this very spectacular act of his, to create a climate of feeling. If he thought that much about it, that's how far he went. He certainly didn't intend any rampant militarism. He must have known, being the kind of man he was, being that intelligent, exactly how these army oafs would react by shouting back *baka yaro* [fool], and sitting down, and things like that, which is exactly what they did. He knew all this, but it was a grandstand play, something you do for the crowds, it was a grandstand play for the nation of Japan. Proving what he believed: this is very, very Japanese, this is why people commit *seppuku* throughout history. This is to prove—it's not just lip service—that they really mean it, and they really mean it by slitting themselves open. And this act proves their intentions.

He had so many motives; I mean, you have to talk about them all to understand his suicide. One of the motives that comes out very, very clearly now is that it wasn't only going forward that motivated him, it was the fear of going backward. He was very narcissistic and he didn't want his body to go bad on him as it had already started to. He didn't want to go bald and have wrinkles; he wanted to be as he always had been.

RB:    All he had made himself to be.

DR:    Precisely. Once I wrote an article about him for *Playboy* or *Esquire* or something, and I showed it to Yukio and he was so upset about it that I never did publish it. One of the things I said was that one of the ways to understand Yukio Mishima was to understand that everything he was was predicated upon what he had not been. That is, a boy so shy that he couldn't speak and who stuttered becomes a public speaker and speaks several languages very well, a boy with writer's cramp turns into a great writer, a boy with spindly legs who is pigeon-chested becomes a great bodybuilder. He was a self-made man in the existential sense of the word; he deliberately made himself into that which he was not. He made himself into what he most admired—and one always admires what one is not.

Since he created his life there is no point in caviling about the way he chose to end it, it was his from the beginning. This act of his fit perfectly, it was the single stone that was needed for the arch of his life, which is the way I perhaps too poetically put it.

RB: Until he did it, it was difficult to take his acts seriously.

DR: Oh, he knew this very well. He talked about suicide often, and who among us believed what Yukio was going to say about suicide? The last time I saw him, which was three or four days before he killed himself, he talked about nothing but the Meiji-period hero Saigo Takamori and his friend Okubo, and talked about the last of the samurai, knowing full well that *he* was going to be the last of the samurai. And talking with his other friends since then, I find that they received telegraph messages up to three or four years earlier which they can now decode.

Nobody took him seriously, and he knew this, and he proved his seriousness. And now one must reassess everything he did or said in light of that act, which is precisely what he desired. Will it have any effect? I don't think so. He had some imitators and his ashes got stolen, but I don't think in this headlong economic rush, leading lemminglike to the sea, that Japan is going through now, I don't think one single man's act can stem it. After all, part of the shock of the act was the very anachronistic quality of it.

RB: Then what he said about the death of the Japanese spirit is true, not mere opinion? And if this act has no reverberations, you feel it must be true?

DR: It is true. In 1950, it would have shaken Japan like an earthquake. Now, Mishima's act shook it, it shook it very much, it turned the whole place upside down for a day or two; but that's all it did. So he proved the truth of the basis for his beliefs.

体験
# 4

## IWAO HOSHII
Naturalized Japanese
Financial Researcher

He first arrived in Japan in 1935 from Germany as a missionary of the Society of Jesus. After a period of study at Fordham University, he returned to Japan in 1940 and, except for occasional trips abroad, has resided there since. Peter J. Herzog, as he was known before acquiring Japanese citizenship, left the Society of Jesus in 1957 and presently works as a financial researcher. Among his publications are *The Economic Challenge to Japan, The Dynamics of Japan's Business Evolution,* and *Japan's Business Concentration.* He is the coauthor (with T. M. F. Adams) of *A Financial History of Modern Japan.*

RB: The most famous naturalized citizen of Japan is Lafcadio Hearn, and the anecdotes most often heard about him concern his disenchantment with his adopted country. Have you experienced any disenchantment with Japan?

IH: I would not use the term "disenchantment" because what is foremost in my mind are my own insufficiencies. For example, I cannot write in Japanese or make Japanese-style speeches. What this means is that I could not become a politician, and I am very interested in politics and very dissatisfied with the present political system. My ability to communicate in the Japanese way is inadequate, although I have been reading and speaking the language for many years. It is not that

I cannot communicate efficiently, it is instead the flavor of my speech. I cannot make the right kind of jokes, nor can I select the right literary or historical allusion for the occasion.

Another problem is that of identifying with Japan and the Japanese. My feeling for Japan is very strong—although not for everything, of course. But I am not regarded as a Japanese by the Japanese. My face does not fit. This does not mean they do not trust me; they do. But the foreigner in Japan remains outside the usual social framework. The Japanese belongs to a certain family and has gone to a certain school, and he is classified socially according to these things. He has no separate identity from them. On the other hand, I am classified by the bank I work for. The Fuji Bank is a large, well-known, respected bank, and when I am introduced as an employee of the bank, people can feel secure about me; they know Fuji would not take on a disreputable foreigner. But in certain senses, though I work for Fuji, I am not integrated into it; I am an alien element. This means that I do not have that social position which is essential to any Japanese.

When I meet my former pupils, they call me *sensei*, teacher. But I am not a *sensei* in the Japanese sense, with all those peculiarly Japanese teacher-pupil connotations. They treat me with deference, of course, but the relationship is not the true Japanese teacher-pupil relationship, it is something different, a hybrid.

With my wife's family, too, there is the problem of how to classify me. Considerations arise like how to address me.

For my children there has been some of the same problem. Although their mother is Japanese, they look foreign. They attend local schools and several times have had trouble: children calling them names, and once an incident of mistreatment. I was able to straighten the matter out, fortunately, by talking to the teachers and one boy's parents. Now they are accepted, they pretty much belong.

RB: Because they have a background to which they can be referred?

IH: Yes, even though they don't look Japanese. They have the necessary credentials; I do not. You see, for many years I was on the faculty at Sophia University in Tokyo and I was identified as belonging to that institution. Although it is no longer as true as it once was, Sophia is not really a part of Japan: it too is an alien element. And so for the many people who still identify me in their memories with that institution, I am part of a foreign organization.

RB: Did you at any point think that someday you would be accepted fully in Japanese society? I think this is what lay behind Hearn's disenchantment.

IH: No, I never did. I liked the ordinary Japanese people very much, and I still do. The Establishment? That's a different story: I feel very strongly against it. The Japanese social system, the political system, the economic system—all are completely corrupt.

RB: As a Japanese citizen do you feel an obligation to try to reform the society?

IH: I don't feel an obligation, but I would like to reform it. If I were truly Japanese, I would like to become a politician or even a political commentator. If I could think and express myself as a native-born Japanese I would like to write about Japanese politics. I have written in English about Japanese politics and economics, but it is no use, it has no effect. And this makes me feel handicapped.

RB: Why did you become a Japanese citizen—why Japan?

IH: When I was in Germany as a novice, I thought I would like to be sent to Japan, although I knew very little about it. Later I volunteered to go to Japan and was sent here in 1935. Later, many years later, they wanted to send me back to Germany, and so I quit the order. I wanted very much to stay in Japan and my reasons for becoming a citizen were practical. There is the problem of renewing visas every three years, of being restricted to certain kinds of work, and I wanted to marry a Japanese woman.

It wasn't difficult to become a citizen. You have to have

resided here five years, have two people vouch for your character, and submit the proper papers. The procedures only took about six months.

RB: Almost every foreigner who has spent some time in Japan has mentioned the difficulties of adjusting to social relations there. Arthur Koestler put it this way: "[the system of *giri* and *on* puts] a considerable strain on professional and private relationships, and not only the foreigner walks constantly on thin ice over the unstable crust of brittle superegos—the Japanese must use equal circumspection, but he has the advantage of having learned to skate."[1] In Koestler's sense, have you mastered the art of skating Japanese style?

IH: My impression is that all of this *giri* and *on* business of reciprocal obligations has been overemphasized by foreign observers. This system—it is partly concerned with deep human relations and partly with etiquette—it does not cause everyday problems. I have to admit that I am in an advantageous position in this respect because my wife can tell me what the proper thing to do is. So I never feel any anxiety about my social obligations. My wife will tell me to whom I should send a gift at midyear or yearend, and how to behave at weddings, funerals, and so on.

In Japanese society you must always be sure to pay due respect. In the office, for instance, you must remember that there are proper ways of showing the man in a position superior to yours that you are aware of his position. You must show deference. You don't go over a person's head: you use the proper channels.

RB: What this means, of course, is that before you can take any action you must stop to consider the positions and feelings of everyone concerned.

IH: Yes. As long as you don't want to be a crusader, as long as you don't want to impose your views on anyone, there aren't any great difficulties.

1. Arthur Koestler, *The Lotus and the Robot* (New York: The Macmillan Co., 1960).

RB: In your opinion, then, the people who would feel the strain that Koestler speaks of would be "individualistic."

IH: Individualistic or impatient or selfish or those who can't stand things as they are. If you want to reform things or do them in a hurry you will have trouble. You must respect the Japanese way of doing things. Getting along presupposes that you know what to do and conform to the rules of social behavior.

As I said, Sophia University is a place *sui generis*. When I was there I did things pretty much my own way and did not care much what the Japanese thought. But since I left it I have had to learn to conform to the Japanese way of doing things. It is not that you cannot speak your piece: you can, but you must learn to do it in the Japanese way.

RB: A few minutes ago you said that you were dissatisfied with the social, political, and economic systems here. Does criticizing them cause you any difficulty?

IH: My work has nothing to do with this. There I do my work, do what the bank wants me to do. The other—talking or writing about these things—this is my private life.

RB: You can do all the criticizing you want without jeopardizing your position in any way?

IH: Sure. For instance, if someone asks me what I think of the national budget, I just tell them it's phony. Or if they ask me about Prime Minister Tanaka's plan to "remodel the Japanese archipelago," I say it's crazy, a cheat.

I don't feel constraint. At the same time I don't go out of my way to offer my opinions, but when I'm asked I don't conceal my true opinions.

As foreigners, we sometimes feel that a confrontation is necessary, that it will clear the air. But this will never do in Japan. Confrontations are to be avoided. And they are ineffective.

RB: Relatively speaking, would you say that the Japanese way of handling social relations is better than the Western way?

IH: I wouldn't say it's a better way, but in Japanese

society if you are going to make an impression you must do things the Japanese way. You should not kick up a row in Japanese society. Of course sometimes I must do things my own way. When someone is smoking on the train I go to them and tell them to put out the cigarette. My wife always tells me I should not do it, but I do it anyway. And when someone in a crowd pushes, I push back.

RB: What has caused you the most difficulty in adjusting to Japanese society?

IH: Thinking. You see, the Japanese way of thinking is analytical: they are always preoccupied with detail, they are meticulous. They stick to fixed forms and concepts, they are always cataloging things and so they put things neatly into boxes and label them.

RB: And one of those labels is *gaijin*, foreigners!

IH: Yes! And they are very great for repeating slogans and for using catch phrases without thinking about the meanings. Journalists, for example, repeat endlessly the same phrases, the same clichés, without any consideration of what the words in them mean. There is great concern for the form of language. And a foreigner can only make a contribution to the work in a cooperative effort as far as language is concerned; they do not want anything substantive from him.

Another problem is the Japanese value system, their system of priorities. Considerations which we Westerners would assign a very low priority they make first, considerations of form that we feel have no relation to the substance. For example, in school your student does not study and flunks. But the school authorities will say *kawaiso,* "the poor boy," and they will give him a passing grade. Another example: when a thing must and can be done, they will evade it by raising objections of little or no real relevance and saying *shikata ga nai,* "it can't be helped."

The Japanese are very great for falling for crackpot ideas. Take Prime Minister Tanaka's plans for remodeling Japan: completely phony, completely absurd, but all the politicians consent to it and all the journalists write about it—without really considering its implications. The reason I call Tanaka's plan phony is that it uses the label of national welfare for subsidizing industry. The basic features of Tanaka's plan, the creation of new "core" cities and a new network of super-highways and superexpress railroad lines, is entirely irrelevant to national welfare. It might even worsen present conditions. I don't deny that there are serious deficiencies in housing, sewerage, roads, and other infrastructural facilities. But these deficiencies can be remedied without building new industrial cities and new expressways. If Tanaka wants to give priority to national welfare, he should start by improving the social security system to such an extent that people can live on their old-age pensions and welfare payments. It's ridiculous to raise welfare payments from ¥3,000 [about $11.50] to ¥5,000 [about $19] a month and call this an improvement of national welfare. The country needs more nurses, more social workers, more and better institutions for the physically handicapped much more than new bullet trains.

Tanaka used national welfare only as a slogan, maybe a smokescreen, but the present system of "industry first" remains unchanged. For national welfare, the present system would have to be scrapped. He should abolish all direct and indirect subsidies to industry and agriculture, including preferential tax treatment and financing privileges. As you know, small businessmen, who even now don't pay their fair share of taxes, still get more favorable tax treatment. Because Taro Takemi, the president of the Japan Medical Association, has enormous political clout, the seventy-two-percent exemption of the income of medical practitioners hasn't been changed. It's about time that the wartime rice distribution system, which has been kept alive in order to secure the farm vote for the Liberal-Democratic Party, was scrapped. The Japan Development Bank, the Export-Import Bank, and most public corporations and special companies should be eliminated. Only a few perform a function which is in the public interest.

Tanaka says his plan will solve the pollution problem. His plan will only spread pollution. What is needed first is to solve the technical problem of building factories, steel mills, and oil refineries that won't pollute the atmosphere. If you build more highways before you develop a clean engine, you will only get more foul air. Industry, of course, is quite happy if the government lends it the money at low interest rates for relocating its old obsolete plants from the crowded cities to sites where it can build more efficient plants.

One of the worst features of Tanaka's plan is the system of superexpress railroads he wants to build. It's the same corrupt political waste which has bankrupted the Japan National Railways. JNR must operate local lines not because they are necessary or because they are economically useful but because the politicians want to have them for their constituencies. The politicians prevent JNR from closing unprofitable local lines and force JNR to build new lines which are sure to lose money because they promised them to their people back home. If I remember correctly, only seven out of JNR's two hundred sixty lines operate at a profit. It's the same scandalous waste as the bridge between Honshu and Shikoku. Because the politicians couldn't agree which of three projects should be built, they built all three bridges, a waste of three trillion yen.

Tanaka's plan will enlarge this system of unnecessary and wasteful local lines to superexpress proportions. JNR can make a profit on the New Tokaido Line because you have an extremely dense traffic pattern. But you can't expect to run such a large number of bullet trains between Sapporo and Tokyo or Kagoshima and Osaka. For these distances, air travel is more economical. Even now, JNR has trouble with the noise from the bullet trains. So the noise pollution will be spread to the rest of the country. Of course, industry will make money and the land speculators will make money if you build hundreds of kilometers of new expressways or railroads, but anybody who thinks that building superexpress railroads or superhighways in order to attract people to depopulated areas is in the national interest should have his head examined. Tanaka, of course, knows on which side his bread is buttered.

For another crazy idea, take the five-day week: what the average worker needs is not more time off—he doesn't know how to use his free time now—but more money to improve the quality of life. Another thing is the government's international prestige projects: the Olympics in 1964, Expo '70, and the Winter Olympics in 1972—absolutely crazy! Look at the schools: many are prewar buildings, firetraps. Or housing and sanitation, which are in very bad shape: instead of building low-cost houses in Tokyo, each ward has built or is building a new multistoried ward office. How unrealistic can you get! And the public hospitals are revolting. The government puts no money into them.

It's this ordering of priorities that upsets me. The Japanese have no sense of social consciousness, of social justice. This is what makes it difficult for me to adjust to Japanese society.

RB: An acquaintance of mine recently remarked that modern technological societies have a tendency to produce people who are "like fat sexless laboratory rats," and of all the places he'd visited in recent years, Tokyo and Tokyoites displayed this tendency to the highest degree. He said this was because of the "general widespread docility of the Japanese before authority, their materialism, their easy acceptance of overcrowded and terribly inadequate living and working conditions, and their low-keyed lifestyles." Does this view correspond in any way with your own?

IH: I'm not in a position to compare Tokyo with other cities, but I've observed modern life in Tokyo for many years. Nowadays you have no pleasure, because of the noise, the crowded conditions, the pollution. Second, we have lost the old way of living, the old amenities, the old landscapes. In speaking of the impact of technology, we must take into account at the same time the Japanese social structure and their way of thinking.

There has been a technological revolution of sorts in Japan, but the changes have been confined largely to the technological sphere: they have not changed the social system much or the way of thinking. In rural politics, for example, you still have the boss system, and everywhere there is still the feudal social stratification. Technology has not touched that.

There is greater social mobility now: one out of five young men can go to the university and enter a company where he can move automatically up the ladder. And of course material goods are far more plentiful than in the prewar, wartime, and immediate postwar periods. But you still have a stratified and monolithic social structure.

One reason you have had no change is the political immaturity of the Japanese. The ordinary people are indifferent to politics. Even the communists seem to have given up the idea of reforming society. Nowadays they talk of working within the social framework.

About the likeness to fat sexless laboratory rats—well, the people at the top, the government and business leaders, they give this impression, and they don't do much. The people who do the real work are those at the lower levels. They are very studious, very serious, very knowledgeable, and they remain anonymous. They don't give this impression of being laboratory rats at all.

The Japanese government is one of the most corrupt in the world. Not so much in the sense of graft and bribery—although there is enough of that, too—corrupt in the sense that it is one-sided, biased, unfair, detrimental to the common good. Government works in the interest of big business and the large agricultural organizations, the latter largely to get the votes.

The ruling alliance of the bureaucrats, government, and big business is what has shaped present-day Japan. The alliance started with Prime Minister Ikeda. The object of the game is money. Big business wants the politicians to make policy favorable to them and they need the high bureaucrats to see that the policies are carried out. They are willing to pay very

well for this. The politicians are paid by direct political con-
tributions, the bureaucrats by sinecures in public corporations
expressly set up for this purpose. Each ministry has its own
private fiefs of public corporations into which its chiefs can
move. And when a high government official reaches retire-
ment age, he leaves the government and moves over into a
position that big business has saved for him. These positions
and the public-corporation sinecures are payment for the
help given to big business.

This system, you can see, is not the result of technology's
impact but of the peculiarities of the Japanese social system.

RB: This, then, is an instance of the highly prized group
harmony working to the disadvantage of the majority.

IH: Yes. Technology did have an impact, of course. Without the technical growth we would not have had business and
corruption on the present scale.

RB: What do you think of Herman Kahn's remark that
the twenty-first century might be Japan's century?

IH: Since Kahn made his predictions, certain premises
upon which they are based have changed. Take, for instance,
the American approach to China, which Kahn did not take
into consideration. This accelerated Japan's approach to
China and the subsequent loosing of her ties with Taiwan.
This has introduced completely new possibilities to the world
power scheme.

In ten years' time Japan was able to become a leading
economic power. Because she could do this, she has become a
disturbing element in international trade. China can repeat
this growth pattern—and on a much larger scale. Japan could
do it because she had a closed economy; consequently, she
could finance her growth with domestic credit without inviting inflation or bankruptcy. The Chinese can do the same
because they too have a closed economy and can shut off any
foreign penetration that might prove disturbing. And like the
Japanese, the Chinese can buy all the technology necessary
for economic expansion.

The greatest difference, to my mind, is the education level. Japan's was very high when her expansion began. This made it possible to bring mass industries to a very high level of efficiency in a very short time. But I don't think that Chinese education, as mass education, is at that level. They may, however, be able to raise their educational standard in a very short time. If they do, then we may have a situation in the next century very different from what Kahn had in mind.

RB: Do you think Japan should scrap the constitution imposed—or bestowed—on her by the Americans and, as has been suggested, "devise one based on the realities of her social system"?

IH: Any amendment to the present constitution or any new constitution would be less democratic, therefore less desirable. Unless there is a wholly new process to replace the present one of representative government, it is better to keep the present system. The representative system is an anachronism, a relic of the time when Americans were spread widely across their country without adequate communication facilities. They needed agents to represent them to their government. Nowadays, representatives are no longer necessary; the system is obsolete. Because all that it does is give certain people a chance to make money.

I don't mean by this that the present constitution could not be improved. For instance, there is a need to clarify Japan's right to self-defense. You could have stronger popular elections of local executives. You could have some form of proportional representation. You could have strong laws against business making donations to political parties. You could have a clarification of judicial review; for to my mind the Supreme Court completely neglects its duties. The Japanese justices have said that politics is not their field, and to my mind this is a disaster. You could eliminate the present meaningless referendum of Supreme Court justices. You could regulate state subsidies. You could abolish the House of Councillors or reform it into a completely different body.

But reforms aside, if you made a constitution based on Japan's present social system, that would be the worst thing you could do, because you would perpetuate the present monopoly of power of big businessmen, politicians, and the top-level bureaucrats.

RB: Is there any justification in your mind for the epithet "economic animal" as it has been applied to the Japanese?

IH: The Japanese have a certain singleness of purpose, and when they want to make money they make money. They want that now. In the postwar period there has been a lack of national values because the older values were discredited because of the disaster of defeat. Consequently the only values the present-day Japanese know about are economic values.

RB: In addition to loyalty, honor, and respect for one's superiors and inferiors, one of the old values most esteemed was austerity, wasn't it?

IH: Yes, but now money has become the only measure of success. There are other values, power and pleasure, for instance, but these can only be purchased with money, so that the only conscious goal is amassing money. Politics is a good example: the politician considers his investment of himself in politics as a business investment. He needs money to get a position and then he needs to concentrate on making that position yield a big profit. In that sense he is not a statesman but just another businessman.

What I've said so far does not mean that the individual Japanese does not have other goals. He does; he wants a respectable position, he wants a house and a small garden, and he wants to send his children to good schools so that they may succeed in life. But these are not national values, they are, in a sense, primitive values and haven't much to do with national purpose. So, when you look at the Japanese, what sticks out is the quest for more and more money.

Americans, too, want to make money. But as a people, they don't give the impression that this is the only thing they are after. They want power, and perhaps they want to dominate the world. But as for the Japanese, you don't know what besides money they want.

RB: Do you think the Japanese work too hard?

IH: Traditionally, the Japanese attitude and way of working is different from that of Americans and northern Europeans. They have a more relaxed way, they don't put every ounce of strength into the work at hand. This does not mean that they don't work diligently; they do, but they take their time about it. The construction workers that you see every day in Tokyo and all the big cities are a good example. They come to work early in the morning, but the first thing they do is build a big fire and stand around talking and warming themselves. When it gets dark they are still at the building site, still working, but still going at a leisurely pace. Nobody is killing himself and still the work gets done.

It's the same in many offices. In our office the only man who quits at five is me.

RB: No wonder you're still considered a foreigner.

IH: Yes! But about this business of the Japanese working hard: it's necessary to make a distinction between kinds of people. Take the office workers you see on the trains every morning; almost all of them will be reading something. They occupy that time in this way—

RB: They do read a lot, but not much can be said for the quality of most of the reading material.

IH: That's true. And when they have leisure time they spend it in watching television, going to the races, or perhaps playing mah-jongg from morning till night. The point is that they put in long hours at a relatively relaxed pace and they take things easy outside the office.

The factory workers are another good example. They think of little else but recreation when their eight-hour day is done. Very few factory or office workers know how to make good use of their leisure time. However, an important consideration here is that in the present system it would not do them much good to study on their own and try to put to practical use what they learn. They would not be promoted any sooner; they would still have to wait their turn in the seniority system. So, you see, there is little incentive to work hard or to learn how to make good use of their leisure time.

Of course there are quite a large number of sincere studious people who read a great deal, who study English or other foreign languages, who try to use their minds. But they are the exceptions; most people search only for amusement.

RB: Do you think that as the Japanese go on to greater economic achievements, they will lose their sense of inferiority toward the West?

IH: They certainly have an inferiority complex, but it is only partially conditioned by economic factors. The present-day inferiority complex developed during the Meiji era [1868–1912]. In early Japan, in different periods, there was great admiration for China because so many cultural imports originated there. But this admiration was restricted to small groups of people, Buddhist priests, scholars, and the aristocracy. The problem of the late nineteenth and the twentieth centuries, however, was largely technical and military inferiority. There were also racial factors involved. In the prewar and wartime military mentality you can find overcompensation for feelings of racial inferiority in the fanatical insistence on the racial superiority of the Japanese.

RB: It's interesting that while the Japanese are nowadays being accused of excessive materialism, the people who before the war insisted on Japan's innate superiority pointed to her "spiritual superiority as opposed to the West's materialism."

IH: Yes, but today's young Japanese are not affected by this. They have great admiration for the West, but not for its technology or its military accomplishments. They admire the Western human form—the young men find Western girls more beautiful than Japanese women. The young people admire Western fashions—clothing, cosmetics, hair styles, music—and imitate them. The older people remember and are affected by the old sense of inferiority, but not the young.

RB: So there is admiration but not inferiority?

IH: Yes. The modern buildings you see in all the Japanese cities, to the young Japanese these are not Western buildings but Japanese buildings. Lipstick is an example: to the Japanese who have grown up seeing Japanese women wearing lipstick, it is Japanese. And Western-style clothing and foods, many of these are everyday items and so are considered Japanese. The older people make distinctions between "Western style" and "Japanese style" that the young people do not bother with. So many of the elements that comprised the Meiji and prewar inferiority complex are no longer present.

RB: As a consequence of this, do you think that as the generation that came to maturity in the postwar period move into positions of influence and have to deal with foreigners they will be able to do so less emotionally than their predecessors?

IH: I think so. An important element here is language. Very few of the older Japanese can speak a foreign language, and this makes it difficult for them to associate with foreigners. Of the postwar generation, however, thousands upon thousands of them have learned and are learning foreign languages, particularly English. What this has meant is that the older people seldom had a chance to deal with foreigners, and, in fact, in the old system they did not have a real social slot for them, as they have for each Japanese, and consequently they did not know how to deal with them. Many of the young people, on the other hand, have had opportunities to associate with foreigners, large numbers visit foreign lands every year, and they are becoming confident in their international experiences. The old feeling of inferiority and discomfort is giving way to one of ease.

RB: One source of anxiety about Japan arises from the question of whether or not when her leaders no longer feel they have to assume a low profile internationally they will display the restraint necessary to avoid conflict with other nations. What answer would you give to this question?

IH: There are two sides to it: one is Japan's objective position, the other is her leadership.

First, more than any other nation Japan relies on international relations for essential raw materials, for fuel, for foods. She also needs them for export markets, not only to pay for the imports but also to maintain her industrial structure. In some product lines more than half of what is produced is sold abroad. Another aspect of her international position is her political and military relations with the United States, a very tenuous relationship. Actually, it is a strange, a historically and culturally perverse alliance. You see, in history Japan has always been in confrontation with the United States.

RB: Except for that short period at the start of the Meiji era.

IH: That was forced cooperation; she cooperated out of necessity. So basically her present relationship with the United States is against the historical pattern. And it is also against her economic position because they are great rivals.

I would say that Japan is fundamentally isolated. If such schemes as the Pacific Basin Plan and the Asian Common Market were to work out, it would be good for Japan, but I don't think the United States would support an economic bloc that would give advantages to Japan, organizations that would include the U.S., Canada, Australia, New Zealand, and Japan.

Also, none of the small nations of Asia will follow Japan's leadership; they are wary of Japan. They want Japan to do things for them but they don't want to join any alliances under her leadership.

Any kind of policy that might lead to a military confrontation is out of the question for Japan. A military conflict with any of the superpowers is unthinkable. No amount of rearmament would allow the Japanese to challenge the United States, or Russia, or China. And a conflict between Japan and any nation in Southeast Asia or Korea would be stopped by the United States or China.

RB: In other words, Japan couldn't get into a Vietnam-like situation?

IH: I don't think so. What this also means is that other nations do not have to take Japan into account militarily. Not seriously.

RB: And yet there have been cries of alarm about "reviving Japanese militarism" because of her military buildup.

IH: Yes, and this is crazy. The superpowers will not let her engage in military adventures, and the present buildup is useless, a waste of money.

RB: Why do you think Japan is building up her military forces?

IH: On account of American pressure, and because the present leadership wants to remain on good terms with the Americans. The craziest part of this is that the Japanese leaders have not really thought about Japan's defense. They have no independent defense policy: their policy is an adjunct of the American defense policy; it's based on American scenarios and not on Japan's needs. So it's completely phony.

RB: What kind of policy do they need?

IH: Japan needs some kind of arrangement with the superpowers. She cannot do this militarily, however, and I don't know how she could achieve it. For instance, the United States would never let her form an economic alliance with China or Russia. Such an alliance would be too formidable.

The other aspect of her isolation is that Japan belongs neither to the West nor to the East. She is unique, and because she is unique she has been able to assimilate many things from the West without losing her identity. These things have been Japanized, even Western ways of thinking, thinking about art, about life and death. You have a Japanese way of thinking about life and death and a Western way, and the Japanese writers have taken to exploring the Western way, thinking about those problems in a Western way. But still they are not Westernized.

RB: Would you say they are being internationalized?

IH:   No, they remain uniquely Japanese. They don't regard the things they have adopted as Western or international. It's strange to us, but these things become Japanese. Furthermore, though Japan is part of Asia geographically, racially, and even to some extent culturally, the labels "Asia" and "Asian" do not describe her reality very well. This means that she does not belong to the East or to the West.

Financially, Japan has invested deeply in the West. In 1969 she became a creditor nation, and Tokyo is gradually emerging as an international money market. But here again, this market is peculiarly Japanese. It's a very special institution, and if you want to deal in Tokyo you must meet very special conditions. For example, the yen problem: as far as currency is concerned the yen is isolated. You have no complete integration of Japan into the international financial system.

RB:   We could almost say, then, that like the foreigner who lives in Japan and has only one foot in Japanese society, Japan has only one foot in international society.

IH:   Yes, that is Japan's objective position. And there is the second problem of the Japanese leaders. No single Japanese in the postwar period is a leader of international stature. You have astute and able businessmen but not international leaders. None, not even Shigeru Yoshida,[2] who was the only outstanding politician.

Throughout the postwar period Japan's leaders have been struggling with problems that have been thrust upon her, problems that have arisen out of her relations with the United States. They have never taken any initiative in order to make policy; because they haven't the leadership.

RB:   We could say then that she is internationally other-directed.

IH:   Yes. The options are largely forced on her. Decisions are largely ad hoc decisions, made to meet current situations.

2. Shigeru Yoshida (1878–1967) was a postwar leader of the Liberal-Democratic party. He became prime minister in 1946 and held that office until 1953.

This situation is due in large part to the educational system. Their education is largely abstract; as far as foreign countries are concerned, the Japanese leaders always think in clichés. As I mentioned earlier, they do not have much international experience. The businessmen that have been abroad do not have much influence because they have been abroad, cut off from the essential social contacts of their organizations. There are also a number of diplomats who have spent a great deal of time abroad, but they are part of the bureaucracy: if they don't please the ministers, out they go.

You see, the situation in Japan is against the emergence of a strong leader. There exists a climate of conformity, and in order to become a leader, a man must be thoroughly Japanese. Therefore, there is very little chance for an international personality to assert himself in Japan. Most Japanese leaders are leaders of a group, a faction, and a leader must have this foundation or he will have no influence in Japan. Take all the ministers: they are chosen not because they are able individuals but because they represent a political faction. Take the business people, a man like Kogoro Uemura,[3] for instance, who has come up the business ladder and been an executive: he wields his influence for Japanese industry and nothing else.

RB: What you said about both the objective and subjective situations of Japan indicates that she is in no better a position for dealing effectively with international problems than she was prior to World War II.

IH: In many ways the present time resembles the interwar period: the same alliance of businessmen, bureaucrats, and politicians exists.

RB: What's missing is the military power, but that is increasing.

IH: Yes, but the military men are apolitical.

---

3. Kogoro Uemura is the present head of Keidanren (Federation of Economic Organizations), Japan's most influential association of industrialists.

# 体験
# 5

## HUGO M. ENOMIYA-LASSALLE
### German
### Catholic Priest

Father Enomiya-Lassalle was born in 1898 in Germany and entered the priesthood as a Jesuit in 1919. He first went to Japan in 1929 where he taught at Tokyo's Sophia University during the years 1931–38. During World War II, while still in Japan, he began to practice *zazen*, the Zen Buddhist method of meditation. In 1969 he founded Shimmeikutsu, a meditation center located in the mountains of western Tokyo, and there he teaches *zazen* to Japanese and foreigners alike. Originally published in German, his *The Zen Way to Enlightment* has been translated into English, Japanese, French, and Spanish. His *Zen Meditation for Christians* will be published in English in late 1973.

RB:  What elements of Japanese culture do you think could be successfully transplanted in the West?

HL:  Zen has a great appeal for Westerners now. And I don't think this is simply a fad, a boom; the interest will continue for a time, I believe. Of course there are people who try the *zazen* method of meditation and they soon realize that it is difficult and they give up. At the same time, you know, there have been a number of foreigners who have persisted and have achieved *satori,* genuine enlightenment. So Westerners do not have to worry that Zen meditation is for the Japanese only.

Many people look at Zen as a means to gain composure, to quiet their nerves. I will not say that there are not other ways to do this—in Europe, for example, there is the autogenic method discovered by Professor Helmuth Schultz, which is well known and much practiced in Germany. And there is a long tradition of meditation in Christianity for religious purposes. But most people who know something about Christian meditation think that the only form it takes is thinking about some matter. There are forms of Christian meditation, however, that are close to that of Zen, in which you do not think.

Many people are very surprised when you show them the parallels between Zen and Christianity. I have known people who became Buddhists and who later told me that they learned what Christiantity is through Buddhism. It was while studying Buddhism, for example, that they heard for the first time that there were Christian mystics.

RB: The Catholic church has deemphasized mysticism, hasn't it, since about the time of the Renaissance?

HL: It hasn't been emphasized because there were abuses and mistakes and because the influence of rationalism became very strong.

RB: Why did you choose the Zen method of meditation rather than one of the traditional Christian methods, for example, the methods suggested by St. Ignatius in his *Spiritual Exercises?*

HL: It is not that I have chosen between the Zen method and Christian methods; I have used both. I was brought up in the Christian tradition and I have discovered that Zen meditation has helped to deepen this Christian experience.

RB: What kind of response in Japan has your work in Zen received?

HL: As you know, it is rather difficult to get genuine criticism in Japan—it is not the polite thing to do, especially in a face-to-face situation. It is often quite difficult to know with any certainty how people feel about matters.

In any case, the Zen masters I have spoken to have been

encouraging. Zen Buddhist monks have visited us at our meditation center, and I think that this can be accepted as a kind of acknowledgment. One master even told me that he had read parts of one of my books to his students. And no one has protested—at least I have not heard of any protests. My master, the late Sessui-roshi—encouraged me and wrote an introduction to the Japanese edition of my book *The Zen Way to Enlightenment.*

The Rinzai sect, however, is very strict about who teaches about Zen. They feel that only a master who has had an enlightenment experience and who has had that experience certified by his master should teach Zen meditation. But Harada Sogaku-roshi said that anyone can teach about Zen as far as they have experienced it; in other words, a person who has not had an enlightenment experience should not decide on it but should send a disciple who seems to have obtained enlightenment to a master who has had this experience.

I ought to add that Zen masters are not narrow-minded. But between Rinzai and Soto and even between single masters there is a lot of criticism. But it seems they don't mind it too much. Also, they do not try to make conversions and do not engage in any kind of progaganda. They simply wait for people to come to them and then they try to help them. If a person who comes to them is sincere in learning about the Zen way of life, they will teach him, but they do not try to persuade people to become Buddhists.

RB: How has the Catholic church responded?

HL: There have been a few individuals who are not happy about what I am doing, but I have received a great deal of encouragement. The Pope told me personally, "I pray for the success of your work." And the Superior General of the Jesuit order has encouraged me to continue my investigations. As you might know, the church has been encouraging some experimentation in recent years, so I have not met with any difficulties of this sort.

RB: In *The Lotus and the Robot* Arthur Koestler has written that Zen is the necessary complement to the severe restrictions of Japanese life. This suggests to me that Zen might not fare so well in less restrictive societies or in societies whose restrictions are quite different from those of Japan. Do you agree with this?

HL:  I should say only one word in answer: no. But perhaps we can talk a little about it. I believe Koestler was sincere in his criticism. But I have the feeling he was seeking something spiritual when he visited the Orient. Don't you agree?

RB:  Yes, and I think that because he did not find it he was greatly disappointed, and that disappointment affected his objectivity.

HL:  One important thing to keep in mind is that while present-day Zen is Japanese in many ways, the Zen communities still follow many of the old traditions brought from China. And they still use, for example, the koans that were developed hundreds of years ago in China.

At the same time, there are elements of Zen today that probably were not present before it came to Japan. The tea ceremony, for example, although it has roots in China, is very Japanese now. And the mixture of Zen and the arts is distinctly Japanese, as is the cult of cleanliness which they brought into Zen. So there are special Japanese features, but the Zen that came to Japan was largely Chinese. It is also perhaps true, as has been said, that there are no two people more different in the world than the Chinese and the Japanese.

RB:  Do you think that the essence of Zen can be separated from its attributes? For instance, can the *zazen* method alone be adapted by Westerners without taking at the same time Buddhist beliefs, the rituals, and the lifestyle with which it is intricately interrelated in Japan?

HL:  That is exactly what we are doing at Shimmeikutsu, our meditation center. We are not Buddhists here, although Buddhists may come and meditate with us, as anyone else may. We have a chapel here and we celebrate Mass; those who want to can attend. We follow some Zen methods, for example, the rule of silence at mealtimes, sitting in the meditation center in the Japanese style, and the use of koans, while at the same time there are many customs which we do not observe; for instance, instead of reciting sutras we recite psalms.

One of the leading Zen masters has said that you must distinguish between Zen and the Zen sect—they are two different things.

Zen is something general; it can be found in all religions, while the Zen sect cannot. Perhaps Zen "sect" is not such a good term: what I mean is Zen Buddhism. Zen means "meditation," and is originally from the Sanskrit *dhyana*. The meditation method can be separated from Zen Buddhism. Even within Zen Buddhism a distinction is sometimes made; for example, during meditation you are not allowed to think of the teachings of Buddha. In *zazen* you must stop thinking completely so that a deeper mental activity can take place, so that intuition can come forth.

RB: Then the *zazen* system is compatible with Christianity?

HL: It is compatible, yes, even though the West has not developed this particular method of meditation. The Eastern Catholic, or Orthodox, church, has a method similiar to that of some Buddhist sects of meditation by invocation—in this case they invoke the name of Jesus, whereas some Buddhist groups invoke the Lotus Sutra. The Eastern Catholic method of invocation seems to have come from the East; it's not a part of traditional Christianity.

RB: Do you think Zen will be Christianized or Christianity Zen-ized, or will nothing of this sort happen?

HL: I don't think anything of this sort will happen. It smells a bit of syncretism. I think there will be no mixture of the two. There should not be; the Japanese Zen Buddhists don't want this, either. The first fruit of the meeting between religions should be to learn one's own religion. By studying other religions, you get to know your own. This kind of meeting is not for the purpose of comparing religions to see which is better. No. One of the fruits received by many Christians who have studied Zen is that they have learned of the existence of the Christian mystics and something of Christian mysticism.

RB: In *The Japanese and the Jews,* the author says that many Christian missionaries who come to Japan to convert the Japanese end up being Japanized themselves. It is they who are converted; the Christian Japanese become Christian less than the foreign missionaries become adherents of Nihonism. Have you observed anything like this?

HL: No, I haven't, although I'm not sure what's meant by "Japanized." The missionaries who go to Japan of course use the Japanese language and many of them learn to live in the Japanese style, but this can hardly be described as conversion to a religion.

RB: I think he overstates his case and is really describing the phenomenon whereby some zealous missionaries go to Japan believing they are going to save the "pagans" and end up with a sympathetic understanding of Japanese religions and lifestyles and are able to see things from Japanese viewpoints. Ben-Dasan would probably think that you have become an adherent of Nihonism because of your present lifestyle and use of *zazen.*

HL: I suppose so, but I don't think any of this has much to do with religious conversion.

Being Japanized can, of course, have good meanings. It's necessary in a sense to understand how the Japanese think if you are to introduce Christianity to them. Christianity has to be made comprehensible to the Japanese so that it will be acceptable. This is accomplished on more than one level. Someone once said to me that we expect a Japanese to learn Western philosophy before he becomes a Christian; in a limited sense this is true, but we should teach it so that they do not have to think in a Western way.

RB: Do you think that Zen is a religion best suited for an elite, that it is a way of life too esoteric for the great mass of people?

HL: When Zen was brought to Japan it was taken up by

the warrior class, who were socially above the masses of the peasants and the townsmen. The masses were converted to other, simpler forms of Buddhism, especially to Shinshu. These "popular" religions, as they have been called, did not make many demands on the people. In Shinshu, for instance, the worshipers only had to have faith and to recite an invocation in order to gain salvation. These forms of Buddhism had great appeal, especially for the outcast class, the *eta*.

On the other hand, Zen was severe and its appeal was strong for the warriors, who were taught from earliest childhood that austere living was a great virtue. During the Edo period, when there were no wars, many members of the warrior class had time for study and practice; they took up Zen as their religion. The peasants had no time for sitting in meditation because their lives were filled with work, and the townsmen were more inclined toward business. And Zen was very demanding—physically and psychologically.

The appeal to intellectuals was strong before World War II, and nowadays you find that most of the young people who practice Zen are university students. The workers have other interests.

It is in a way an elite religion—because it is difficult. But there are quite a few people who want to practice *zazen*, both Japanese and foreigners.

Let me give you an example. Recently, a young European came to me. He very much wanted to enter a Zen monastery and practice the Zen way. Because he was sincere, I sent him to a monastery where I knew the master was a good master. Not much time passed before the young man came back and told me that the conditions in the monastery were very severe. He said that although it was winter there was no heat at all and the doors and shutters of the meditation hall were wide open all day. He said that as soon as a meal was prepared, the cooking fires were put out so that no one would be tempted to try to warm themselves. It is difficult, but I'm happy to say that this young man is learning to bear it.

RB: Is *satori*, the sudden enlightenment of Zen, unique to this religion or is it basically the same as experiences recorded by *yogis, sufis,* St. John of the Cross, and St. Teresa of Avila?

HL: In general, enlightenment is something that has been found in all times, in all religions, and even without religion. Great philosophers have had enlightenment experiences. Plotinus, for instance, had it—Japanese who know of his experience do not doubt it.

Catholic mystics have had the mystical experience of the absolute as a person, as God, whereas Zen enlightenment is not described in that sense. This does not mean that the Zen meditator does not experience the absolute being in his enlightenment, however.

So enlightenment is realizing absolute reality, though not necessarily as a person. In Christian mysticism the experience is bound up with faith; therefore, it is different from the Zen experience. And Buddhists do not speak at any length about enlightenment experience. Often they will describe it with only a single sentence or they'll write a haiku about it.

RB: Buddhists speak of absolute reality in negative terms, don't they—using terms like "void" and "emptiness"?

HL: Yes, that is a major difference—how it is described. Through both Zen and Christian mystical practice, you can receive visions. Zen says that you should ignore all such visions, that they rise up from the unconscious and are not expressions of true reality. St. John of the Cross also says to ignore all visions, even if you think they are from God. And the first rule of Christian spirituality is that you should not want visions. Because if a meditator wants visions, he will perhaps get them, and he may easily be deceived by what he experiences at that time.

There is one major difference between Zen and Christianity, however, one that concerns visions. Catholics believe that because God is a person he can send messages and make demands in the form of visions.

RB: Catholics believe that Joan of Arc received orders

from God, but Zen would say these were illusions—is that right?

HL: Yes. Theoretically Zen and Christianity differ about such experiences, but they are very close to each other in a psychological sense. Zen says that you must lose all attachments to perceptions and sensations if you are to experience absolute reality, and Christianity says you must do the same if you are to experience God, because God is absolutely without division.

RB: Do you agree with Sol Sanders that each Japanese is "an island unto himself. There are no more solitary individuals on the face of the earth; unable to communicate except in either clichés or bursts of emotion among themselves, much less with foreigners"?[1]

HL: No, I don't agree. Communication between a Japanese and a foreigner is difficult if the foreigner expects the Japanese to follow a logical line of thought. The Japanese mind does not go straight to the point; the Japanese prefer the discursive or roundabout way. Some people say Japanese thinking is collective, others say it is individualistic. Both descriptions are true. Because of course we are talking about a very complex thing, something too difficult to describe so simply. And nowadays, because there are so many foreign influences in Japanese life, it is even more difficult to define them—what is pure Japanese, what is the foreign influence?

I have known many Japanese with whom I could communicate well, so I can't agree with this part about "clichés and bursts of emotion." If the Japanese really had this difficulty communicating, I don't think they could have made the tremendous progress they have. They would not have made the great technological and economic advances that everyone can see. It's true that rules of courtesy require them to use many polite clichés, and they are often not spontaneous for the same reason, but they can communicate well enough.

RB: What has caused you the most difficulty in adapting to Japan?

HL: I never had any difficulties at all.

1. Sol Sanders, *A Sense of Asia* (New York: Charles Scribner's Sons, 1969).

RB: Really? You must be highly receptive to Japanese ways.

HL: Nothing bothered me—eating, sleeping, dealing with people. Of course, it was hard to learn Japanese.

RB: You had no difficulties with social relationships?

HL: No, but this is perhaps because I belonged to a missionary group and have spent much time with Europeans in Japan. I was not a young man thrown alone into Japanese society: I was past thirty when I arrived in Japan, and I had the social framework of the church and my fellow missionaries to advise and support me. And of course I was always busy, in the beginning with learning the language. Japanese is a problem, but not too much of one if you continue to study and practice.

An old Japanese man who lived abroad for many years said to me that most foreigners when they come to Japan like it. Then many of them discover the human weaknessess of the Japanese and they are disappointed. But those who stay for twenty or thirty years seem to genuinely appreciate it. These longtime residents—not all of them, of course—understand how complex Japan is and because they are usually deeply involved they don't make many generalizations about the Japanese. You know, it is very difficult to speak about such broad matters as Japan and the Japanese when you have been here for many years. When you make a generalization, you can always think of so many examples that do not fit it.

RB: There is a saying that if you are going to write a book about Japan, you had better do it in your first few years of residence, otherwise you will know too much.

HL: I must say that it is true.

RB: During the many years you lived in Japan you have observed the ambition and failure of the Greater East Asia Co-Prosperity Sphere, World War II and Japan's humiliating defeat, and, recently, her rapid rise to economic prominence. How do you think the Japanese will adjust to their present venture into the international sphere?

HL: Since I'm not a political scientist I cannot go very far into this. There is no doubt that Japan is now a great economic power. Japan is now a rich country and, whether it is out of envy or not, she has caused many people from poorer countries, particularly in Southeast Asia, to dislike her.

Japan is now so deeply involved with other countries that she must take great care in how she deals with them. Japan's future depends on her relations with other nations. Until the end of World War II, Japan was very much for herself alone. The Japanese were poor then; they had little food and not many natural resources. Now they have risen in the world. They have solved their agricultural problems—they produce so much rice that they do not know what to do with it—and they have found out how to import raw materials and export finished products. They have risen very high, but I think they have not given up their former mentality. They still think in terms of people from a poor country. Perhaps they do not see themselves as being *in* the world. Instead they look out at the world—it is *outside* Japan; Japan is not inside the world in their view. There are some Japanese people who do not look at international relations from a strictly Japanese viewpoint, but I do not think there are many, at least not enough. I do think, however, that this way of looking at international matters will change.

One thing that bothers me is that I do not think that they show much concern for the welfare of others in their international economic relations. They do not seem to show much responsiblity for other peoples, unless it will bring them a profit.

Of course, some people may say that Europeans are just as selfish in such matters. But I do not agree that that is true. I believe that Europeans have changed in regard to accepting this kind of responsibility and I attribute this change—accepting the obligation to help other people, even when they are not your countrymen—to some extent to the influence of Christianity.

RB: I have found that the Japanese do not tend to think

that "all men are brothers" but that "all Japanese are brothers," although by this I certainly don't mean that they are not kind to foreigners, because I've often been kindly treated by Japanese. What I mean is that it takes an effort of will on their part to reach out and consider non-Japanese in the same way that they consider their countrymen.

HL: A Japanese acquaintance of mine lived in Europe and America for quite a few years before World War II and returned to Japan in the early years of the war. When the war was over, he told me, some Japanese came to him and asked him to make speeches on the theme of democracy and liberty. This is a difficult topic to talk about before a group of people who have not experienced such things. But this man solved it, in a way. He said to the people, Until now you always said *ware ware Nihonjin,* we Japanese. Now you must say we men. He had learned this lesson, as have other Japanese who have lived abroad, but it is a difficult thing for others to learn. It is not their customary way of thinking. However, this is changing too; the island mentality is gradually beginning to fade.

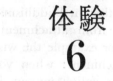

体験

# 6

## BRIAN VICTORIA
### American
### Zen Priest

Born in Nebraska thirty-four years ago, he went to Japan in 1961 as a Methodist missionary. In 1965 he entered the Zen priesthood.

Victoria Ryojun, to use his Buddhist name, describes himself as an ardent peaceworker and an active opponent of the U.S.-Japan Security Treaty and the Japanese government's proposed revision of its immigration control bill. In 1971 he wrote and had published in Japanese a brief autobiography, *Gaijin de Ari, Zen Bozu de Ari* (Foreigner and Zen Priest). He is at present located in Yokosuka, Japan, where he counsels American servicemen on their rights.

RB: Tell me something about the basic tenets of the Buddhist sect to which you belong.

BV: I belong to the Soto Zen sect. And perhaps I should start from the Zen aspect of it. That is, this sect perhaps could be simply described as *shikan taza,* which means "earnest sitting." The reason for this emphasis in the Soto Zen sect is that at the time the sect was founded—in the thirteenth century —by Dogen, a Japanese priest, he wished to stress the fact that *zazen* was not a method of becoming enlightened—that is, you did not train in a monastery, you did not do meditation, in order to become a Buddha. Rather, the training is an aspect of a Buddha. Because a man originally has the Buddha nature he can, as a real Buddha, express himself through activities such as training and meditation. Perhaps another way to say this is that in Buddhism the most important thing is to free oneself from attachment to things, to ideas, to concepts. Take for example the wish for enlightenment, in itself a kind of attachment: when you are attached even to this wish, because enlightenment is nonattachment to ideas and to things, it is impossible to realize enlightenment. And too often, especially in other sects, methodology itself becomes an end. People see methodology as a way of getting something they want, in this case enlightenment. They use the methodology as a means of getting their ends. But from the view of the Soto sect it is important to see that the methodology is an expression of the ends, of enlightenment, rather than a way of achieving enlightenment.

RB: Why did you turn away from Western religions?

BV: If Christianity can be reduced to its essentials, one of these essentials would be that it is concerned primarily with the relationship between man and God. This has been expressed primarily, at least, as the relation between oneself and another, something other than oneself. This generally means that man himself has been taken rather uncritically. The nature of man, especially the concept of the "I" in Western society, has been accepted uncritically, and while the relationship between man and other, especially between man and nature, has produced great progress in the scientific realm, I feel that as science has progressed there has been the alienation of man from his environment and of man from man, and this alienation and the feeling of alienation have increased a great deal. I think that in Hinduism and Buddhism and Taoism, where the essential factors are an understanding of oneself and introspection, and through these an understanding of one's relationship to reality in reality—these features make them very attractive as religions to Westerners.

Actually I don't think that I have really turned away from Western religions; it is not so much that I don't believe in Christianity, but that I feel that Buddhism offers a deeper insight into man than Christianity in its Western form does.

One aspect of Christianity to which I react is its exclusive claim to truth. I think this is no longer as true of modern versions of Christianity, but at least Christianity traditionally has said of itself—to paraphrase the Bible—that it has the only truth, way, light of the world. When I looked around and saw human beings in other religions, and in no religion at all, fulfilling their lives, why, then, Christianity was no longer acceptable.

RB: What religion were you brought up in?

BV: I was not really brought up in any particular sect. That is, my father was a Mexican who was sent to the United States to become a Catholic priest, but was unable to accept the ecclesiastical structure of the Catholic church and their

restrictions on intellectual freedom. So he quit the seminary
and became a lawyer. My mother was from a very fundamentalist Protestant background, one which would not allow the
women to cut their hair or to wear lipstick, and so forth. When
she grew older she reacted against this fundamentalist inter-
pretation of Christianity. My parents met in revolt against
particular restrictions of Christianity and so I was raised in a
religious atmosphere but of no particular sect because my
parents were concerned that I be able to choose freely the
particular creed by which I was going to live. When I was in
high school, I did join the Methodist church and I became a
student-minister in that church and eventually came to Japan
as a missionary.

RB:    Why did you choose the Soto Zen sect?

BV:    At the time that I began my Zen training I was not
very well informed about the differences between Soto Zen and
Rinzai Zen. So, in fact, I had not chosen to enter Soto Zen in
the beginning but was first introduced to the monastery at
Eihei-ji temple in Fukui Prefecture, which is a Soto Zen
monastery. I trained there for several weeks while I was still
a Methodist missionary and did most of my early reading on
the differences between Soto and Rinzai Zen—the two major
Zen sects in Japan—and it was through reading that I became
particularly interested in Soto Zen. This was because of its
emphasis on "earnest sitting." This is a very nondirected type
of sitting, in comparison with Rinzai's method. In Rinzai,
for instance, the master almost always assigns to the disciple
a particular koan, a particular Zen riddle. The koans are divided on the basis of their difficulty, and when a student is
able to solve one, he moves to another one, from a relatively
easy one to a more difficult one. However, in Soto Zen, during
meditation periods, generally no koans are given to the disciple.
Rather, a student's entire training is considered as a koan.
That is, he is to consider what is the nature of washing his
face in the morning, what is the nature of eating, what is the
nature of sleeping, et cetera. Your entire life is considered to

be a koan—and not only during training. As Dogen expressed it, this is the *genjo koan*, that is, to see reality itself as a big question mark, rather than to limit oneself to one particular aspect of one particular question, as in the Rinzai sect. I felt this was particularly meaningful to me in my training and because of it I chose to become a priest in the Soto Zen sect.

RB: Do you think that the term "radical," in a political sense, can be justly applied to you?

BV: Of course that depends on who is doing the applying. For instance, if I were in China, which after all contains from one fifth to one-fourth of the world's people, I would not be considered radical at all.

RB: True, and how about from the viewpoint of Western democracy, particularly the United States?

BV: To call a man a radical in Western terminology means generally that he believes society should make some kind of drastic immediate change, some kind of drastic immediate progress. And since the "common-sense" point of view is that things change very slowly, that progress is slow, even before this man opens his mouth he is labeled "unrealistic," and in a sense emotionally immature in his thinking, because—people will say—things don't work out that way. This kind of thinking is, in a way, a means of putting him in a box, to take care of him so that you really don't have to give serious consideration to what he has to say. But still, I understand that the term "radical" has a certain meaning. From the particular Buddhist point of view from which I work, I see that individuals have the potentiality of a Buddha, which I can express in English as the capability of being a true human being, of realizing one's humanness. In this sense we are progressing toward a goal, yet the goal is really existent within us, if only we would realize it, become aware of it. So, in one sense, I can say that I am an ultraconservative, because I believe that this awareness of what we already are is the important aspect. I think that there is too much of the kind of thinking in the West—even among so-called radicals—that society will be changed and taken—even forced—to progress to a particular point in the future. In one sense, I believe that this goal is not a future thing at all, but it is rather in our natures as human beings, if only we realize our natures. At the same time I feel that I should say that in Western capitalistic societies—and also in Western Marxist societies—there remains the concept of the "self," the "I," and of the things that are done for "me," or for "my family," or even for "my nation." And, particularly in Western capitalistic societies, where everything revolves around the "me," if there was a realization of the Eastern "nonself," this could not but help to change drastically the conditions in which people live. In that sense I think that I could be called a radical.

RB: How do Japanese radicalism and Western radicalism compare?

BV: There are many kinds of radicals, as I think I've indicated: there is the kind of radical that conforms to the stereotype of radicals. In America, of course, there are many kinds of radicalism. I think, for example, the kind of radicalism expressed by the leaders of the blacks is quite different from the radicalism expressed in recent years by student leaders at American universities, particularly different from that of white leaders, although in a very deep sense they share a common cause, they both feel the need for change, abrupt social change. In the case of the blacks there is a very pressing physical need arising from life in the ghettos. This need is generally not so acute for most whites, and in fact is often absent. Also, the repression directed against the two groups is very often different.

Similar to the position of the blacks is that of the military-base workers in Okinawa and the Japanese *eta* outcasts and the Koreans in Japan. On the other hand, the struggles of the Japanese students are similar to those of the white students in America.

RB: And are their methods similar?

BV: Well, recently there haven't been any major uprisings

by, for example, Korean residents in Japan. However, several years ago, almost every summer there were uprisings in the slum districts of Osaka and in Tokyo's slum district—Sanya— by the day laborers. These were small-scale uprisings. The leaders of these struggles are aware existentially of what they are doing—that is, they are deeply conscious politically. They cannot afford the luxury of anarchism in their organization; they cannot afford the luxury of egoistic thinking in which every man is the leader of the group and every man does his own thing in his own way. For these people the struggle is much more a life-and-death one than it is for the students in either Japan or America.

I've stressed the similarities of the American and Japanese movements but perhaps the differences are greater. For example, in the Japanese student movement there is the *sempai-kohai* relationship—the relationship of senior and junior students —which differs from the more individualistic relationship among American students. Another aspect of interest here is that the forms the Japanese movement takes are far more limited than those of their American counterparts. That is that the demonstrations, the scuffling with the riot police are— well, after having participated in a number of them, I've come to think of them as being almost balletlike, almost a kind of a dance on both sides. They are like set pieces in which each side knows how the other will act and how it will end but they go through the performance anyway. In America you don't have this conformity to forms; for instance, the demonstrations against American corporations and banks or those in which the students broke into the induction centers and poured blood on the records. There is what I might call creativity, a greater range of expression, in America, whereas in Japan the forms of expression and the forms of repression are clear-cut and the results known even before the operations begin.

RB: As a peaceworker, what kind of activities have you participated in while in Japan?

BV: For a number of years I took part in many of the activities of Gaikokujin Beheiren, which, as the name indicates, was an anti–Vietnam war movement.

The immediate cause for the formation of the movement, however, was concern about the new immigration bill which was advanced in the spring of 1969. There was concern among some resident Europeans and Americans as to how this bill would affect their status in Japan. As more became known about the bill, our concern grew, and as we studied the bill we came to know how it would effect the Chinese and the Koreans living here and the particular way in which the bill would repress them. We also felt that in order to promote unity among the foreign residents of Japan it was necessary to express our opinions in regard to the bill.

So these were the two main causes of the movement—its immediate cause and its underlying cause. But there was also a third cause and that was the Japan-America Security Treaty. The problem, as we saw it, with the treaty is the effect that its existence has upon the United States' ability to conduct its war in Indochina and its ability to support the Chiang Kaishek military dictatorship in Taiwan and the Park military dictatorship in South Korea. We were also concerned with how it strengthens the Japanese government's ability to repress some of its own citizens.

RB: How many members did it have?

BV: As does Beheiren, the Japanese anti–Vietnam war movement, our group claimed to be a movement rather than an organization, so that in one sense there were no members. There were only people who participated in activities in Gaikokujin Beheiren, and there were between fifteen and twenty of these. Unfortunately, the movement is now defunct. Seven participants have been or are in the process of deportation; that is, they weren't all thrown out physically, but a number were not allowed to remain in Japan, so it comes to the same thing.

RB: What activities did Gaikokujin Beheiren engage in?

BV: The most extensive activity we participated in was with

Beheiren and with other groups in anti–Vietnam war demonstrations, in anti–immigration bill demonstrations and
meetings, and in anti–Security Treaty meetings. We also helped
Beheiren to publish a GI newspaper, *We Got the Brass,* and
an English-language newspaper called *Ampo* [Security].

RB: Did you aid American deserters?

BV: No, we didn't actively do that. Beheiren has a group
called JATEC for aiding deserters—of course there is a three-
year jail penalty and a fine of several thousand dollars for
aiding and abetting American deserters—so we wouldn't get
involved. Fortunately, the movement in America and also
here in Japan decided that deserting was no longer a good
way to struggle against the American armed forces. Rather,
what we did here, and what was being done in America, was
primarily to encourage soldiers to stay in the military and
organize groups and to secure what we feel are their fundamental human rights. We wanted them to organize and express
their opinions on issues like the war in Vietnam and American
activities throughout the world.

My present work with Pacific Counseling Service is aimed
at these same goals.

RB: How did the police treat Gaikokujin Beheiren?

BV: Well, they have treated us in a number of ways. There
has been no direct repression, but let me say this, that they have
been concerned about the activities of Gaikokujin Beheiren can
be shown from the fact that there was a young Canadian man
who participated in Gaikokujin Beheiren activities just before
he went home. And he informed us that when he applied for
a new visa just three months before he left Japan the immigration authorities had questioned him closely and they said that
they—the immigration authorities, but I think that you can
say that they were working with the police—would extend his
visa if he promised to give reports on our meetings. And he
did go ahead and give reports, but at the end of that three
months he confessed to us that they had forced him to report
in order to get his visa.

RB: Was he a member of the movement before the police asked him to spy?

BV: As I've said, there were no members: it was a movement. But yes, he did participate in the movement's activities.

RB: In other words, they didn't instigate him to join the group?

BV: No, they didn't do that. But they evidently do try to intimidate people through immigration control.

RB: Many people both in the Orient and in the West think of Buddhism as a quiescent, passive religion. How does this square with your political activism?

BV: I think that that is a rather shortsighted view of Buddhist history. It's true that during the middle ages Buddhism entered a stage of decline throughout Asia, and in China and Japan it became closely associated with the ruling classes. However, before that time, in China for example, Buddhist priests were the teachers of society. They often ran orphanages and they did many of the charitable works that are associated with Christianity in the West. And in Japan the famous Buddhist prophet Nichiren had a very definite political influence on the government of his day. While his influence was perhaps not as great as he had hoped, at least it was political as well as religious, and his followers through the ages have also been politically active.

However, I would say that the main point of Buddhism is a realization of one's unity with other people and the realization of one's unity with the universe. And within this realization there cannot help but be a concern for other people. This is especially true of Mahayana Buddhism, where it is expressed in the ideal of the Bodhisattva. A Bodhisattva is a potential Buddha who sacrifices final entrance into Nirvana in order to serve others, in order to lead them to enlightenment.

I feel that, as Buddhism has developed, the spiritually related elements have been given great stress, while the physically related elements have not. By this I mean that a worker or farmer who is bound to his job or to the soil has no time for

reflective thinking and cannot be expected to practice meditation or to study Buddhism. It is only a person who has a full
stomach, who has some kind of security, who is able to reflect
upon life and upon the meaning of his own life. My own
feeling is that while human beings cannot be enlightened by
a change in social structure, at the very least a just society
is a prerequisite for a wider understanding of Buddhism and
of oneself. You cannot expect a hungry, sick, or insecure
person to understand his own position in society in a Buddhistic
sense. It is necessary, therefore, that when we say that these
conditions exist—that is, so many people being ill-housed,
ill-clothed, and sick—in many parts of the world, it is part of
a Buddhist priest's role to help people realize their human
potential, their Buddhahood.

RB: How have the temple officials and the clergy of your
temple, and the university officials reacted toward your
espousal of radical causes?

BV: Some temple officials—and I stress the word "officials"—especially in Komazawa University let me know that
I should desist. At Komazawa University some years ago there
was a student movement in which the students barricaded the
university. Although I was not openly a participant in the
barricading, I did feel that students in the Buddhist faculty
should become aware of these problems and should try to
find solutions as Buddhist students and find some as Buddhist
students to relate to these problems. The university officials
felt that I was agitating the students, the Buddhist students,
and they indirectly threatened to have me put out of the
Buddhist priesthood. Also there were pressures put on other
Buddhist students, who were members of a group we had
formed, to break up the group. However, my master and
several Buddhist priests at Komazawa, as well as several
younger priests in the sect, while they have not always agreed
with the methods I have used, also feel that if Soto Zen is to
be relevant to the present day, then the priests must become
concerned with the particular social problems which young

people are facing. And so many of them, although they do not always support my methods, are sympathetic with my objectives.

RB: How about the American officials here, the embassy people and the CIA, how have they treated you?

BV: When I came to Japan twelve years ago I was a Methodist missionary and I was a conscientious objector fulfilling my alternate service duty. I did not know it at the time, but when I served as a missionary English teacher several years ago at Aoyama Gakuin the CIA investigated me. I was later informed of this by a Mr. Matsumoto, a former CIA agent. He has since quit the CIA and is now under the protection of the Socialist Party in Japan. At that time I was engaged in no political activities whatsoever, but apparently the CIA felt that even a conscientious objector might be a potential threat to the American presence.

I've had little to do with the embassy because I feel that they do not really represent me as an American in Japan. However, when I was put into Immigration Detention at Shinagawa, someone from the embassy came and asked us if we—I and Roger Scott—were being discriminated against. And I answered that we were probably the first Western political prisoners of the Japanese since the end of World War II. Of course, he denied that there was anything political about our case. He said that we were in detention because we had overstayed our visa limits. But then later, they said that maybe there were some political aspects to our case.

Later, when we were in detention for the second time, Roger Scott—who was also a participant in an aborted trip to China and who was also active in anti–Vietnam war movements—put through a telephone call to the ambassador. Ambassador Armin Meyer, when he got on the line, said to Roger, You know, some Americans do not appreciate Americans who come to Japan and make trouble. And he also said, I understand that you not only hate America but you also hate Japan. I was standing next to Roger at the time and heard him reply, Ambassador Meyer, that is a very childish thing to say.

Still later I was put in solitary in the detention center for advising Chinese prisoners to resist the immigration authorities. I demanded that a call to the embassy be put through for me because I did feel that I was being discriminated against. About a week after the call an embassy official visited me to investigate my claim. He said to me right away, Mr. Victoria, you claim that you are being kept in solitary. However, after investigating the matter we don't feel that you are in solitary; you are only living apart from the rest of the detainees here. I asked him what the difference was, and he answered, Solitary is when they put you in a black hole and just leave you there. And we understand that your room has a window. So we don't consider that you are being discriminated against. Well, you can see from this incident that there was no sense in pursuing the matter further. Anyway, the American embassy officials' attitude was rather clear.

RB: Have you found any public officials who are sympathetic with your aims? Any who are actively willing to aid you?

BV: I certainly haven't found any high officials who would. In November of 1968 when I applied for a new visa, the immigration authorities told me that they were going to cut down my visa from six months to three months because I had participated in demonstrations. Now, these demonstrations were legal. They were nonviolent. However, the immigration authorities felt that this behavior was incompatible with my status in Japan and as a punishment they were going to cut down the length of my visa. I then went to the Ministry of Justice to protest this punishment. A middle-aged worker there told me that he had been wounded in the defense of Okinawa, and he opposed war very much and he thought my activities were worthwhile. However, he said that because he was only a minor official, there was nothing he could do to help me. Also, when I was in the Immigration Detention Center, a number of the young guards were helpful and friendly. One young guard who was a Catholic and whose younger brother was active in student movements said that he doubted greatly his actions and the necessity for keeping me and many of the Chinese—some of whom have been detained for three or four years—and he wondered in his heart if he would be able to continue as an immigration official for the rest of his life.

RB: Why were you placed in detention?

BV: First I should explain that I have been placed in a Japanese immigration detention center on two different occasions. The first time was on September 11, 1969, when I was placed in the Tokyo Immigration Detention Center in Shinagawa, the ostensible reason being to conduct an investigation to determine whether or not I had overstayed my period of residence in Japan. This investigation was merely a formality, however, since it was the Immigration Bureau itself which had earlier refused my application for an extension of my visa. Although the Immigration Bureau refused to give a specific reason for their refusal, since I have never broken a single Japanese law in my twelve years of residence here, I cannot help but think that their attitude reflected their displeasure with my peace activities in this country, particularly with my attempted visit to the People's Republic of China.

I was placed in detention for the second time on October 16, 1969. As a result of the investigation it was determined that I had, indeed, overstayed my period of residence and ought, therefore, to be deported. I was placed in the Yokohama Detention Center to await execution of the deportation order. Fortunately, however, I was released by court order on December 2, 1969. The reason for this release, simply stated, was that since I had already initiated a civil suit against the Immigration Bureau for denying me a visa extension, the court made an interim ruling that I should neither be deported nor detained until a judgment was given in my case. The fact that I was a student in the master's course in Buddhist studies at Komazawa University was an important factor in this decision.

RB: When you were in your own country did you participate in any political activities?

BV: Having been born and raised in Nebraska—that is, Nebraska is in the country and is cut off from political movements, especially activist movements—I didn't have a chance. Also, at the time that I was a student, there were not many anti–U.S. government movements in America, especially not in Nebraska, and so there was little chance for me to participate. The only time that I was active was when there was a movie called *Operation Abolition*, distributed by the House Un-American Activities Committee, that purported to show that student demonstrators who opposed a hearing of this committee were led and influenced by known communists. The film was shown throughout the U.S. and at the school I attended in Nebraska. There was a committee of students at the time who sent out information that the students who had opposed the House Un-American Activities Committee were not communists but were concerned with the violation of human rights by the investigators of this committee. I was a spokesman of this national student group when the film appeared at our university, and as a result of my activities I was labeled a "pinko" by the Omaha branch of the American Legion. This was the only political activity that I participated in in the U.S.

RB: Some foreigners feel that their proper role here is that of a guest and like a guest a foreigner should not criticize his host. Would you care to comment on this attitude?

BV: Yes, I agree completely. I feel that I am indeed a guest of the Japanese people. Hopefully, in any country the government reflects the attitudes of the people. In Japan the government does not reflect the attitudes of the Japanese people. Only one in three Japanese actively supports the Liberal-Democratic Party in elections. And when you consider the great financial resources the LDP has—especially through Nikkeiren [Japan Economic Council]—and you consider the amount of money they can spend on elections, you can see the tremendous advantage they have over those parties that don't have much money. Also, we should consider that under the Japanese electorate system, although the majority of the people live in urban areas they are not represented proportionately in the Diet. Rather, the greatest number of representatives come from the country. This system is another way that the LDP has of maintaining their control.

Taking all these factors into account, I don't feel that the LDP represents the majority of the Japanese people; it represents a small number, a certain class.

I make my living by collecting alms and mainly I collect them in the poorer sections, in places like Tokyo's Asakusa. I rely truly on the mercy of the ordinary Japanese. And I think that if the ordinary Japanese believed that my activities—these have been well publicized—are detrimental to their interests, they would not continue to support me with alms. On the other hand, very often when I am collecting alms, they have come to me and said, "We also oppose the war in Vietnam and we support your activities." I have never had anyone of them say, "You should leave Japan. We don't like what you are doing." The only people who have said that are representatives of the Japanese government.

I would also like to say that the people who say we are guests and as such we should not criticize our host are very often foreign businessmen and they are already a part of the system of capitalistic imperialism, if I may use that term, and their presence in Japan is not only an economic phenomenon but is also a political phenomenon. When the Japanese government pursues policies which American businessmen think might endanger their business interests, the American government puts a tremendous amount of pressure on the Japanese government to act to protect those interests. And in places like Vietnam, Cambodia, Laos, and so forth, they have sent troops to insure that the governments of these countries act as they demand.

What this boils down to is that these businessmen mean that

as long as you support imperialistic capitalism there is no need to get involved in so-called internal affairs. This is because you are already involved in them, you are creating internal policies by the pressures you can exert. What they mean by the critical guest is one who opposes this system. Moreover, the American military in Japan is the greatest political tool that the American government has for use here. Without the American military in Japan, Taiwan would be liberated, there would be a strengthening of the people's struggle in Japan—the so-called leftist movement. And these moves would endanger American capital in Asia. For this reason, the American government, in cooperation with the Japanese capitalistic ruling class, is here.

The U.S. government will not let their soldiers make political statements. Ironically, however, the very presence of the U.S. military in Japan is the most forceful demonstration and statement that can be made.

What I'm getting at is that foreigners who support the present economic and political structure here in Japan are allowed to stay. But those people who would unite with the Japanese people who are struggling to change this system are denied the right of freedom, freedom of expression, freedom of speech, and freedom of assembly.

RB: How would you characterize your continuing dispute with the immigration authorities? How do you think they justify their position toward you?

BV: The immigration authorities are simply representatives of the present Japanese government, and since I and many Japanese and many Americans do not support capitalism and imperialism—whether it be in Japan or America or any place in the world—naturally they are determined that we shall be repressed.

RB: What are the chances that even if you win all your disputes with the immigration authorities the government will simply change the laws so that they can retain the control over foreigners to the degree that they want?

BV: In the short run, I think they will do just that. But, unfortunately, I will eventually be forced to leave Japan—as long as the present government remains in control. I do feel that at the present time I am helping to build a unity between the progressive Japanese people and the American people which will one day bring about changes in the governments of both countries that will help to alter the social system as well.

RB: The foreign authors of two recently published books have written that the Japanese do not like foreigners. Do you agree?

BV: In any situation where you have two races or two cultures involved, there is bound to be friction. For example, a three-year-old Japanese child seeing a black man on TV for the first time. She points to him and says, *Kaiju! Kaiju!* [Monster! Monster!]. And this I think is a normal human response, especially for a small child and particularly when she sees something which looks like a human being but which looks unlike anything she has ever seen before. It's natural for her to be frightened, because it is a new and different experience. The important point here is how natural feelings between races are developed and directed, whether for good or bad.

In Japan during the war white people were thought of as *chikusho,* or beasts. The early Dutch traders were called *keto,* a pejorative term meaning "hairy ones." So there is a racial problem here. The relationship between Japanese and Caucasians is much different from that of Japanese to blacks and from Japanese to other Asians. Certainly in Japan because of the *shimaguni konjo,* or "island mentality," there is often a feeling of distance between Japanese and other people that is particularly pronounced. And what I am particularly worried about is that the present Japanese government will use this natural friction, this natural fear, to prevent the unity of progressive Japanese and progressive Americans and progressive Japanese and progressive Asians who are struggling against the unjust social and economic systems which rule in all the so-called free countries in Asia as well as in the United States.

Although I cannot explain my feelings toward Japanese satisfactorily in a psychological way, paradoxically I feel more at home with those Japanese who have had little contact with foreigners. For example, when I'm invited to the small temple which my master has in Fukui Prefecture to read sutras at O-bon. Afterwards when we drink tea together I feel a real warmth from being with the country people. I don't feel this warmth with many of the people I've met in Tokyo, that is, with Japanese who have associated in one way or another with Americans, who have some command of English, or who have studied in America, or who try to keep up with the latest fashions and fads of Western countries and who feel that they are very hip on Western culture—the kind of people who, in regard to the West, say, We Japanese people feel this way, and you foreigners will never be able to understand us Japanese because our language is so complicated and because we have such a different culture from yours. These Japanese on the one hand act as if they are more Western than Westerners and on the other hand act as though they are more Oriental than anybody else in the Orient. I have the hardest time relating to this kind of Japanese. And I feel a greater lack of warmth and concern for the well-being of foreigners among them than I do among any other group of Japanese.

My feeling is that Japan, in order to support its social and capitalistic structure, cannot help but exploit other countries. It needs raw materials and under the present economic system it must search for sources of raw materials and for markets. In other words, it cannot help but exploit other Asian countries. South Korea and Taiwan are already sources of cheap labor for Japan's capital and Indonesia is becoming an increasingly important source of raw materials. And in South Korea, Taiwan, and Indonesia, and other Asian countries, the people are struggling against an unjust social system. Taiwan is a complete military dictatorship; the fundamental freedoms are denied there, especially to the native Taiwanese. In South Korea there is a military dictatorship operating under a very shallow mask of democracy. Indonesia is a military dictatorship. Thailand is a military dictatorship. South Vietnam is a military dictatorship. And Japan and America are supporting all of these—if I may use the term—reactionary governments. This policy cannot help but eventually bring Japan into conflict with the movements of these people for a just society in their countries. As Japanese capital increases its penetration of these countries, naturally when a revolutionary situation arises that threatens Japanese capital's interests, they will feel forced to rearm—and they are rearming now—in order to protect Japanese interests in these countries. Eventually this pursuit will, I feel, bring Japan into conflict with her Asian neighbors.

RB: As a Buddhist, what is your opinion of the Soka Gakkai? Is it a force for good, as it claims, or is it dangerously opportunistic, as its critics claim?

BV: Soka Gakkai has too many aspects to it for me to give a simple answer. However, its good features are that in the present Japanese social system, which is very hierarchic, the classes are divided very sharply. Soka Gakkai has given a new meaning to the lives of the people at the bottom of the social scale, particularly to workers in small businesses, small shopowners, employees of nonunionized small companies, people who do menial work, and even bar hostesses—all of these people have a low status in Japanese society. By becoming members of Soka Gakkai they can break out of their isolation and they can feel they are a part of a large important group. In Soka Gakkai, if they apply themselves to study, they can take tests and become assistant professors, professors, and teachers of others. They can achieve a social position that they never could through their jobs or in the general society. In giving these people a new sense of their worth, a sense of belonging, and a sense of purpose, I think we can say that the Soka Gakkai is a force for good.

However, I feel the dangerous aspect of Soka Gakkai is that as with so many organizations in Japan—even with some of the so-called leftist organizations—it is a hierarchically structured organization in which the directions for the movement come from the top. Daisaku Ikeda, its leader, has not been elected by anyone; he is not chosen by the members; instead he was chosen by the former head of Soka Gakkai. The leaders of the organization are chosen by other leaders and at Ikeda's instigation. This means that as long as he makes wise decisions, ones that help the people, the setup is fine. Claiming to be no god, and certainly he is no god, he is subject to error. Since Soka Gakkai has a hierarchical structure in which the instructions flow from the top down, this means that if the leaders become corrupt or change the policy the effect could be terrific. Especially because Soka Gakkai also maintains a political arm, Komeito, a change in direction could have a tremendous effect on the direction of Japan's policies in the future. As has been pointed out in the newspapers in their accounts of the repression of publishers of books that are critical of Soka Gakkai, the leaders of Soka Gakkai can exert a tremendous reactionary pressure if they choose to do so.

The danger of Soka Gakkai is that one can never be certain of its leadership. Since it can change its position in the future, it could easily have tremendous repercussions. Because of its hierarchical nature there is the danger that in certain situations it could become fascistic in its operations.

RB: What do you think about the future of the radical left in Japan?

BV: I think that in the immediate future it is going to be repressed severely. The New Left especially has isolated itself and it has been isolated. Its members have isolated themselves by not taking the steps for building necessary support among the general populace. They—especially the students—have been too naive in their use of violence. They have not used violence in a way which the general populace could understand. The radical left is unable to reach the ordinary Japanese to explain to them the purposes of their violence. To be successful they would have to bring the people to feel that violence is directly connected to their daily problems. In addition, the Japanese government has isolated the students and workers through its control of the mass media, making them appear to be violent for the sake of violence. By isolating the radicals in this way, the government will be able to repress them. For the students it is important that the right questions be raised. In general, the students' solutions are better than those of the present Japanese government. Eventually, when the present expansionist policy of the present leaders produces conflicts in other Asian countries as well as within Japan, people will be more receptive to the student radicals' ideas.

# 7

## DONN DRAEGER
### American
### Martial Arts Exponent

He has spent almost thirty years in the Orient, first as a U.S. Marine officer, then as a research historian, author, and lecturer on Asian martial culture. He is widely regarded as the leading Western scholar and exponent of the Japanese classical martial disciplines, in which he holds a large number of expert ranks and teaching licenses. Among his published works are included *Judo Training Methods, Asian Fighting Arts, Classical Bujutsu,* and *Classical Budo.* He is the technical director of the journal *Martial Arts International* and an editor of *Judo Illustrated.*

RB: I've heard people say that practice of the martial arts increases aggressive and warlike tendencies, and I've heard other people say that—because of the asceticism and humility demanded—the martial arts increase masochistic tendencies. Do either of these opinions agree with your observations?

DD: Bluntly speaking, I don't think these people know what they're talking about.

Anything that we use as a training method is designed to help us to improve a skill, say a motor skill or a mental process. But I don't believe that warlike or aggressive tendencies are developed by the martial arts. Sociologists, one in particular, Maurice Davie, have found that racial characteristics are at the base of aggressiveness, black being the most aggressive, white second, and the yellow race being only moderately so. These findings have been substantiated by other scholars.

In the case of the Japanese and their martial arts—not their martial ways, an important distinction I'll explain later—other than that these practices develop technical skills and the spirit that supports them, I don't believe they lead necessarily to aggressive tendencies or a warlike manner. They do help to make a person a better fighter, just as when you practice kicking a football over and over it can make you a better punter. But the tendency to apply the skill, the thing inside you, I believe, isn't affected; the martial arts are external to it. The results you'd get from training, for instance, a Caucasian, a black, and a Japanese would, I believe, be different. That is, if you train them with the same instruction, same method, same teacher, you'd get different results.

Perhaps the people who've said that warlike tendencies were increased by the martial arts were thinking of competitive sports, activities like football and modern *budo*—judo, karate, aikido—but that is something else entirely.

RB: And you don't think, then, that masochistic tendencies are increased?

DD: No, not at all. I've known hundreds of people in the

martial arts and if masochistic tendencies were affected by that kind of training I think I would have noticed it. In fact, the characteristics of the men who really practice these arts are quite different. The many people I've met who have undergone training in the Japanese classical martial disciplines— *bujutsu*—are some of the most stable people I've ever met in any society. What they've been studying, what they've been practicing has engendered this composure in them and this has taught them not to be aggressive, not to be warlike, but to be very emotionally stable people. The proof of the training is here to be seen in the men who practice these arts, the *bujutsu*, not the competitive *budo* and sports like that.

RB: I've read that in America karate contests are bloodier, more violent than they are in Japan. Do you think this points to any fundamental difference in temperament or approach?

DD: I think it's both. In America the contests are bloodier; you're right. There is, literally, a thirst for blood: the spectators want to see some action. The same spectators will go to automobile races to see the cars turn over, to see the racers get splattered. They'll go to a boxing match to see cut faces and athletes battered senseless, and so on. This is not exclusively an American thing, of course, but it's quite prevalent among American fans. Without this violence, I doubt that you'd have much enthusiasm for sports, say for two boxers simply but skillfully touching each other to score points.

Anyway, karate contests are definitely bloodier in America than in Japan, and the fundamental differences are located in temperament—again, this is the racial difference I mentioned, the Oriental being only mildly aggressive as compared to the white man. The approach in training is different, too— I don't think the American has the genuine approach to karate as the Japanese have designed it. He has *an* approach; he has his way; he's developed an American approach to karate.

RB: One that is fundamentally different from the Japanese way?

DD: Yes, fundamentally different. Even technically it's

different. The Westerner is muscle-centered on the chest and arms, while the source of the Japanese athlete's strength is in his stomach, his waist, and his loins, and he's generally less strong than the Westerner in his arms and shoulders. So the movements, the techniques they emphasize are different.

RB: Japanese and Chinese masters say the essence of the martial arts is proper spirit, and I've often heard Japanese wonder aloud whether foreign students of the martial arts were actually being imbued with this spirit. How would you answer them?

DD: I think their criticism of the foreign exponents of these disciplines has a lot of merit. But let me limit myself to the Japanese sphere in this discussion. The Japanese experts do wonder, sometimes aloud, whether or not we can learn to understand the Japanese spirit. This is simply saying that if you cannot imitate a Japanese doing something essentially Japanese, you cannot achieve the true spirit of the martial arts—it's impossible. You cannot separate the spirit from the technique.

In considering a trained exponent, you can point to aspects of his development that are physical and others that are mental or spiritual, but actually man functions as a unit and you can't really separate these two in nature.

RB: Then you don't think someone could become a master of judo, aikido, or kendo without the proper spiritual development?

DD: Impossible. Mastery includes the spiritual element. Oh, he can become a technician, skilled in the sense of mastery of motor skills, but the real essence will be missing; the whole idea behind the training is absent.

RB: What about the achievement of Anton Geesink, the Olympic judo champion from Holland?

DD: Now we're speaking about a sport contest—judo is not a martial art by any stretch of the imagination. Geesink was a tremendous competitor, a sportsman. He still is. Sports—no matter which one, running two miles, throwing a man down

judo style, hurling a javelin—are based on a fighting spirit.
And Geesink was a killer sportsman, he had the killer instinct.
He did not believe in making any concessions to his opponent.
This is the same with a good miler—he hopes the guy closing
up on him will drop dead. Anything else, any concession,
according to Percy Cerrutty, one of our most famous coaches
for distance runners, is hypocritical humbug. This idea that I
wish my opponent good luck is nonsense. I'm going to beat
him. This is the kind of man Geesink is: If you get on the mat
with me and I break your neck, that's your tough luck. Why
did you come up here?

Geesink once ripped a man's shoulder out of its socket.
Not maliciously. In a legitimate technique. The man resisted
and didn't have the strength to resist enough and he lost his
shoulder muscles—they were all pulled loose.

So this type of spirit in Geesink is the sportsman's type.
But put Mr. Geesink in the martial arts—unless he put a
tremendous amount of time in swordsmanship, or in using one
of the other traditional weapons of *bujutsu,* I don't believe the
spirit he displays would carry him very far. *Bujutsu,* the true
martial arts, require far more than a competitive spirit, far
more.

The killer attitude of sport is let loose within certain legal
limits, of course. And the fighting spirit developed in a competitive spirit can help you, to a certain extent, on the battle-
field. There must be a carryover of ardor, courage, endurance,
and so on. But getting back to our question, unless a foreigner
is prepared to spend a tremendous amount of time living in
Japan and learning in the Japanese manner, he will not succeed
in becoming a master of any of the *bujutsu.* He may become a
skilled technician—a lower level—but not a master.

RB: Then the spirit has to be developed in the Japanese
way, and this way is not simply a kind of social adhesive, a
tactic of Japanese groupism that can be ignored?

DD: The Japanese did develop the spirit out of a need for
collective security. In that sense it is a kind of social adhesive.

Yes, and therefore an individualist, a person committed to maintaining his individuality, cannot succeed. This is the stumbling block to foreigners—individualism.

RB: In other words, the foreigner, particularly the American, has to learn to control his ego, his striving to make his identity highly distinct, and become part of a group?

DD: Right, he must become part of a group. And he must serve a sort of apprenticeship to the group and learn subservience to it. And as he gets experience, he'll be able to feel this, that what he's doing is for the good of the group, not for himself. This is a very important point. Not too many foreigners are able to find any reason for doing so.

RB: Or probably are not even willing to try.

DD: That's so. And the willingness not being there, the mastery will not develop. Except in a technical sense, and then usually only to a limited degree.

RB: And this particular inability or unwillingness must make it hard for them to function with Japanese in the martial arts world?

DD: Very much so. Even at a social level, the foreigner not wanting to put up with or adapt to the customs or manners—divorcing themselves, literally, from the spirit of the idea—will in fact affect their total progress.

This is the limiting factor, this is what a lot of foreigners are not prepared for, are not equipped to put up with, this purely Japanese approach.

RB: Morihei Uyeshiba, the originator of aikido, has told of his training experience in this way: "The fundamental principle of the martial arts is God's love and universal love. . . . martial arts training is not training that has as its purpose the defeating of others, but is the practice of God's love within ourselves." Has your own practice of these arts led you to any conclusions of this sort? Do you think his experience is unique or do you know of other martial arts practitioners who have had experiences like Uyeshiba's?

DD: What Uyeshiba is saying here is not original but was

first put forth about three hundred years ago by Kaibara Ekken, a physician and a Confucian philosopher. It's something that has been echoed down the years by Japanese thinkers.

My own practice agrees with what Mr. Uyeshiba has said. I believe that the principal purpose of martial arts training requires the development of tolerance and understanding. This may sound strange or contradictory, but let me explain it like this: unless you have undergone the experience yourself to a considerable depth, you cannot begin to understand what is being said about it. It's like my showing you a road map and saying you can go from here to here and at this place you're to turn, and at this place you'll come across a town, or you must cross a bridge here, and so on. You can get the idea of the journey from this map-reading session, but until you've made the journey you don't really know the lay of the land. In the martial arts, unless you have undergone the training—as in the case of Mr. Uyeshiba, who had tremendous experience—the need for doing things in a particular way doesn't register.

Mr. Uyeshiba's experience isn't really unique. All martial arts people who delve deeply enough go through it.

RB: This sounds as though it's related to Zen thought, where it's taught that in order for the Zen acolyte to understand enlightenment it is absolutely necessary for him to experience it.

DD: It sounds to many people as though a barrier, an arbitrary obstacle, had been set in the way of people trying to understand, as though the masters are trying to hide their teachings with a kind of mystique to give it prestige or something. But I have been on both sides of that fence, so to speak, and there is an important difference between thinking about it and undergoing the experience.

RB: Have you studied Zen in relation to the martial arts?

DD: The Zen we see today, with all respect to the people doing it, the people who claim to be following the old traditions, has very little relation to the martial arts. There is little true connection between modern Zen and the modern martial arts and ways. When Zen came to Japan—in spite of what the Zen master Dogen has written—it was controlled by the warrior class. The warrior class was the police of its clergy. Zen had to fit a social mold then.

What people were getting out of Zen then and what they're getting now are quite different, I believe. At that time, Zen made a great impact on the warrior class. Nowadays, for instance, at the Soto sect's Eihei-ji temple, you're not allowed to bring a weapon into the premises. Several hundred years ago, nobody told a warrior he couldn't carry his weapons while in the temple grounds.

RB: At that time there was a close relationship among *bushi,* or warriors, Zen, and the martial arts, the classical *bujutsu,* wasn't there?

DD: Yes. Zen was used to discipline the warrior's mind, to prepare it to function efficiently in the environment in which he had to survive.

RB: It was used by the military leaders, then, on the warriors?

DD: Yes, and by the warrior himself. It was a way for him to learn how to become a better warrior, for the sake of the group. He had to learn to develop *fudoshin,* translated roughly as "the immovable mind." Zen was to teach him this. Zen monks like Takuan, from time to time, took warriors and trained them in mental disciplines.

But this relationship between Zen and fighting systems no longer exists. In fact, the Zen people decry it.

RB: Then you wouldn't recommend to the foreigner beginning martial arts training, either *bujutsu* or *budo,* that he practice, say, Zen meditation.

DD: I wouldn't say not to, but I'd tell him that he can get all the Zen-like discipline he needs from any legitimate training in any of the traditional fighting systems, the *ryu.*

RB: Some foreign students of karate and kendo have expressed bitter disappointment about what they feel to be the wide disparity between the ideal martial sports practitioner and the Japanese who teach and practice them. Generally speaking, would you say that this is true, or do the practitioners as you know them actually live up to the strict codes of their arts?

DD: I've had the same experience. Some of the worst people, the worst examples of what we expect from people who are supposed to be highly disciplined, are in the modern entities—in judo and karate, particularly karate. And in the true martial arts, the *bujutsu,* I've met some of the nicest people in the world. The difference has almost shocked me. I've thought a lot about this during the last ten years and have focused my attention acutely on it in the last three or four, so that I've become disgusted with those who fail to live up to their stated ideals. These people, these Japanese teachers, do not live up to the ideals that sincere and dedicated trainees expect of them. I don't know why some Japanese fail, but I feel that they don't go deep enough into the spiritual training, don't care enough about it. Perhaps it's the growing competitiveness of the sports. And most likely the increasing commercialism. Whatever the causes, it's a very bad situation, a cause for shame upon those who are responsible.

RB: An acquaintance of mine, a long-time resident and observer of the Japanese, says that they cannot accept the necessity of being good losers as well as good winners because losing is like an acid bath to their sense of inferiority. Do you think he is right?

DD: There's some justice in what he says, but I've competed against many Japanese and have found them some of the most gracious and humble losers that I've met anywhere in the world. No one likes to lose, nobody likes to come in second in any endeavor. And I don't think the Japanese have a monopoly on being oversensitive about losing. I recall a championship judo match in Brazil—we needed police protection to get back to the locker room because the Brazilian crowd came out of the stands and was attacking us. And at their soccer games, the Brazilian spectators try to injure each other, and they sometimes tear the stadium apart. You get some of this at European sports contests, too.

I don't think your acquaintance is completely wrong, however. Let me put it this way: outwardly the Japanese lose better. It hurts like hell inside, of course. It's a kind of acid bath to anybody, particularly to them, but at least they mask their feelings well. Not like some Westerners I've seen in Japan who literally cry out in anguish before the spectators and who curse out the judges and whose "I was robbed" statements are seen in the newspapers. No, the Japanese competitors do much better at covering it up.

RB: This same acquaintance says that in sports, as well as in all competitive undertakings with foreigners, the average Japanese cannot separate himself from strong nationalistic feelings, that to root for a foreign athlete in competition would be close to treason for him. Do you think he exaggerates?

DD: I don't think they are any more nationalistic in regard to sports. They're certainly not as bad as the Brazilians. When a Brazilian team loses, it's not just the team, not just Pele or whoever, but all of Brazil, and they want to "kill" the foreign victors! And I've seen this in other countries, in Cuba and Costa Rica. The Japanese may be high on the list of people with strong nationalistic tendencies, but they're way behind the Latins.

RB: What my acquaintance pointed to was the fixed kickboxing matches and the wrestling matches with their foreign villains and Japanese good guys, and the inability of the Japanese sports announcers to restrain their partisanship on the airways.

DD: I'm not sure how serious an imperfection this is. And, again, the Japanese are by no means alone in this way. But here you've got to remember the strong Japanese sense of the *nakama*, the group, and the need for group security. And if group loyalty is displayed too strongly, if it raises the ugly head of extreme partisanship, at least we can see why. But as far as nationalism goes, the Russians—have you ever been at a match when a Russian loses? You'd better not be too close to the Russian crowd then. Pro matches are fixed the world around. The Japanese may have more national pride than peoples of other countries, but I don't think they go to extremes with this so much that they stand out internationally.

RB: Foreign businessmen have complained that they cannot compete with Japanese businessmen abroad because of the united front Japanese business and government presents. That is, while Japanese businesses compete with each other at home they help each other abroad and receive substantial support from their government. In the martial arts, do the Japanese pursue national solidarity and exclusivity in any way?

DD: A foreigner can get into either the *budo* or *bujutsu* worlds. The catch is, however, that you almost have to become a Japanese to do well in them. Because you're doing something they developed you have to do it their way; not the Brooklyn way, not the French way, but the Japanese way. You may think that you get the same result doing it differently, but it's not the same.

The exclusiveness of martial discipline groups goes back to the need for collective security. The outsider will be accepted only to the extent that he can approximate to the best of his ability, sincerely, the Japanese way. This is the only real stumbling block to the foreigner who wants to learn the martial disciplines.

RB: This exclusivity, it's manifested in the custom that dictates that a master will pass his group's secrets on to specially selected people only, isn't it?

DD: Yes, and of course that means only certain Japanese, too, get to learn these. The purpose of keeping things secret in the martial arts is to keep the group stronger than other groups, and it helps preserve the identity of the group.

Every *bujutsu* group today has *okuden*, secret arts, which are given only to certain people. You know, you must walk before you can run. If you don't have the foundation, the secrets will do you no good because they are based on the first steps.

RB: How do foreigners fare in the Japanese martial arts world?

DD: If the foreigner is willing to play the role, he will be accepted as a brother. The Japanese are very tolerant and will understand that you make mistakes as a foreigner, but they'll help you to succeed.

RB: By "play the role" you don't mean to fake it in any way, do you?

DD: No, a sincere attempt. You could fake it for a couple of weeks if you're a skillful actor, but this kind of training takes years, and the Japanese would read you before long. They'd catch you when you're relaxed, they'd catch you when you're tired, they'd catch you when you're disturbed about something else.

You have a "hand-untying" or probationary period, in which you're watched and observed—both foreigners and Japanese go through it. And when the headmaster thinks, Yes, this man can do it, then you are accepted.

RB: Are foreigners accepted as martial arts masters?

DD: In a strict sense there is no master in *bujutsu,* except in a technical sense. You have an emphasis on spiritual mastery in classical *budo,* but not in the fighting systems. But to this day there is no foreigner who has achieved mastery in a *budo* form, not in the minds of the Japanese anyway. In the *bujutsu,* some foreigners have reached the middle levels of technical skill, but that's as high as they've climbed.

As far as the Japanese are concerned, foreigners with the proper license teaching other foreigners is permissible. There are a few—a very few—foreigners who have achieved this. And all of these have had more than ten years' residence in Japan.

RB: Many observers have remarked on the amazing change in the physical stature of the postwar generation of Japanese— they are much taller than the previous generation and have longer, straighter legs. At the same time concern has been expressed about the growing incidence of obesity, since before and for a while after the war fat people were rarely seen here. Do you think that the Japanese are getting soft physically or is the traditional desire for gaining self-control through austerities still strong among them?

DD: The length of my experience in Japan is just a bit over twenty-five years, and I believe that I can see a softness setting in. It's obvious that the mode of life has changed, what with the increasing conveniences. The Japanese are getting soft physically, but more important is the mental flabbiness. My teachers tell me that the young Japanese are less interested in the traditional austere ways—the martial arts, flower arranging, the tea ceremony, all of them. And I find now that in some of the classical *bujutsu* organizations there may be as few as three young students. And the majority of students are over forty. Teenagers just aren't interested.

RB: Recently I've read about complaints made by people in the Sumo Association because they can't get enough recruits.

DD: Yes, and the recruits aren't as strong as they were even ten years ago. This most likely has to do with the food they eat—too much cake, too much ice cream and candy.

RB: Yukio Mishima said that the spirit of Japan is dying and the Japanese of today does not care if his soul dies. Is this a good capsule summary of the present-day situation in Japan?

DD: There does seem to be a spiritual decline. Mishima was a very sensitive man and certainly he knew the Japanese better than I do. If by spirit he was referring to *Yamato-damashii*, "Japanese spirit," I too find very little of it in the youth of today.

By *Yamato-damashii* I don't necessarily mean the warrior type of physical or moral courage; any Japanese can have it, I believe. But I don't see it in the young fellows today.

RB: Do you mean perseverance and endurance in any way of life?

DD: Yes, it's not there. I see complaisance; they've had life too easy, especially in the city. If you're going to look for spiritual strength, you'd do best to look in the country. But of course the young people are leaving the rural areas in great numbers every year. How you gonna keep 'em down on the farm? as the song goes.

But, really, we can only gauge *Yamato-damashii* in an emergency; it comes out in emergencies, crises. And maybe crises are necessary to humans, to keep them in spiritual balance. I think Mishima may be right.

RB: Because he practiced and was an influential advocate of several martial ways, Mishima's sudden death by his own hand must have had a shocking impact in martial ways circles. Will you tell me what some of these reactions were?

DD: When he killed himself I was at a *dojo* about eight hundred meters away from the incident. The teacher in midstride, literally, said, Oh, Mishima committed *seppuku*. And that was that. We went back to practicing. I don't remember the teacher saying any more than that about it, although I never did question him.

In only one of the other three or four *ryu* that I'm involved with did I hear the incident mentioned. The teacher there simply said that it was a waste.

RB: They didn't think that by this action he had manifested the way of the warrior?

DD: If they did, I didn't hear them express it. It's rather strange, I know, because I'm around a lot of people who are involved with the sword.

RB: What about your own reaction—for you did his ritual suicide manifest anything extraordinary?

DD: Obviously he was trying to tell us something, and to do it in the way the warrior of old did, the way he did when he disgreed with his superior. At that time you didn't argue with him, you killed yourself. This was your right, the correct way to protest.

I think that Yukio felt that because he was well known and

because of the method he chose, his message would get across to people. And I think he was sincere. I don't think he was deranged or anything like that. Most likely he thought this was the best way he could serve his country. In that sense he displayed *Yamato-damashii*. But whether he made any real impact or not, I can't say. At this time, it doesn't look like he did.

RB: What criticism can you offer of the present-day martial disciplines?

DD: I think that most Japanese don't understand very much about this part of their culture. Very few of them—even educated people—can tell you what the constituents of the martial culture are. This is a sad thing.

Also I don't think there is enough technical professionalism in the field. Not enough of the teachers are as good as they should be and the people they're teaching aren't being taught well; they're not getting the meat. The quality of teaching has definitely gone down.

Another criticism I'd make is that Westerners are not approaching the martial disciplines correctly. They are confusing the sports and the true fighting arts, and these are not compatible. The classical disciplines must be separated from the modern sports.

What Westerners do is to learn something like aikido, go back to their own country, and set themselves up as teachers of aikido as self-defense. But aikido as they learned it in Japan isn't really a method of self-defense. When you work back through the sports and try to construct systems of self-defense, you don't do justice to the sports or the fighting systems. There are very few foreigners, really, who know what's what about the Japanese martial disciplines. And, generally, what Western teachers teach is not correct. A whole lot is lost in the jump from Japan to the West.

体験

# 8

## JOHN NATHAN
### American
### Scholar

Born in New York City in 1940, he first went to Japan in 1961 to study Japanese literature at Tokyo University. His translations include Yukio Mishima's *The Sailor Who Fell from Grace with the Sea* and Kenzaburo Oe's *A Personal Matter.* Mr. Nathan is currently lecturing at Princeton University and writing a book on Mishima. He has written several screenplays, including one in Japanese and English for a film that was released in 1971 as *Summer Soldiers.*

RB: When you were making *Summer Soldiers,* you no doubt came in contact with numerous Japanese who actively opposed the American presence in Japan. What is the nature of their opposition? Is it simply antiwar feeling in general or does it arise from pity for Asians being killed by white men?

JN: The people in the underground movement—and they are not what we would consider radicals—those who aid GIs who desert, have in common very strong antiwar feelings, as do all Japanese, I believe. This is for various complicated reasons. For one, their own martyrdom, as they see it, during World War II and the kind of guilt feelings they have about Japan's own behavior in Asia during the Second World War, which they tend to compare continuously with what we've done in Vietnam.

The part of the question that refers to racist feelings—about white men killing yellow men—is something I've never encountered. Even if we suppose this operates subconsciously . . . well, if that identification had ever existed it has greatly decreased because, I think, the Japanese don't really consider themselves Asians. I don't think the Japanese of today is any quicker to identify with a Vietnamese, because he's an Asian, than, say, the average American would with a Welshman because he is Anglo-Saxon. In any case, the racist slant applies, I think, much less in Japan than it would in parallel circumstances in the U.S., or the West in general.

RB: Were you aware of any special problems in your work on *Summer Soldiers* that arose out of differences of viewpoint between Japanese and Americans toward artistic creation?

JN: There were enormous problems. It's hard to isolate those problems because the making of a film tends to be something tremendously divisive and destructive—even when you are working with your fellow countrymen. But obviously, in this case there were some special pressures. I'm hesitant to say too much because I'm not convinced that the problems weren't something that arose between two individuals—myself and Teshigahara.

The movie we were making is about Americans, and about American deserters in particular. And of course we were talking about the Vietnam war, on one hand. On the other, we were talking about the Japanese who harbored the deserters. My view of both the American deserter and the Japanese group was radically different from that of the director, Hiroshi Teshigahara. I don't think that he was analytical enough about the problems. And when he did analyze, I think he was wrong. I don't know if this is a Japanese problem or just his. Of course there were a lot of superficial problems—language and approach. We were working in Japanese, but the screenplay was seventy percent English. Since no one else read English, my script had to be translated into Japanese and that made for misunderstandings of all kinds. There was a certain amount of difficulty because of this, but I think less than in other cases, given my bilinguality and our—Teshigahara's and my—long association together. I found that not only Teshigahara but also the other Japanese associated with the project were surprisingly reluctant, no, unable to view themselves with the kind of detached ironic humor that seemed to me necessary to the film. I had trouble convincing them—and ultimately failed to convince them—that there were aspects of the movement that were grotesquely humorous and should be, and correctly would have been, satirized. And so I've come to feel that the Japanese have a rather limited capacity for self-satirization and for objective, negative criticism of themselves.

I've made a sweeping generalization here which I'm not sure I can defend. I could point to several examples from Japanese literature which suggest to me that there is no real tradition in Japan of satirical literature—unless you consider Saikaku[1] a satirist, and he is of course, to an extent, but he is a rarity who was not understood in his time. What strikes the Japanese as funny, or tolerably funny, is very different from what strikes us as tolerably funny. Humor is bred of despair in the West, frequently it is anyway. I have a feeling that it isn't here. That is, despair, the kind of deep unrest and discontent that people feel about their lives; this I think the Japanese are not prone to or even capable of handling artfully. They're capable of being serious about them, of course, and they're capable of lamenting them in, say, the Dazai[2] manner, but they are not capable really of stepping back from these feelings and seeing that there is in fact humor here. There is, for example, no real theater of the absurd in Japan, Kobo Abe[3] notwithstanding. Nor is there any black or gallows humor.

1. Ihara Saikaku (1642–93) was an author of realist novels, chiefly about Japan's rising merchant class.
2. Osamu Dazai (1909–48) was a popular novelist who wrote of the degeneration of Japanese society.
3. Kobo Abe is a contemporary novelist and essayist.

RB: I've heard more than one student of Japanese literature express regret and disappointment about the quality of work produced by Japan's leading modern writers. The opinion generally expressed is that one can find very few works that justify the very arduous task of learning to read and translate Japanese, and that there is a depressive sameness of theme and treatment. How do you think Japanese literature rates in the world's literature?

JN: Without exception every Japanese writer overproduces—outrageously. The effect of this certainly is that page for page—I'm talking also about the writers of large talent— there seems to me to be less density, less value really, than we would expect to find in the West, where standards are, I believe, maintained at a higher level and where a writer is expected to re-prove himself on each performance. There are several things about the Japanese literary establishment which in America are essentially unthinkable. For example, once a writer is accepted, has his debut in the Japanese establishment, which results from his having won a prize or having been taken on by somebody with authority and prestige—and this is all very formal and clear cut, it's not vague when this happens—a party is thrown, for example, and the man has become a writer, officially. In America a man doesn't write something, and is then given a coming-out party and a badge and a French fountain pen; but in Japan he is. And this has been going on, oh . . . certainly since the nineteen twenties. What happens thereafter is that the man begins to write all the time. That is, the novelist is a kind of craftsman. His publishers expect him to produce a novel in a certain period of time, which he does. At the same time he is constantly writing: essays, stories, diaries, travel articles, everything, in popular magazines and such, and he is serializing, really overproducing. Literature, of course, is very seriously affected by the expectations that are directed at it. The idea that the writing of a novel is a very arduous task, which requires—even of a man of large talent—an enormous amount of his time and

effort, this is an idea that is in some way understood certainly
by people in the Japanese literary world but is in some ways
subordinated to these other anticipations and pressures having
to do with his place in society as a writer.

This is a very strange phenomenon, one I've been interested
in for years because I know a lot of writers and I can never
understand why they do what they do and turn out such shit
when they could in fact turn out better work if they took
themselves more seriously. The fact is that they do, even the
greatest ones, put themselves through these extraordinary
paces in order to convince and  persuade their publishers
and their literary fellows that they are professional novelists.
That's the very important part of the whole business. That is,
according to this idea, a professional novelist is a man who can
sit down and write a novel. And, by God, he can do it in time
and regularly—and does—and at the same time he has the
leeway—emotional and intellectual—to produce all kinds of
other things. So what happens is that you get all kinds of
people who . . . well, all the writers have opuses that are
unthinkably large. Compared with anyone in the West.
Balzac is considered an extraordinary case in Western literature, but there are any number of Japanese writers who have
tripled Balzac's production during the course of their lives.
The sad truth is that as a result of this situation, a lot of this
writing is just not any good.

And so I sympathize with foreign students who say that they
find it difficult to justify the time and effort they put into
learning Japanese because of the literature that awaits them.

Certainly there are many more novels in modern Japanese
literature than in the literature of any nation in the West, but
a great many of these are second rate, at best.

RB: Which ones would you consider first rate?

JN: I myself would consider very few as first rate. Of course,
I would say the same thing about American literature. But
there are fewer books to mislead the Japanese student of
modern American literature, whereas in Japanese there are

so many books, the student is almost inevitably going to come up with a bummer.

Books that I would value highly are Kawabata's *Sound of the Mountain,* which I consider to be a beautiful and important book and one that anyone who has an interest in Japanese literature is well advised to read. I also like Dazai's *No Longer Human* very much, because of its passion, something not often encountered in Japanese literature; that is, passion which communicates itself to me and moves me. Tanizaki's *The Makioka Sisters* is another book which I prize.

Those are the three that I think are best.

RB: Much of the opinion I've heard about Yukio Mishima's suicide can be grouped into two general categories: he was crazy; he was an extraordinary narcissist. What do you think moved him to make such an extraordinary exit?

JN: In the West when a man commits suicide it's almost taken for granted that he's crazy in one way or another. I don't think that Mishima was crazy, by my definition of that word, except that I do believe that for most of his life he was very alienated from reality and therefore under modern definitions could be considered insane from about the time he was a boy of fourteen. He was certainly a very unhappy man all his life, and he was indeed a narcissist. The reasons for his death—of course these will never be explained away, and there will always be some mystery about why he did it—seem to have to do with a whole lot of complicated things centering on an attempt to come to terms with himself in a way that he hadn't been able to do before. The man had been obsessed with death since he was a small boy, had in fact been eagerly waiting to die since he was about nineteen, waiting in his fantasy life, and had found in the last four or five years of his life something that heightened the aesthetic beauty of his long obsession with death, not as a reality but as a kind of aesthetic state, by which I mean his association with those young people in his Tate no Kai [Shield Society]. And he can be considered to have finished his final masterpiece on the day that he went into the Self-

Defense headquarters. The only problem is that this act can't be considered to have any validity with his audience; but the same thing can be said with almost everything he ever wrote, so that I feel that he rationalized the death in various ways; that is, there were reasons for it that he entertained at various times and told people about at other times. My feeling is that essentially he was doing the thing for which he had waited for years and years and had decided that now was the time. He had pretty much written every kind of book he'd wanted to and had put himself through most of the extreme paces he had anticipated going through, and the one thing he had not done which he had talked about all his life was to become a hero. Of course, to him a hero meant very special things, but generally, it meant a very glorious, a very erotic death. Since life was never particularly meaningful to Yukio Mishima and he never succeeded in participating in it in any successful way, it was almost inevitable that this should have been something that he would have done.

RB: He seemed to have been obsessed with becoming a man of action—

JN: Well, there's a tremendously complicated mythology that is surrounding Mishima, and the reason it is complicated is that he created it himself. This "action" business comes up rather late in his life and to me is extremely unconvincing. First of all, he didn't take any action, he didn't do anything. And he never entertained for more than possibly a fleeting second the notion that he was going to provoke a coup d'état, for example, which is one of the things which we hear. He was going there to proclaim himself and to die. That isn't really action in the terms he was talking about it in his last years. He was cloaking it in all kinds of philosophical garments and invoking *yomeigaku,* a Chinese philosophy of action, and this and that, but it went against everything he'd believed till then. He was a man committed entirely, intellectually and emotionally, to art. And he knew that art was not action, not of the kind he was talking about in his last years. I don't believe that he had ever renounced his art. I believe that his death was the final affirmation of his art, and therefore had nothing to do with action.

There is an opinion about him current in Japan that runs along the same lines, but which says that he didn't believe in anything, that he was essentially a nihilist, which, I feel, is essentially true. He wasn't a man who had what we would consider ideological ideals and objectives, convictions. His whole life is explainable in terms of his erotic disposition, and it was an erotic experience that he was searching for.

This is a view that is extreme and it's offensive to anyone who wants to believe that Mishima stood for this and that having to do with Japanese nationalism or the threat of annihilation that hangs over us. In fact, it doesn't mean that the man is not to be taken seriously, it just means that he died for reasons that were extremely aesthetic and personal and had nothing to do with what he claimed they had to do with.

RB: Do you think Mishima was in the first rank of the world's novelists?

JN: No, I don't think he was of that first rank, by any means. I think he was an extraordinary genius of a special kind, and he did master something which at times was beautiful and always was very impressive, but I don't think he was ever able to get close enough in touch with himself to be a really great novelist. His novels are relegated to second-classdom by what I consider to be their artificiality and their essential emptiness.

RB: I find that they lack what the Japanese often refer to as "humanness." They seem to be all idea, ideal, and style, with no truly human feelings behind these.

JN: He had strong feelings, but he was terrified of them for most of his life and did everything he could to camouflage them in his writings. This is probably the greatest tragedy for him: he was never able psychologically to get in touch with the psychic energy, the passion, he had. The passion was all redirected, hidden, and cloaked in other robes in his work.

RB: People talk of him as a self-made man. Do you think that in making himself he got away from himself, his essence, the essential person inside himself?

JN: Yes, I think that essentially he tried to rebuild the surface of his system cell by cell, and did in fact do that, was motivated to do it by an overwhelming, overriding fear about what he really was. However, I don't believe that he ever really changed—I don't believe that anyone changes radically. I believe that what he really was was what he was when he was fifteen or sixteen, which possibly was what he tried to become again by his death.

体験
**9**

## JUNE SILLA
### Korean
### Writer

Born in 1928 in what is now South Korea, where he was raised, he arrived in Japan as a young man during World War II and worked there as a reporter for a French news agency for seventeen years. He has also written for the *Washington Post* and for European and North and South American newspapers. Presently he is a free-lance writer and translator.

RB: Do you think that the changes to be observed in Japanese society since World War II are superficial and that the social structure remains fundamentally the same?

JS: The basic social structure during this time has remained unchanged. However, change is going on all the time and I feel that the future is pregnant with more change. In judging Japan, as well as any other nation, we should give careful attention not only to the basic structure but also to these changes and to appearances. We should ask: What do these changes mean to Japan? How will they effect Japanese society? How will they effect Japan's relations with other countries? And we need to try to understand whether they are temporary, semipermanent, or permanent changes. The problem with focusing any investigation on the basic structure is that there are changes that do not affect this structure and yet have serious consequences.

Although there is strong scholarly support for the idea that the changes to be observed in Japan in the last twenty-five or so years are not fundamental, I don't entirely agree with that view. We've got to consider appearances more deeply; we ought to remember what Oscar Wilde said, that it is only superficial people who refuse to judge by appearances. The changes that have occurred and are occurring—some of them at least—may not be as superficial as they first appear to be. Take, for instance, the family system. It's disintegrating. It's disintegrating rapidly in the cities, more slowly in rural areas. While the larger framework, the vertical, hierarchical structure, has remained fundamentally unchanged for centuries, within this structure is the family system, and the fact that it is crumbling may very well have a serious effect on the larger structure.

Language too has been undergoing great changes. Of course this affects social behavior. The people born after the war speak a language that is different in many ways from that which the older generation uses. One important change here is the use—I should probably say nonuse—of honorifics. The young don't pay much attention to this nowadays. Television and radio with their need for rapid speech cut out a lot of what used to be *de rigueur* polite speech. Of course, the younger people in business, for instance, have to observe many polite social forms, but outside of business hours or when they are not dealing with their bosses or important clients they are more relaxed in their speech. It will be interesting to see what courtesies today's young people will demand when they occupy the important positions in society.

RB: Something important to watch, I believe, will be how the new time limits on telephone use will effect the use of honorific language. Since telephone users will no longer be able to talk for twenty or thirty minutes for the same price that they now talk for one minute, they will probably limit their calls severely. And the thing that will probably be reduced the most will be courtesy exchanges, that seemingly endless stream of polite language that begins and ends most telephone conversations, especially between women of middle age or older.

JS: This will of course affect both the sense of hierarchy and the sense of order.

Not only is the use of honorifics decreasing, but the language is being changed by the great number of English and European words being brought into daily use. The newspapers and magazines are full of these. Many of these words will probably become part of the Japanese language; they'll be adapted, Japanized. This change will occur in a manner similar to that in which the Japanese have adopted Western clothes. Older people wear Western clothes somewhat clumsily, while the young people dress very smartly. Western clothes are part of the culture now, they are no longer something imported. To the young they are as Japanese as kimono, perhaps more so. Most young Japanese girls today don't know how to wear kimono and rely on the help of their mothers on those special occasions when they have to wear kimono.

Another important change is in eating habits. Since the medieval days, when Buddhism frowned on the killing of animals, vegetables and fish along with rice have been the chief foods of the Japanese. Today they eat more meat than they ever have before—perhaps with the exception of the neolithic period, when their ancestors, unacquainted with wet-rice agriculture, relied on hunting.

Many of the changes to be seen in modern Japan, then, may very well not be superficial, I believe.

RB: What do you like most and least about Japan and the Japanese?

JS: What I like least is the inferiority complex toward the West, which takes the form of blind admiration for anything Western. This is especially true of Japanese intellectuals and artists. They carry it so far that it smacks of masochism. And I wonder often if there isn't a streak of masochism in the Japanese psyche.

This inferiority complex also takes the form of what I call "racial snobbism." I think that there are among Japanese intellectuals remnants of Yukichi Fukuzawa's[1] idea of inter-marriage with Caucasians to improve the quality of the Japanese race. Now, no one says anything like that these days, but the feeling of inferiority toward the West is still very strong. Japan is now heavily indebted to the West and has been thriving on Westernization. As a result she has become a major economic power. And, among Japanese intellectuals at least, there is almost indiscriminate admiration of anything Western: not Western policies that affect Japan, or things like America's Vietnam war, but Western culture, Western science. For instance, they find it difficult to speak of Japanese culture or Japanese values without juxtaposing them on Western ones. They are obsessed with making this kind of comparison. They seldom use a completely Japanese standard, never mind a Far Eastern one. French intellectuals will often refer to ancient Greek mythology and sages, and this is fitting because French culture is deeply rooted in ancient Greek thought. You might expect the Japanese, who have received so much of their culture from China and Korea, to refer to the values of these countries. But oh no, they won't! They would rather quote the ancient Greeks and Europeans!

The intellectuals revel in feelings of inferiority; they even

1. Yukichi Fukuzawa (1835–1901) was a famous educator and the founder of Tokyo's Keio University.

seem to derive pleasure from them. The other side of this coin is their indifference to, really their contempt for, things Chinese and Korean. Of course, there is a constructive side to Japanese masochism; it is in large part responsible for the emergence of the Japanese state. They thrive on their feelings of inferiority, you see. Snobbism, of course, always contains an element of aspiration, and like snobbish bourgeoisie the Japanese want to attain the level of the people they admire.

The Chinese and the Koreans don't have this inferiority complex. Because they don't "worship" the West as Japan does they haven't imitated Western ways nearly as much. Consequently, they haven't made the technological progress Japan has. They feel that they are as good as Westerners and therefore they don't need many Western improvements. They are willing to go back to their own roots, while the Japanese intellectuals turn their backs on theirs. The Japanese are, I believe, barking up the wrong tree. So much so that it looks like they are trying to become yellow Caucasians or yellow Europeans.

A Japanese writer recently published a two-thousand-page novel about a Roman emperor. This strikes me as a good example of what I mean by trying to become Western. Mishima was able to do this successfully in his play about de Sade, but that was because he and de Sade had similar sensibilities.

I don't mean, of course, that tradition is all good and Westernization all bad. Not at all. Obviously it has brought a lot of good, particularly in the material sense. What I do not like is the uncritical acceptance of Western things and ideas and the unthinking assumption that Western things are somehow innately superior.

What I like most about Japan is the emphasis given here to beauty and order. People give a lot of time and effort to rituals and ceremonies. Not only at weddings and funerals, but they also observe them in everyday life. The relationship between the living and the dead, for example, involves a lot of ritual. Commoner examples of their love for beauty and order are the tea ceremony, flower arranging, and their gardens. When you observe a Japanese family of a certain social level you find a degree of preoccupation with beauty that is not to be found in their counterparts in other countries. It's usually on a small scale, but they do pay a lot of attention to beautifying life.

Human life, after all, is a very chaotic thing. And the Japanese, with their concern for beauty and order, are able to create at least a semblance of order. I appreciate this very much, this establishing of rituals and observing them. Art is not separated from living in Japan.

RB: What do you think of Prime Minister Tanaka's plan to remodel the Japanese archipelago?

JS: It's vandalism! For me the most important element of Japanese culture is the aesthetic tradition. This tradition, responsible for producing all of Japan's artists and great art works, is so deep-rooted that it generates a kind of metaphysic. The artists, painters, and poets, like Sotatsu, Korin, Basho, have all been very much concerned with nature, with their country's natural beauty. The indigenous Shinto religion, a primary root of Japan, is a kind of nature worship. Linguists tell us that the word "nature" did not exist in ancient Japanese. There was no need for it; the ancient Japanese saw no need for such a distinction because he felt himself to be a part of nature. In the West, nature was often presented as something hostile, a thing to be conquered. Hence, the rapid growth of science and technology in the West. The Japanese, on the other hand, felt that nature was in their bloodstream, a part of their psyche.

What Tanaka proposes to do is to tear the country apart and destroy its natural beauty for the sake of economic growth and for conveniences which we don't need. For this beauty he intends to exchange more cars, airports, highways, and superexpress trains, and we have more than enough of those. What we have is creating great problems. By consensus Japan is the most polluted country in the world. Redeployment of Japan's industries will mean that all natural beauty will go, the way it has gone in the Tokyo-Yokohama area, the Nagoya area, the Kita Kyushu area.

This destruction of natural beauty may very well put an end to the art that thrives on it and to the very essence of the Japanese spirit.

In his book, Tanaka says he wants to get rid of pollution, but the reason he gives is not because it is detrimental to human life but because it deters the growth of industry.

RB: Why do you think the Japanese people are allowing their natural beauty to be destroyed without much of an outcry, with hardly a murmur of dissent?

JS: The newspapers are campaigning against pollution, although their effect on the government seems inconsequential. I think the majority of people are against Tanaka's plan and their opposition has been shown in the dramatic increase in the number of seats the Communist Party won in the recent elections. It's not so much that people think the communists are competent, but they voted for them because their politicians violently oppose Tanaka's plan.

I've wondered why some ardent patriots have not committed *seppuku* in protest against the plan, because it really is a colossal mistake. You know, once you destroy nature you don't get it back; it's an irredeemable act.

RB: How has your being a member of the largest minority group in Japan affected your relations with the Japanese?

JS: I'm bitter about the way Koreans are generally treated in Japan, but I have to admit that I have not personally experienced prejudice. I was able to attend a Japanese university and I did not try to enter a Japanese company. Consequently, I didn't feel I was barred from these things. Perhaps because I worked for a French news agency and am familiar with European culture and languages I was identified in some way with what the Japanese admire. For me, the racial snobbism has worked in a strange way.

Japanese prejudice against Koreans and Chinese is of rather recent origin. It belongs to Japan's expansionist period, which followed soon after the Japanese opened their country to Western penetration and began to feel inferior to the West.

When they took the West for their model they turned against the cultures that had nurtured them. They westernized themselves in a few decades and turned around and defeated the Chinese in the Sino-Japanese war of 1894–95. Very soon after that they occupied and annexed Korea. Because they were able to do these things rather easily they became contemptuous of Koreans and Chinese. Though with the emergence of Communist China as a major world power, the Japanese are quickly modifying their attitude toward the Chinese.

The Japanese prejudice against Koreans isn't like the prejudice of whites against blacks in the United States. The Koreans look like the Japanese, being of the same racial stock. When the Koreans were bringing the Asian continental culture to Japan, they were very highly regarded and they occupied important posts in the imperial court. Professor Namio Egami maintains that the rulers of the Korean Kingdom of Paekche were probably the founders of Yamato, the paramount Japanese state in ancient times. This means that the imperial Japanese family is descended from Korean kings. And it's well known now that Emperor Kammu's mother was of Korean origin.

It was in art and religion that the Korean influence was the strongest, and anyone who knows anything about Japanese history knows how important art and Buddhism have been to Japan. An important point to remember here, however, is that most adult Japanese are ignorant of these early ties. They have not been taught such things in their schools. It's being taught now, but not much importance is given to it. Recent archaeological finds are revealing how very important the early ties were and these have been getting a good play in the press. Until the last decade this relationship was an unpopular one, but now some scholars are able to support it with enthusiasm. They couldn't do that before.

RB: With Korea on the rise technologically and economically, do you think Japanese prejudice against Koreans will decrease?

js: It's diminishing now. The three leading Japanese newspapers seem to have decided to educate the public about Korean-Japanese relations. This will help, I believe, and may improve the lot of the more than 620,000 Korean residents of Japan. The popular Japanese view of Koreans has been that they are a people of an inferior culture with inferior abilities. One reason for this is that the Koreans who came to Japan to work in this century—those who came voluntarily and those who were forced to come—were of the lowest strata of their society. They were mostly uneducated farmers and laborers, and these, as you know, do not make good cultural ambassadors. Once in Japan, they had to work so hard to survive and were the lowest paid people that for a long time they remained uneducated and unskilled. This is why so many Japanese were prejudiced against them and spread derogatory stories about them.

Prejudice against Koreans remains today even among some of the best-educated Japanese scholars. For example, some of them cannot bring themselves to say "Korean influence"; they always say "continental influence."

rb: Which of your Japanese contemporaries, individuals or groups, do you respect the most?

js: Yukio Mishima, as artist and individual. For me he was the only Japanese to achieve an authentic synthesis of East and West. In him was the crystallization of one hundred years of Westernization. It's a shame that it went to waste at his death. He was passionately interested in the West, but he didn't stop there, for he outgrew this interest, went back to his Japanese roots, and came up with something new. He was one of the very few Japanese writers whose work was an asset to the world as well as to Japan.

Mishima's return to his own roots is in marked contrast to the path followed by most Japanese intellectuals. He was scornful of them for blindly absorbing Western culture while ignoring the Japanese tradition. His emperor worship and his patriotism were in part directed against the trend of worship of the West. He himself had been imitative of such Western writers as Radiguet and Mann, but he outgrew this early stage and continued to develop himself. I think he is the only modern Japanese writer to have put the Japanese metaphysical tradition to good use in his work.

It's interesting to me that by turning back to the Japanese tradition, Mishima became universal. One example of this is the response his suicide drew from Malraux and other French intellectuals. Malraux was tremendously moved by Mishima's death. He felt an affinity with Mishima for his concept of death.

It was interesting to compare the reactions of the French intellectuals and the intellectuals of Anglo-Saxon cultures to Mishima's suicide. The British, for instance, were horrified. It was a barbaric act that recalled to them the acts of sword-wielding Japanese officers against British prisoners of war during World War II. As I said, Malraux admired Mishima for his act. A French painter did a painting in honor of Mishima and a poet wrote a poem eulogizing his act. They felt he was a man of superior sensibility who had great insight into the concept of death. The same act offended British sensibilities; they thought it a great violation of common sense.

RB: What was your own reaction to his suicide?

JS: I have nothing but admiration for him. You see, all his life he had been obsessed with the idea of death. In the years before his death, when we met he used to say that the time had come for him to write "something cosmic." "Something cosmic" turned out to be the tetralogy *The Sea of Fertility*. We talked often of death, though Mishima rarely chose a subject like that for ordinary conversation. I tried to get him interested in Taoism, while he tried to get me interested in *kendo*. He was fascinated by Taoism, but he said he would rather not get involved, because, he said, Once I get into it, I know I'll never be able to get out of its labyrinth. *Bushido*, on the other hand, offered a heroic confrontation with, and the ultimately masculine solution to, the problem of death. Therefore I regard his *seppuku* as a metaphysical act in the guise of a samurai. He wanted to die as a samurai, but he was deceiving himself in a way, and he knew it, because he was an artist *par excellence*. In spite of his bodybuilding and *kendo*, and his seemingly impregnable façade, he never ceased to be extraordinarily sensitive and vulnerable. He was really a tormented soul.

Another important aspect was his effort to get out of the shell of the novelist. He felt that as a novelist he was chiefly a voyeur, standing outside reality. The stuttering arsonist in *The Temple of the Golden Pavilion*, his masterpiece, for instance, is portrayed as a youth who is unable to get into reality. In his last years, Mishima went out of his way to appear in movies and on the stage, because he was fed up with observing other people—Honda, one of the chief characters in the tetralogy, is portrayed as an incorrigible voyeur—and he wanted to reverse the position by being seen by others as a man of action.

There's also the question of his affinity with the mind of the criminal, who is also outside reality and life. It was no coincidence that legally speaking, he committed a crime when he broke into the office of a high Self-Defense Force official. These things show the working of an extraordinarily complex mind and sensitivity, which he found futile and wanted to get out of. Through *bushido* he was trying to transform himself.

His suicide can't be explained from a single viewpoint alone. It encompasses, I think, the whole history of Japan, going back to *bushido*, the warrior ethic of medieval Japan, and even the *Man'yoshu*.[2] I believe Hideo Kobayashi, the eminent critic, said something along the same lines. For all that, Mishima had a strong affinity with thinkers like Georges Bataille and André Malraux.

He was a bundle of contradictions. As a personality, he was fairly simple; but intellectually he was extremely complex. He used to call himself a mixed-up kid. He was more knowl-

2. The *Man'yoshu* is a long poetry anthology compiled about 760. The poems it contains are from the Asuka (552–646) and Nara (646–794) periods, and number 4,516.

edgeable about Western culture than most of the Japanese intellectuals and artists. He lived in a Western-style house and practiced a Westernized life. But this didn't blind him to his own roots.

RB: Why do you think he chose the time and the place he did?

JS: He had a strong resentment against modern Japanese society. He disliked intensely the Japanese worship of the West and of technology. For instance, he abhorred television. And he hated commercialism. You know that in Japan even well-known writers and composers appear in commercials. He despised them for that. I admire him for never accepting any of the tremendous offers he received to appear in commercials. He invariably rejected them.

Spiritually, Mishima was an aristocrat. He felt estranged from modern society because of that. He had no friends in the literary world, except Yasunari Kawabata, who was also not really a part of the literary establishment. He didn't like the intellectuals and felt that they didn't understand him or his work. *The Sea of Fertility,* for instance, he felt wouldn't get a good reception in Japan because it was too Japanese, too Buddhist, for the critics.

He wanted to shock them into awareness of their own tradition, from which they were estranged. In a way, Mishima was playing with time and history. By committing what was in appearance a shockingly anachronistic act, he distorted time and took the Japanese, though only for a moment, back to the days when *seppuku,* probably the most peculiarly Japanese tradition, was not an anomaly.

At the end he felt he had exhausted his literary energy. He could have written more works, of course—he had written nearly one hundred works—but he felt he had written everything he wanted to write. It was as though he had lived eighty years during his forty-five years of life. At the end he also felt that writing was futile: he spoke often of the emptiness of words. He wanted to act, to be done with philosophical considerations. As I've said, death in the *bushi* way provided a heroic confrontation. So he acted in that manner.

RB: Do you think that Japan is truly changing for the worse, or is this merely more of the kind of sentiment that is always dragged up by people who yearn for the "good old days"?

JS: Romantic nostalgia must be one of the most persistent habits of man. In any age, in any society, the older generation deplores the present and looks back to the "good old days." Only the other day I read one of Jun'ichiro Tanizaki's novels, in which one of his characters laments the ugliness of the Tokyo of the 1950s and reminisces about how wonderful a city Tokyo was in the prewar days. If Tanizaki found Tokyo ugly in the 1950s, what would he think of the city today, with the streets smothered in smog and cars?

I myself believe, nevertheless, that Japan is definitely on the decline. While economically the country is among the richest in the world, she is producing less and less in the cultural domain. No young people in their twenties of notable talent have appeared during the past decade or so in most artistic fields: cinema, literature, fine arts, architecture, et cetera. In cinema, only a handful are really functioning, directors like Shinoda and Oshima, but they are in their late thirties. Otherwise, moviemaking is almost dead, a far cry from the days when Kurosawa, Ozu, and Ichikawa were active. In literature, the "new faces" nowadays are almost entirely writers in their late thirties and forties, and many of them are housewives. There isn't a single novelist of note who is in his twenties. This is a peculiar phenomenon in a country where novels are still widely read. It's as though with the younger generation Japan has stopped her creative activity. I don't know what really accounts for this creative hiatus. It may be that their creative instincts are being strangled by technology, the computer, and environmental pollution. It seems to get less and less interesting, and one has to go back to other times in history in the search for stimulating ideas.

# 体験
# 10

## DANIEL OKIMOTO
### American
### Student

Born in a wartime relocation camp for Japanese-Americans at California's Santa Anita racetrack in 1942, he first visited Japan in 1962. As a graduate student at Tokyo University, he studied in Japan for two and a half years. He is the author of *American in Disguise,* and is currently a Ph.D. candidate at the University of Michigan.

RB: From your own experience, would you say that the nisei's physical resemblance and family relations open any doors for him in Japanese society?

DO: Yes, they do. Japan is a self-enclosed society from the perspective of most of the foreigners who reside here. And the nisei's physical resemblance and family connections give him openings which are denied the Caucasian or other foreigners. Having relatives here is a very good thing for nisei who do want to reside in Japan for some time because through associating with his relatives he is able to get himself accepted into kinship groups and make inroads into the society that are closed to people who have no such opportunities.

But even without relatives, it's easier for the nisei. The Japanese feel a sort of racial bond with nisei which makes them much more at ease with us. Often my Japanese friends have remarked on how much easier it is to talk to me than to other foreigners—because I'm Japanese. They've said they feel tight and unnatural around foreigners who are not of Japanese origin.

RB: What problem is the nisei faced with when he comes to Japan?

DO: The greatest problem is caused by the expectations of the Japanese. If the nisei wishes to break into this tightly knit society, he must conform to Japanese social forms; he must behave as they do to a much greater extent than other foreigners. This is because he does have some ties, however remote, to Japanese culture, and the Japanese feel that he should have had some training in their ways. If he should break indigenous customs, therefore, he is subject to a great deal more criticism. It works two ways, this racial link.

RB: Have you ever encountered any Japanese animosity toward nisei?

DO: Generally, no. I have come up against individuals who have seemed to be somewhat threatened by, or are jealous of, the nisei experience, and they may sometimes try to put the nisei at a disadvantage. But the Japanese are much more tolerant and accepting of the nisei than the nisei in America are of Japanese.

RB: What about the nisei community in Japan—the business and professional people and the U.S. civil service workers— do they tend to form their own groups or cliques? How are they integrated into Japanese society?

DO: It's natural perhaps for nisei to congregate together here. There are clubs in Japan composed entirely of nisei; there is a Canadian nisei club, an American nisei club, a Latin American nisei club, and so forth. Often the nisei also feels alienated here, I think, because the society is a closed one in so many respects. And it's natural for the nisei to seek the company of people who share a common background. However, by and large, nisei are probably better integrated into Japanese society than most other foreigners. They tend to have more contact with Japanese in their business and social lives.

RB: How have your Japanese friends reacted to your marriage to a Caucasian?

DO: The Japanese seem to think it's natural for me to have married a Caucasian in view of the fact that I was brought up in America. I have sensed no implicit criticism to my marriage among Japanese. However, if I were a Japanese and had to get along in this society, it would be much more difficult for me with a Caucasian than with a Japanese wife.

RB: How about your Japanese-American friends?

DO: They accept it. There are the Yellow Power types, however, who feel that a Japanese-American should marry his own kind—that is, a Japanese-American or a Japanese. They may feel that I've copped out on them, in a way, by marrying a white.

RB: Japanese often say that Westerners can never understand the Japanese way of life. Do you think this is true?

DO: No, I don't. Perhaps the Japanese have taken the old saying that East is East and West is West more to heart than Westerners have. They have probably been persuaded that there is more to the matter of Japanese inscrutability than is the case. Japan certainly has a very different culture, one that has to be understood from the inside, one that presents a number of special difficulties in understanding. But the problems have really been exaggerated, I feel. The remarkable insights of such people as Edwin Reischauer, Ruth Benedict, and Ronald Dore, to name just a few, into the nature of Japanese society prove that Japan is by no means an inscrutable nation—even though it is hard at times to understand.

RB: There are those who say that Japanese and Westerners are so different that no real bridges of affection can link them. Their thesis goes on to say that neither side is willing to change its ways enough to effect cultural links other than on the economic, political, and sometimes artistic levels. Do you agree with this?

DO: It's too pessimistic. It doesn't do justice to the bridges that have been built. Despite differences in culture, Japanese and Westerners can, I feel, come to a deep understanding and affection for one another. Of course, relations are always in danger of cultural misunderstandings, but it's much too pessimistic to say that groups of human beings can't be bound together by a commonality of interests and affection.

RB: Then would you say that the nisei is in a unique position to serve as a cultural link between Japan and the West?

DO: No, I wouldn't. The nisei is in no better position to serve as a cultural link than other Westerners who are deeply interested in this country and are willing to make the effort to understand it. The nisei does have a special advantage when it comes to breaking into Japanese society, but sadly the nisei is sometimes hung up on identity problems that stand in the way of his serving as a link. Some of the nisei I've known here are turned off by Japan and have rejected it because it hasn't come up to their standards of what a society should be.

RB: What are the least and most attractive elements of Japanese society?

DO: The tremendous pressures against individual freedom I find is the least attractive feature of Japanese society. It comes out in a number of different ways; for example, I can't wear shorts on the streets as I can in America because it's something that people simply don't do here. I can't suddenly call upon people unless I have a formal introduction. I can't do a lot of the things I'm free to do in the States because this society is structured more formally. The repressive nature of Japanese society in terms of individual freedom is very unattractive. On the other hand, this very aspect is also one reason why I enjoy Japan. That is, once you are part of a certain group, you are accepted fully and relationships with other members of that group can be extremely warm. This group solidarity gives a person a real sense of security and belonging.

RB: In *American in Disguise* you have written about your observations on the Japanese student movement and have been scathing in your characterization of the Japanese political leaders. Can I say that, in general, your sympathies lie with the students?

DO: Yes, very much so. Perhaps it's because I'm a student myself. But I do feel that the grievances of the students are justified. If you look at what is happening in Japanese society— the corruption, the tightly knit elite group, the divorce from popular rule in many respects—then I think you can understand why the students were up in arms about the nature of their society and the problems that confront the universities. The students really have been protesting against the basic weaknesses of Japanese society, ranging from the university to politics. Educational priorities have long been neglected in Japan. Public universities receive less money from the Ministry of Education, for instance, than business spends on entertainment. This is a gross distortion of values. I sympathize very much with the students in their protest against this failure to right social wrongs.

RB: What do you think of the means of dissent the students have employed?

DO: I feel ambivalent about this problem. On the one hand I see that the students have very few other means by which to make their opinions heard. I don't think the government would listen to what they have to say if they presented petitions in an orderly manner to make their case known. I think it would be very hard for them to go through established channels to make their voices heard. This is one reason the student movement took to the streets.

On the other hand, violent tactics are leading Japan slowly down the road toward a reaction. I hope it won't lead to a fascist sort of repression, but I can see that violence has been very counterproductive for the liberal cause here. I feel some concern for the future of liberalism in Japan.

RB: What do you think of the Yellow Power movement?

DO: It's a recent development that owes a great deal to the Black Power movement. It arose in response to the racial tensions in the U.S. It's an interesting movement, one that is trying to give Orientals in the United States a sense of solidarity and to politicize a rather passive group of people and to make them active in the fight for civil liberties. In this respect, I stand behind it. But realistically speaking, I don't think it will ever become a major movement in the United States; it will never gain the influence, say, of the Black Power movement. Nor will it ever become as militant. But within the limitations of small numbers, the Yellow Power movement can achieve a lot, giving Orientals a sense of pride in their culture and in their past and motivating them to participate in the great issues at stake.

RB: Several black leaders have said that the reason the U.S. dropped the atomic bomb on Japan and not on Germany was a racist one, born of the same impulse that caused the imprisonment of thousands of Japanese-Americans but only a few German-Americans. Do you agree with this charge?

DO: I don't think the individuals who made the decision to drop the bomb were solely motivated by racist sentiments. It was a very complex decision, and I think it would be a gross simplification to reduce their motives to racism alone. It is interesting, though, that it was a "yellow" people that the bomb was dropped on. A lot of Japanese-Americans feel that this choice was no accident. And increasingly as I talked to more and more Japanese who were angry about the Vietnam war and who saw it as a war to exterminate yellow people, I discovered more and more of them interpreting the dropping of the atomic bomb on Japan as a racially inspired decision.

RB: Do you think that blacks and Oriental have a common cause against the white man?

DO: I'm afraid the situation might possibly degenerate to the point where they would have to band together against the white man. It's unfortunate that things have to be considered in these triangular categories of black, yellow, and white. There are a great many white people, I feel, who are sympathetic with the Third World movement and who will try to do all they can on behalf of the blacks and Orientals. Their assistance is necessary for blacks and Orientals to get what they seek.

RB: Then you believe that those people in the Third World movement who say there is no place for whites in the movement are wrong?

DO: I disagree with them very strongly. From practical imperatives alone, blacks and yellows can't hope to achieve their goals without the assistance of whites. Not only that, rejection of the whites who are concerned with this struggle is unjust. Consciously or not, it conveys a flavor of the same kind of racist sentiments I deplore in American whites.

RB: Do you think the American whites will ever face up to the consequences of their racism?

DO: By God, I hope so! I can foresee no hope for America—or for the world—if they don't.

RB: Do you see any signs that they are waking up?

DO: Yes, I do. In the past decade significant progress has been made, especially in the area of black civil rights. This may signal the start of broader reforms in the United States. Particularly through the efforts of America's young people some encouraging signs of progress have been made and more promises to be made in the future.

RB: Have you found any racism among the Japanese?

DO: Not in the same sense that it exists in America, largely because the Japanese don't have America's kind of racial mix. But I think the Japanese are as *conscious* of race as any people I've seen. Japanese make a very sharp distinction between "us" and "them." This comes out often in their relations with foreigners. For some this comes close to racism—especially among some of the older Japanese, who entertain unfavorable stereotyped images of Koreans, Southeast Asians, and Chinese. Even some of the younger ones have told me that they feel strange around Negroes or frightened by being near Pakistanis or Indians. Racism doesn't exist here as it does in America because you don't have the same racial heterogeneity, but if a time were ever to come when Japan did have large racial minorities to contend with, the problem of social assimilation could conceivably be worse, believe it or not, than it is now in the United States.

RB: What dangers must Japan avoid as she enlarges her role in international affairs?

DO: Right now Japan is playing the role of political eunuch. In a sense, she's having her cake and eating it too; she has been largely relieved of international responsibilities commensurate with her economic position. I think that in the future Japan will find herself less able to enjoy such freedom from global responsibilities. History shows us that there have been few nations heavily involved in economic investments abroad that have been able to stay out of political—or military—entanglements. Southeast Asia as a region is extremely important to Japan as a trading partner, and it is likely that this market will become increasingly important in the future. There may be situations when Japan will be very tempted to get involved in the internal affairs of nations in that region in order to protect her interests. The Straits of Malacca, for example, are vital to Japanese national security; if Japan were ever denied access through the straits, her flow of oil would be delayed and perhaps made prohibitively costly.

RB: Japan would feel it necessary to protect herself from whom?

DO: A hostile power in control of the area.

体験
# 11

## ANTONIN RAYMOND
### American
### Architect

Born in Czechoslovakia, he went to the United States from Prague in 1910 because he wanted to work with Frank Lloyd Wright. In New York he worked with Cass Gilbert on the Woolworth Building, met Wright, and was invited by him to travel together to Japan to build the Imperial Hotel in Tokyo. Mr. Raymond arrived in Japan in 1920 and, except for the years 1937–47, he and his wife Noémi have lived part of each year there. Among his numerous architectural works in Japan are the original Reader's Digest Building, Nanzan University in Nagoya, the Gumma Music Center, St. Anselm's, and the U.S. Embassy. The emperor of Japan has conferred on him the Order of the Rising Sun, Third Class. *Antonin Raymond: An Autobiography* was published in 1973.

RB: Which of your experiences in Japan has made the most profound impression on you?

AR: When I came back to Japan after World War II, in 1947, I landed at Yokohama and rode up to Tokyo through an area with which I had been very familiar. The total destruction, even the smell of the place, is something I can never forget. And when I met the people, I was amazed at how their moral character had degenerated. Even women from wealthy families sold themselves because they had no food for their hungry children.

*162*

Not only the terrible effects of the war made a deep impression on me but the attitude of the people was something I can't forget. They were not complaining; nobody said a word but you could see the horror: they acted it and looked it. You could see in them the effects of a terrible downfall. I would not have believed it if I had not seen the change myself.

Because of this great change their coming up again is just as amazing. They really are an astonishing people.

When I got back to Japan, the Socony Oil people asked me to inspect their installations along the seashore to see how to restore them. In the last days of the war, ships of the American fleet had sailed up and down the coast bombarding it indiscriminately. It was a terrible thing, but it was war, and the spirit of revenge for Pearl Harbor was very strong then. The complete destruction of the areas they hit was unbelievable. I could not see, from a technical viewpoint, how we could rebuild the area. Just getting rid of the concrete wreckage seemed impossible.

The suffering and the almost fatalistic attitude of the Japanese impressed me most. They were ready for any sacrifice. Their attitude was, Let's get on with it; let's do the work we must do. They were ready for anything—anything except more war.

Another impression that is almost as strong is of the day after the Great Kanto Earthquake of 1923. Again what I remember strongest was the attitude of the Japanese people. They showed very little emotion. They were quiet. You take the Italians, for example: when something like an earthquake happens they wring their hands, they scream and run about, they make a great deal of noise and trouble; for them a crisis is the end of the world. Not the Japanese. They got quietly to work organizing themselves. They immediately started to help people who needed it, and there were very many of those.

The amazing thing was that there was no panic. Well, there was one thing, the hunting of the Koreans. For some strange reason they thought the Koreans would attack them and would poison the wells.[1] There was almost no public water supply then, so that everyone depended on the wells. The Japanese got me to patrol the neighborhood carrying a bamboo spear.

I had a little French Ford at the time and I was able to get all the gas I wanted because I was driving people all over the city, helping those who were hurt. Sometimes I'd be carrying so many people they would be clinging to the sides of the car like bunches of grapes.

Nobody bothered me because I was a foreigner; just the opposite. The manager of the Imperial Hotel was worried about the safety of his guests, however. Hibiya Park is just across the street from where the hotel stood and there were many people of the lower strata there and they were very hungry. The manager was afraid they would attack the hotel and steal what they could. He asked the army to station guards around the hotel. At first they wouldn't do it, but later soldiers came to protect it. But the poor people never bothered the hotel or its guests.

On the day of the Great Earthquake my wife and I were not hurt at all. Our house was at Shinagawa, very close to the bay, and part of it slid into the water. At the time I was working in an office building in downtown Tokyo and my wife was in Shinagawa. We immediately rushed to get to each other and, fantastically in all that confusion, we met on Shinagawa Bridge.

RB: How has living among the Japanese affected you, your personality, your outlook on life, and your basic approach to living?

AR: Being an artist and an architect, I was very interested in tracing the fundamentals of the Japanese design philosophy. I found it very sympathetic to my own ideas and feelings. Over the years as I studied this philosophy, the more I became con-

1. Japanese vigilante groups armed with bamboo spears, clubs, kitchen knives, and other weapons set up roadblocks and stormed Korean settlements, capturing and killing thousands of Korean residents. The dead numbered 4,000 and included some Japanese who were mistakenly murdered.

vinced that what we consider truly modern in Western architecture the Japanese had had for millenniums. Exactly the same principles: the simplest, the most natural, the most economical is the best, they said. And they are creative, not copyists as is thought in the West. When I came here the Japanese were thought to be mere imitators because of the things they exported. I found just the opposite to be true: they are a truly creative people. Today I believe that I have been proven right.

This study put me on the right track. It made me, I believe, one of the most creative architects of modern times, even if I receive no fanfare for my work, as Frank Lloyd Wright has. Frank was also in Japan, but he really did not understand it. He liked Japan, and its influence on him was strong, although he was affected differently from me. He was a fantastic genius of ornamentation. In his mind, when he saw an empty space, he would create an extremely imaginative design. In Japan he found much ornamentation to stimulate him, but where for the Japanese ornamentation was a byproduct, for Frank it was the principal thing.

I think the influence I received from Japan was more fundamental. It came not through my eyes but through my soul. I was truly impressed—and I still am—by true Japanese architecture, like the Grand Shrine of Ise. The opposite of this is the baroque influence of Nikko. Frank Lloyd Wright loved Nikko, you see. The beauty of Nikko is accessible to almost everybody, while the beauty of Ise is comprehensible to only those who have spent all their life trying to find out what is good or bad. It's not for those who take a casual look and say I like it or don't like it.

The design philosophy of the Japanese was very sympathetic to my own. They had what I was seeking, and that made our stay in Japan extremely pleasant. I never had the slightest difficulty with the Japanese in any way! I have worked on hundreds of architectural jobs in Japan, projects involving thousands and thousands of dollars, and I never used a lawyer, never had a strike on any of my jobs, and I've never had trouble with the tax people. I think this is because the Japanese know that I understand them more than most foreigners do. We, my wife and I, are sympathetic to them. Why, we even liked Japanese food from the first day we ate it!

RB: Did these good relations continue even during the immediate prewar years, when the militarists had taken power?

AR: The Japanese military people knew that I had been an intelligence officer in the American army in World War I and they knew I was still a reserve officer, but their officers shook dice and drank with me in the Tokyo Club.

My true friends amongst the Japanese said to me in 1937, Antonin, you'd better go home, because if you stay here it will not be pleasant for you. So we packed up and went home.

An interesting job I worked at during the war was building mock Japanese workmen's houses. Because I was the only architect who knew how the Japanese built their buildings, the Pentagon had me design them. We got cypress wood from Russia and tatami mats from Hawaii and we prefabricated the buildings in Fort Dix, New Jersey, and sent them to Nevada, where the air force experimented on them with different kinds of bombs. Finally, they came up with the kind of bomb which they wanted. When my workmen were digging the pond in my garden after the war they found one of those bombs.

RB: Do you feel that you have been integrated into Japanese society?

AR: You know, after fifty years in Japan, I am still a *gaijin*. That is understandable. The Japanese think—no, they know— that they are a chosen people, more so than the Jews. They are chosen to dominate the world; not dominate physically so much as being above every other nation.

One of the problems of being a foreigner is the Japanese language. It takes a young Japanese about fifteen years to learn his language well and it takes a foreigner a lifetime to learn it and then he dies. The language is formidable and few foreigners learn it well.

But it's absurd for a foreigner to worry about always being a *gaijin* in Japan. A *gaijin* can never be a Japanese, just as a gentile can never become a Jew.

RB: Did you ever mind being a *gaijin?*

AR: No, it's the proper thing. We have a place and we fit into it.

RB: How would you characterize the Japanese ruling class, the rich and powerful, the top business and government leaders?

AR: They know how to run the country. They have a wonderful organization and the people have to follow them. I have my best friends among the aristocracy.

The Japanese ruling class is like any other ruling class except that they are better organized.

RB: Do you think their organization is a good thing?

AR: It's marvelous. They have real strength. It's also very dangerous to the world. We Americans have nothing to match it. Americans could not work together the way the Japanese can. I wish I could live another fifty years to see if they will dominate the world. I think they will.

I admire their organization and I have organized my office in the Japanese way. Nobody ever gets fired and the employment is for life. If you don't do it that way you will not get really good employees. I have in my company several people who have been with me for fifty years. These people run the company now. If they wanted to, they could easily break me because they have the power. But I never have to worry about them. My manager is a marvelous man.

I have sixty men in my office and often I can't get them to go home because they are so interested in their work. In our office in New York the men get good salaries and they are good men, but to them five o'clock is five o'clock, weekends are weekends, and overtime is overtime.

RB: Have you found anything you dislike about the Japanese?

AR: I dislike—though I can excuse it—the fact that we

can never be fully accepted in Japanese society. We have Japanese friends, many of them, but we are not accepted as part of Japanese society. In the United States you have the opposite situation. Americans are happy to make you an American, they accept you. So, at the end of fifty years, we do not really belong to Japan.

RB: You've mentioned that in architecture the important thing is integrity, and I would think that for you another important thing would be to be an integral part of the society in which you work.

AR: That's true. And that is why it's a disappointment not to be accepted in all senses. I think that there must be very few foreigners who want to die here. They all want to go home in the end, I think. So do I. I am ready to give it all up, my home, the security, the comfort I have in Japan. All of it.

RB: In your relations with the Japanese ruling class have you ever come across any corruption?

AR: No, I never did. No one ever tried to bribe me, and I have dealt with hundreds of big businessmen, politicians, and bureaucrats. I've never lost any money: I'm paid when I send the bill, and I can't say that about America.

RB: You don't think that everything in Japan is organized primarily for the benefit of a very small group of people?

AR: Of course it is. But from my point of view that is the proper way. I don't believe that democracy ever existed. There is no such thing. Even Plato has said that. Don't tell me it exists in the United States, because it doesn't. The people don't govern there. I don't know why people bother about democracy or its absence in Japan.

RB: Do you think the Japanese are losing their artistic traditions?

AR: They are losing some of it, but they are still making beautiful things. Fifty years ago when you went into a department store like Tokyo's Mitsukoshi, you found it was full of beautiful things. Now the stores are full of fantastically ugly things. They have become chambers of horror.

By moving into apartment houses the people have lost their artistic understanding. Completely. I think that it will come back in time, but it's gone now. They will adjust to the new environments they are creating and they will make beautiful things for them. But at present they are buying antiques and such from Europe and they are filling their homes with abominable trash.

RB: How does Tokyo compare architecturally with the leading cities of the West?

AR: The Japanese are the best architects in the world today by far. I don't mean that everything in Japan is beautiful, of course. There are many ugly buildings and ugly towns and cities. There are any number of ugly buildings in Tokyo, but there are also some good ones, while we have no good ones. We are at a middle level making mediocre structures. The Japanese are making buildings that are unbelievably ugly or truly beautiful.

In the United States you have many people who have the money and who want to contribute to building a beautiful environment, but there are no architects who know the true way of building, from the inside. The American architects, even the top men, are picture makers. They make a picture of the building they intend to build and they sell the idea to the unsuspecting, well-meaning client. Afterwards, they will try to fit the inside of the building to the picture they have sold. Take the Kennedy Memorial in Washington: it's unbelievably ugly, Hollywood decoration. Rockefeller Center in New York is not great architecture, but at least it has some idea at its base. The Lincoln Center in New York is a complete flop. It's a typical example of what I call picture-making design. The architect made it for people whose understanding of architecture is zero. They were sold a picture, and the acoustics in it do not work. This way of building is so childish. The acoustics are the first thing that should have been solved, and the building should have been built around that in the simplest way. Every architect should know that you must build from the inside out. Probably most of them know that, but they ignore this principle because they want to get the big jobs and become famous quickly.

RB: Who do you think are the best Japanese architects?

AR: There is no such thing as best, just as there is no such best writer and so on. There are outstanding Japanese architects, a few, like Junzo Yoshimura and Kenzo Tange, Maekawa, Sugiyama. Some of them came from my office.

The Japanese architects are having difficulties, though. Take Yoshimura's work on the new Imperial Palace, a truly superior design, an amazing performance for a modern architect! For a while he worked in perfect harmony with the Imperial Household Agency and everything went well. Then he wanted to go as far as designing the court dress for the imperial family because up to now, you know, they wear a weak imitation of the dress of British royalty. He wanted to make truly modern court dress in Japanese style. That was the commencement of his downfall. The bureaucrats in the Imperial Household said, That's going too far. And maybe a lot of the other designs go too far! So they started to change things. Yoshimura's overall design is marvelous, truly inspired; but they started to put things inside the building. Yoshimura, being a real architect, resigned, even though it was the Imperial Palace he was working on.

Another magnificent example of modern Japanese architecture is Tange's Olympic swimming pool in Yoyogi. It is so well integrated with its surroundings! But it is being spoiled now because it belongs to the city and they respond to the public wants—they have put in Coca-Cola stands and other things! It's an example of democracy, which doesn't work of course. But the building is still a splendid thing. We have nothing like it and neither has Europe.

In America, technology is the principal mainstay of culture. The creativity of the Americans is expressed in technology. Someone there is always creating something technological. They do it for profit, and that is a legitimate goal. Some American artists don't care about money, of course, but in Japan there are many creative people who don't care much about money. And architecture is vital here. In America there are only two architectural magazines. Neither of them is critical; they are mostly only interested in getting advertisements. In Japan there are about a dozen good, beautifully printed architectural magazines, and each one has a good critic who will tear to pieces an architect who thinks he's somebody. Of course it's done for his benefit. If they criticized an architect that way in the U.S., he would sue them!

RB: Do you think that there is any basis for long-lasting, deep, and peaceful relations between your two adopted countries—America and Japan?

AR: What stands in the way of such relations is the increasing rivalry in technology and business. Japan will surely try to surpass the United States economically. Even today the relations are becoming precarious, and I'm afraid they will become worse as the United States relinquishes to Japan domination of certain markets. America won't give up those markets easily, so there will be intense economic rivalry.

Culturally they can have friendly relations. They should be able to share each other's cultural wealth, but economically things do not look good for the future.

RB: Do you have any regrets about your relations with Japan?

AR: Just the other way, I think my most wonderful piece of luck was Frank Lloyd Wright's taking me to Japan. I'm grateful to Frank. I'll never forget the day. He came to our office in Greenwich Village and he said, Antonin, I've got forty thousand dollars in my pocket. Let's go to Japan and build the Imperial Hotel. We went together; he left and I stayed on, all these years.

体験

# 12

## CHARLES F. GALLAGHER
### American
### Scholar

He served during World War II as a Japanese-language officer in the U.S. Navy and was resident in Japan during the period 1945–49, for over three years of which he was Cultural Properties Adviser. Since that time he has made frequent visits to Japan. Mr. Gallagher has maintained academic interests over the past three decades in both Far Eastern and Near Eastern studies. He currently serves as Director of Studies of the American Universities Field Staff and as Consultant on International Relations at the University of Hawaii. He is the author of *The United States and North Africa* and contributes to such journals as *Foreign Affairs, Politique Etrangère, The Muslim World,* and *Oriental Art.*

RB: Japan's advances in international business have been accompanied by cries of "miraculous" and other epithets of wonder and astonishment, and, pejoratively, by "economic animal" and "economic slave." What would you say are the prevailing opinions of Japan in the world today?

CG: I think there has been a gradual drift in the climate of opinion in the world over the past approximately fifteen years —which is really when people first began noticing the Japanese economic performance—and this drift has gone from, in the beginning, a measure of surprise and a certain amount of admiration to a tendency now to look askance at Japan and then, finally, to be somewhat disturbed and unsettled by what is going on. In a way, I think that you have to remember that the world is used to economic miracles—there was the German miracle in the early and mid-fifties and the Italian miracle that preceded the Japanese, not so much chronologically as in the world's awareness of it. People weren't very aware of what was happening in Japan in the late fifties. Both the German and Italian miracles more or less petered out. Both of these countries are parts of the Western tradition, with all that that implies, and this makes them easier to understand.

Japan suffers from a certain feeling that it is not fully a member of Western civilization. One of the problems is that there is a certain air of mystery about the Japanese social, economic, and political structure which has produced the achievement that is there for everyone to see. And this mystery, this lack of understanding on the part of Western observers, contributes to the general feeling of unease. They don't really know how this has come about, in what ways the Japanese have done it.

I think that now we have reached a point where there is a great deal of distrust of Japanese economic and political behavior because the roots of it are not understood. Perhaps at the moment it is not so much distrust in the actual sense, as there are all sorts of institutional ways in which discussion and cooperation can be and are being furthered, but the basis of the feeling is that Japan doesn't fit into the fundamental sets, I would say, of the developed world.

RB: What would you say the pace of this growing unease is?

CG: It has grown very rapidly in the last year or so. I know this is the case in the United States. I'm not so certain that this is the case in Europe, but the indications I've noted during a recent trip are that it is growing there, too. The Europeans have watched Japan's exports to the United States, and it is widely expected that the Japanese will shift the burden of their exports to Europe. This is already happening: in the first six months of 1972, exports to Europe went up over thirty percent compared to the previous year, to West Germany they went up forty-one percent, and these rates of increase are much higher than in the case of the United States. This is going to cause more problems for the Japanese in their overseas relations.

RB: In conversation recently you remarked on the growing animosity—perhaps that's a stronger word than you used— toward the Japanese in Southeast Asia. Would you expand on this point?

CG: "Mistrust" is probably closer to the attitude I was describing. I think we ought to divide the feelings about Japan into several categories. One is those of the developed countries, with whom Japan has numerous relations: she's a member of OECD, the Group of Ten, and so on. Another area of reactions we should consider is that of the developing world, and we should include here countries like Australia, which supplies Japan with raw materials, and we might even include the U.S. here too, since the bulk of our trade is moving that way, toward supplying Japan with raw materials. Again, I would use the word "mistrust" to describe the feelings of this group. Some people in this area feel that perhaps their natural resources are being exploited by Japan. This, however, is a common feeling the developing countries have toward the industrialized nations: the countries that produce primary products have been complaining for many years that the prices they are paid for them do not increase proportionate to the increases they pay for the finished products. This feeling is not specifically directed toward Japan, then, but the feeling in Southeast Asia—and this has been widely reported—is that the Japanese are considered as greedy and ruthless exploiters of what they want. The Japanese, of course, deny this. They throw a different light on the problem by saying that there is no country that has such a fragile economy as theirs, no country that is so completely dependent on an outside source of raw materials. This is one of the reasons why they have to tread so carefully in the Middle East: they can't afford to offend the Arab countries, which supply about ninety percent of their petroleum.

You could look at it, I suppose, from the Japanese point of view. You could say the Japanese need Australia for a source of raw materials more than Australia needs Japan as a market.

There is a third area of feelings we should consider, that is, those of the communist-socialist bloc: China and the Soviet Union. I think we had better separate these, however. The Soviet Union is not afraid in any way of Japanese military revanchism; it's far too powerful a nation for that. It doesn't look upon Japan with quite the same degree of suspicion that China clearly does, at least as that expressed in statements by Chou En-lai on several occasions. I think that there is a genuine worry about Japanese militarism among some Chinese leaders, and it has been openly expressed that Japan's economic needs may drive her to certain overt political acts that the Chinese would not welcome.

RB: Do you think the trend in Japan since the Occupation has been toward an increase or a decrease in democratization?

CG: It depends on what you mean by democratization. If you're talking about a formal kind of democratization which is stated in a constitution or in laws that surround a constitution, that is one thing. But if you are talking about a *sense* of democracy having become imbued in a people, that is a different thing. You can have formal democracies, which look awfully good on paper, but in which there still is a great deal of hierarchical behavior and which do not correspond with our most advanced notions of social democracy. There is a great difference between Italy, on the one hand, and Denmark, on the other. And yet really the constitution and the legal and political processes, on the surface, are much the same in those countries.

In the Japanese case, the Occupation did introduce a formal idea of democracy and attempted to indoctrinate the Japanese in this. Perhaps some of this has taken, but I'm not so sure the Occupation ought to be looked upon as a very potent force in Japanese history of the last hundred years, except perhaps in such special fields as land reform. This is one area that comes to my mind in which permanent results have possibly been obtained. Perhaps to a slight degree this is also true of the area of women's rights.

If you look back at the period since the Meiji Restoration of 1868, there was another formal presentation of a kind of democracy in the Meiji constitution of 1889. We don't look back on that constitution as being very democratic, but by the standards of its time it wasn't really too retrograde, and by the standards of Tokugawa-period [1603–1868] Japan it was really a great improvement. The provisions of that document took root in their own way during the next generation—and I think we can safely say it takes almost a generation for the organic process to work its way out of that kind of formality. So it really isn't until around 1912, or about the time of the socialist movements of the twenties, that you get a certain flourishing of what one might call democracy in Japan. If you look at the journals of the period from, say, 1905 till 1925, there is a surprising amount of free speech, lively controversy, and individual opinion—on the part of a very small elite, of course. Nevertheless, there were roots that perhaps the Occupation did something to revive, and so provided the climate in which the Japanese could reach back to that period. If we take the long view of history, I think that period is more important than the Occupation.

RB:   Coming back to the post-Occupation period, do you think the trend has been toward the restrictions of the thirties or toward a more open society?

CG:   I think there are two trends at work. In no sense, however, is there a trend toward the kind of social control of the thirties and early forties. If anything, it's gone back to a kind of earlier control. This is one of the trends I've mentioned. You see, after the Meiji Restoration—which was a great shaking up of society—there was a period of uncertainty and a desire on the part of the early Meiji oligarchs to create a stable society. Cohesion was a very important value, with everyone encouraged to work for national solidarity because Japan had to catch up with the West. After World War II, especially after the Occupation, much the same thing was true: emphases were put on these same values so that Japan could restore its tarnished image. This trend, of course, reinforces the idea of control. And as is well known, a number of wartime politicians have been restored to former positions and have been raised to even higher positions, including prime ministerships.

The second trend has to do with modernization as a whole, and that is the creation of an industrial, and now a postindustrial, society. This has inevitable concomitants of social egalitarianism and works constantly toward a more open society. In Japan we are seeing this trend, too. I don't think we're seeing a full clash between these two forces, although we may very well see it in the nineteen seventies.

RB: You have written that "Japan's persevering task of selection is really without parallel in our times." How much of the selecting has been done by the people and how much by government and business leaders? In other words, has the great majority of the people had much choice in these matters or have the choices, the pace and forms of modernization, been chosen by a rather small number of people?

CG: Modernization, it seems to me, at the beginning—I use the word "beginning" here to refer primarily to those countries that are outside the Western social and culture sphere, where the importation of modernization has been in most cases rather brusque—has always been the work of a small elite. This was true of the Meiji elite for about twenty or twenty-five years. Mass journalism did not begin in Japan until about the time the Russo-Japanese War made it popular, that is, after the turn of the century, when universal education had come about.

The same thing is true of a great many other countries in the non-Western world: Egypt is a good example, for there modernization is still largely in the hands of a small elite.

The real question in modernization is, When does the elite become a critical mass? In the Japanese case the critical mass, bolstered by universal education and by the taking root of a certain feeling about democracy and self-management of one's affairs, came into being at the very end of the Meiji period and during the twenties. Other factors intervened in this process, problems not completely unlike today's problems. Japan's problems in the twenties were a combination of Japanese penetration of the colonial markets, which the Europeans did not like, particularly the British in India, and reactions to them, by which the Europeans shut out the Japanese and made things so difficult for them during the Great Depression. In any case, these are extraneous factors, and the critical mass *was* formed in Japan—in a Japanese framework, of course.

Structural change is almost always determined by a few persons in government and business. This is inevitable. It may be that in the more advanced stages of modernization there is discussion of problems by a larger number of persons; however, the size and effect of the critical mass is hard to determine. You take the polls conducted in the U.S. on people's knowledge of personalities and issues before national elections: the results are always abysmally low. This makes one wonder how great understanding on the part of the educated mass really is.

Particularly intriguing in the case of Japan is the matter of cultural modernization. This is also carried out at first by a few persons. Nevertheless, what is fascinating is how this is spread in Japan. Cultural modernization, you know, cannot really be indoctrinated. For example, who was it that taught Japanese businessmen to go to Paris at the turn of the century and to buy impressionist and postimpressionist paintings? There is a large number of Cezannes, Renoirs, et cetera, in the National Museum at Ueno in Tokyo, as well as a number of fascinating secondary painters who are just coming into vogue again. Obviously it was their own artistic tradition and the eye they had developed from that. Who was it that taught the Japanese to appreciate the merits of Bach, Beethoven, Mozart, Debussy, et cetera, much more than any other non-Western people? The whole Western classical musical tradition has been absorbed by the Japanese—an astonishing thing to me. A friend of mine, Bernard Lewis, who has written a great book on Turkey, has put it that music is the ultimate citadel of Western civilization. It's the most difficult, abstract thing for non-Westerners to grasp. And I think it is significant that in most of Asia and in Africa, for example, there is no popular interest in Western classical music, as opposed to Western popular music.

You can see then that what is involved here is also taste. Somehow the very high level of taste involved in the Japanese classical tradition has been able quite often to extract some of the best things from the Western classical tradition. It has also done some awful things, as well: in architecture you will find, frankly, a great majority of hideous buildings scattered about with a small number of very interesting kinds of construction. On the whole, however, the Japanese have given more in the field of architecture than they have taken.

RB: Critics unfriendly to the Japanese speak of their ethical system as "opportunistic," while friendlier observers have sometimes described it as "situational." How would you describe it?

CG: I really think that most national ethical systems are elastic. There are very few examples in history of countries following totally altruistic courses of action. And I think it is especially difficult for Americans to understand this problem. Because for a long time we've deluded ourselves that we and we alone have followed totally altruistic courses of action. We certainly felt this in World War II, particularly vis-à-vis Japan: what Japan was doing was all bad, and we were restraining them and acting on behalf of poor downtrodden China, and so on.

When I use the word "elastic," I feel it can apply to almost any national ethical system. It isn't necessarily a weakness or a strength; it's the way all political organisms operate.

Beyond that there is another aspect to this question, and that has to do with the fact that national ethical systems, as I see them, are all flexible—and flexible can mean quite slippery at times—and a nation can change friendships and policies. As a British prime minister has said, there are no permanent alliances. We've seen a good example of this in the United States' recent relations vis-à-vis China and the Soviet Union. These things change on the basis of what is conceived to be at the moment the national interest.

Another aspect of this is the problem of how one convinces other nations to act in a common self-interest. This is, in a way, similar to the problems men face; that is, how do some men gain ascendancy over other men, how do they lead them, how are they able to convince them to do certain things? And there is an indisputable moral force involved here. Because of the vagaries of history some countries have this moral force more than others, and they've expressed it in different ways: the British have done it primarily through legal institutions, the French have done it primarily through their convictions about their own culture and language. The great weakness of the Japanese, however, is that they really don't try to convince others, they don't try to lead morally; they never have. I'm not criticizing them for this. I think this, as with many other problems the Japanese face in their relations with the non-Western world, goes back to Japanese uniqueness, their isolation from the rest of the world for long historical periods, their uncertainty about their relations with the world, et cetera. The Japanese think it would be unseemly for them to try to lead the world. Certainly their one effort to do so—under the famous slogan of the Greater East Asia Co-Prosperity Sphere, "Eight Houses"—i.e., the whole world—"Under One Roof"—was such a dreadful failure that it is probably going to inhibit them for a long time. They are followers now; they take no initiative on a moral plane in international affairs. For example, they might have tried to mediate between North and South Korea or in Vietnam or Taiwan. There are many reasons why they were not able to, but I think the basic reason is that Japan has never been historically prepared for this kind of role. In this sense, Japan does not have very highly developed international ethical values.

RB: The French journalist Robert Guillain has asked

rhetorically: "Contradications whose injustice would make us [Westerners] cry out with indignation and which would really be dangerous in our world are accepted as normal in Japan. But even so, is there not a grave risk in the accumulation of these anomalies?"[1] How would you answer him?

CG: I think most people would agree that there is a bipolarity in Japanese thought and behavior. It's something that often baffles outside observers. We see this in the way they separate Japanese-style painting from Western-style painting or the way in which they separate Japanese music from Western music. This bipolarity exists at the expense of synthesis. Japan does bring together almost everything; but whether they synthesize the materials or not is another matter.

At the simplest, most overt level—and this struck me on this visit even more forcefully than before—what is noticeable in an economic sense about these contradictions is that you have here a society which has all the gadgets and baubles available in the world, either imported or made at home, and yet there is no quality to life. There seems to me to be an accumulation of junk in Japan, in both a spiritual and material sense, and I wonder what the result of this is going to be.

RB: And this accumulation, of course, stands in contradiction to the basic aesthetic values of the Japanese.

CG: Yes. But the Japanese still talk endlessly about their aesthetic sense, and it's undeniable that they have had this. I remember well when they had this, before World War II, when the quality of life was undeniably superior to what it is now. There certainly wasn't freedom in the sense that we understand it in the West, and not in the way the Japanese understand it today; and yet there was another kind of relaxed way of living one's life, another kind of freedom that is no longer possible in Japan. It may be merely my own nostalgia and that of my older Japanese friends, but I do remember that period and I think it was very important, and I think that many of my

1. Robert Guillain, *The Japanese Challenge: The Race to the Year Two Thousand* (New York: J. B. Lippincott Co., 1970).

Japanese friends would like to go back to it or find its secrets and in some way amalgamate them to life today.

The bipolarity in Japanese life and thought does create tension, and this tension is expressed quite often in frenetic activity, some of which seems fairly pointless. And in the total picture, there is, I believe, always tension in relations between Japanese and non-Japanese, so that there is a natural tendency for Japanese to accept what are for foreigners intolerable conditions. The Japanese have so often felt that they live in a kind of permanent emergency vis-à-vis the outside world that they never can relax. Even though they've had twenty-eight years of peace, somehow one gets a kind of wartime emergency sense in Japan of *having* to create a brilliant industrial state, of *having* to constantly confront the world because they face tensions and have to get rid of them.

RB: I think that this sense of emergency was greatly accelerated by the preparations for the 1964 Olympics, and the pace appears not to have slowed much at all.

CG: Yes, it's connected with pride, as we've seen in the Olympics, Expo '70, the Winter Olympics, and so on. Adams and Iwao Hoshii[2] point out that Japan spends more money than any other country, proportionately, on such events, on staging international gatherings of one kind or another, on arranging to have its image studied abroad. It does this, I feel, in order to smooth down some of the tensions that it feels constantly existing between itself and others.

RB: Some of the contradictions I could point to are, for example, in the industrial world, the near worship of technology as opposed to the love, in the arts, of the asymmetrical, the unique, original product as different from the machine-made, repeatable product. Another example would be love for so many, many arts versus the almost incredible jumble of the cities, the traffic-clogged streets, and the stinking, repulsive rivers of the cities. The Japanese have a high degree of tolerance

2. T. F. M. Adams and Iwao Hoshii, *A Financial History of the New Japan* (Tokyo: Kodansha International, 1971).

for this juxtaposition of art and garbage, disorder, and they haven't paid any attention to it until now and that only belatedly in the wake of the West's interest in ecology.

CG: Interest of this sort is not part of their heritage; there never was in premodern Japan a civic tradition. Kyoto, for instance, is a miserably ugly city, as a city, with many beautiful things in it, and, as Fosco Maraini has pointed out, you have to seek them out to see them. I think most visitors to Kyoto must feel absolutely horrified when they first set foot in it because they've heard that it is Japan's Florence or Athens, and yet it isn't Florence or Athens at all, because it has no public beauty.

I think there is hope for countering this in Japan, however. I've argued that there are parts of Tokyo that are becoming very attractive, and a sense of public beauty is increasing. The landscaping that one finds in parts of Marunouchi and elsewhere now is among the first examples of this. It seems to me that this is an extension of the Japanese love of gardening, especially miniature gardens. An extension like this takes a long time to develop, but as I return to Japan each year I've been noticing how it has grown. I think if they put their minds to it—and they are going to have to put their minds to it, as well as put a great deal of money into social overhead—they could probably turn out some stunning public amenities and cities.

RB: Some observers have spoken admiringly of the Japanese people's tolerance of, by Western standards, intolerable living conditions—environmental and political, for example. Others speak of this phenomenon with scorn, pointing to the underlying submissiveness and exploitability of the Japanese. What is your opinion on the matter?

CG: Let me start with the well-known fact of the homogeneity of the Japanese. This has, I think, been exploited—in the past by the militarists, and now by the economic power groups—to convince the Japanese that they must work hard, train, build, save, do all sorts of things to protect the image of the nation in order to confront the outside world. This submissiveness was to a large extent built into the system through the more than two and a half centuries of the Tokugawa period. And part did undoubtedly carry over into modern times. But I think the Japanese are much less exploitable today than they were twenty or forty years ago. First, this aspect of organization changes with modernization everywhere.

Let me give a personal example here. When I went to the Shibuya ward office in Tokyo in 1968 to renew my alien registration card, my attention was caught by a sign over the counter at which you are to take a numbered tag and wait your turn. The sign said that if you were not taken care of in—oh, twenty or thirty minutes—you were to go to another specified window and complain. To me this was an extraordinary feature of development because if you've ever stood in lines—or waited in nonlines, I should say—in developing countries, with everybody trying to push money across the counter to their favorite employee in order to get attention, you will understand why I feel this is an extraordinary change.

The general quality of public service—if one removes it from politics—is quite good. It's certainly on a European level and it's higher than in many European countries.

Two factors are working to reduce submissiveness among the Japanese. One is the general process of modernization. The other is that despite the pressures and chicanery of the government mechanism, Japan still is essentially a democracy and people do have rights here. Another very heartening thing was the pollution trial that ended recently at Yokkaichi, even though the sums awarded were very low. The most interesting thing to me was that the people said, We have gotten some money, but we want clean air. This shows that it isn't enough really to satisfy them with just money. In a sense this could have been just a repetition of a feudal pattern: the people are given a tip, a *chadai*, and they are not expected to complain anymore. So it's important that in this case the people know that the money granted is not enough, they need to insist on solution of the problem.

RB: If indeed the twenty-first century might well be Japan's, what kind of century do you think it might be?

CG: I think that the key point here is the way in which the Japanese have been able to effect a subtle—different from the West's—way of relating the individual to the group. It's probably the most important thing the Japanese can teach the outside world. I've spoken already about the decreasing submissiveness of the Japanese and the fact that certain organic democratic ideas are taking root and the people are becoming more demanding. In the past the pendulum most likely swung too far toward excessive compliance with group needs, and the balance is still too heavily this way today. But one of the problems of our advanced technological society is that the individual is going to have to compromise more and more with society, and with the environment, which is a reflection of society as it is changed by society. This is one of the most important lessons that Western man has to learn. Our idea of Faustian man is no longer really possible, as we cannot do unlimited things. I think that perhaps the whole East Asian and Buddhist tradition is very important here. Man has become more involved socially in our time than has ever been the case before. The rugged individualism of the kind that was so popular in America up until 1929 or a little later has gradually declined. This suggests to me that perhaps there is in this a meeting ground for East and West.

Secondly, there is the matter of consensus. It's a difficult matter, one that is too easily passed over by foreign writers on Japan. It is indeed quite often true that Japanese superiors are able to make their wishes known to their subordinates and the subordinates then respond in keeping with those wishes, rather than that the decisions are made by subordinates and passed on to the superior for ratification.

However, I would like to point out that this is also the case in most of the West. There is more consensus in reaching decisions in large corporations in developed countries than is generally known. There are two considerations of importance here. One is the ability of superiors to make their wishes known. The other is the way in which policy can be initiated by sub-ordinates. I know, for example, that during the Occupation, as a middle-level official, I initiated a good deal of policy— things that I just thought up. By subtly suggesting these in the form of memorandums I eventually got something, not everything of course, of what I wanted done. I couldn't force my wishes on my superiors, of course, but I could get things started. Subordinates can whisper things in superiors' ears and then have the superiors order them done, the superiors not always realizing that they are not the true originators of the idea.

Consensus has another side to it, a more political side. There are three kinds of political power that can be expressed. First, through majoritarian rule, in which a fifty-one to forty-nine vote gives you absolute authority to do what you want; we see the extreme example of this in Britain. The second is democratic centralism of the kind you find in the communist countries, in which a problem is thrashed out and once a decision is made everyone must follow unswervingly the line adopted by the majority. The third is the Japanese idea of consensus. In this system, if you win sixty percent of the vote you are allowed to carry out sixty percent of your programs—not one hundred percent. Now this is not stated, of course. This is the reason for the rages the opposition parties have occasionally gotten into in the Diet when the Liberal-Democratic Party has attempted to do exactly what it wishes without giving enough weight to this facet of consensus.

I think it's important to note that it is by no means certain that majoritarian rule or democratic centralism is superior to the Japanese system of consensus. All three are valid alterna-tives.

Let me move from the political to the aesthetic realm. Japan has lost a lot of its beauty, an appalling amount, and yet they still manage to preserve little niches of loveliness. It may be that as the Japanese are losing this they can give some of it to the rest of the world, some appreciation of beauty. The image of Japan in the world may be more important than the ugly reality that is being created. I feel this rather strongly. In Hawaii many of my friends have Japanese-style houses. They have adopted and adapted them and live in an environmental setting that is perhaps superior to what is to be found in Japan. This is true elsewhere, as well. I've been struck by the way in which Japanese gardens and architecture are taking root in California, for example. I think—I hope—that in some way this Japanese capacity for creating and preserving beauty within a technological jungle can be carried over to the West.

RB: It has been suggested that perhaps as Zen is losing its vigor in Japan it will take root in the West. Perhaps, too, just as traditional Japanese architecture is going under in Japan— you see very few homes that are not clogged with appliances and junk they were never intended to hold, that are an affront to traditional concepts of space, for example—that its concepts will find a welcome and useful place in Western architecture.

It may be that just as Japan is reaching her highest peak of material power she is losing her best qualities.

CG: That may be true. It's sad, and perhaps inevitable, as well.

RB: You have written: "Like any society, as we know from the case of Nazi Germany, Japan is not immune to ideological recidivism under specific circumstances, but it is very much aware of the dangers inherent therein." What specific circumstances might you imagine?

CG: We are seeing some of the possibilities of dangerous circumstances right now. I mentioned earlier the growing unease in the world concerning Japanese achievements, which by and large are legitimate achievements, though they may have been pressed too hard and with a great disregard for the interests of the Japanese people. If the trend of uneasiness continues, and if Japan increasingly feels itself to be an unloved "orphan society"—a phrase of Edward Seidensticker, which is very apt—then there might be all sorts of emotional results which would stem from the problem of controlled tension we spoke of earlier. If they feel that trade blocs are being formed that will leave them out—and the formation of the sixteen-nation free-trade area in Europe is going to create further difficulties for them in Europe, as it will for the U.S. as well—and if they feel that political alliances, however nebulous, are being concocted against them, say between the U.S. and China, or the U.S. and the Soviets, then we might have this kind of emotional recidivism, which would lead to ideological recidivism.

The principal task both for Japanese and for foreigners who are friends of Japan, and even for people who don't feel particularly friendly to the Japanese, is to integrate Japan into the world. Japan is not, by a long shot, fully integrated, even though it belongs to GATT, OECD, the Asian Development Bank, and does nothing but praise the U.N., and so on. Integrating Japan is no easy job. It's a task that involves education, for generations to come on both sides. And it will mean changing Japanese character in some ways.

One way this might happen will be through increased Japanese contacts with the outside world. On my most recent trip to Japan, I was talking to a Japanese businessman on the plane about the fact that the Netherlands and Japan have roughly the same per-capita income today. But he had noted that the Netherlands, because of accumulated national wealth, has an infrastructure of social and economic amenities that is far greater than Japan's. You really can't compare them only on the basis of per-capita income. And one of the things that is making the Japanese more demanding these days is that for the first time a great many of them are going abroad and seeing how other people live. Conditions in Japan really are intolerable: they don't have any living space. I particularly took the Netherlands here as an example because it is a very crowded country, too, and yet people live really much better; there's a much higher quality of life there than in Japan.

RB: And the Japanese are learning that around the world

when people want to point to a particulary bad example of a ruined, polluted environment they choose Japan, especially the Tokyo-Yokohama area.

CG: Yes, this came out at the environmental conference in Stockholm in 1972. When I was on my way to Japan last time my office wrote to me, Get a gas mask and have a good stay.

RB: What do you think is the greatest barrier toward Japan's becoming the leading nation of the world?

CG: We've touched on some points concerning this, but the real barrier is that Japan does not have a universalistic vocation. It does not have anything which it really believes in itself. The Japanese, for example, with the rarest exceptions, do not have any program for extending Japanese values to the world— that is, aside from flower arranging, tea ceremony, and such exotica, which, frankly, no one is really interested in anymore.

I'm talking about real values, in the sense that the French, in particular, believe that civilization and French culture are coeval and central in the whole scheme of things. There's no doubt in their minds about this. The missionary feeling that they have about this has enabled them to create the Francophone zone, where the elite really does use French, really does think in French, and has many French values.

As I pointed out earlier, the English did this primarily with law. They have brought into being numbers of countries that practice—however deficiently—a legal system with remarkable similarity. India is a good example.

The United States has perhaps done it with our ideas of democracy, very imperfectly expressed and now very much put to the test, but nevertheless we've built up a great reservoir of credit all over the world over a long period of time.

Japan has nothing like this. Even China has something of this sort. I think this is one of the reasons China appeals to the outside world much more than Japan. Japan has never had it; China has. There is among the Japanese the feeling that the rest of the world might drop Japan like a hot potato if China would allow the world to get interested in it.

I think the reason for this is that it is felt in the world that there are some fundamental Chinese values, and that these relate to the world, and that the Chinese are understandable even though they are very different. The Chinese have been out in the world for a long time, they've lived in great numbers in various Southeast Asian countries, and they are not a mysterious, unknown quality. It is Japan that is unknown and unpredictable and is felt to be so. It is Japan that is the different, strange, queer country. This is a problem the Japanese have to face.

RB: Part of the problem is that the Japanese emphasize their own uniqueness and will often say that their culture is unique, so special that foreigners can't possibly understand it.

CG: Yes, they like thinking that they are unique. I have always felt that the Japanese do not like foreigners to get too close. I shall never forget one party I was at years ago with a member of the imperial family. The conversation happened to turn to the *Kojiki*,[3] a subject I was interested in and had been studying at the time. At one point I quoted some lines from it. Well, the Japanese guests were amazed; they made polite comments but they were very uneasy and they dropped the subject immediately. It suddenly struck me then that they really didn't like it. This same sort of thing has happened to me and to friends quite often.

Among Japanese there is this feeling of the *oku*, the inner heart of Japan, the *naichi* complex, the inner recess of the nation, considered something like a sacred shrine, which they really don't like you to get too close to.

I suppose that what this comes down to is that despite its economic and political power, unless the enormous task of integration into the world really works, Japan may be condemned to being forever a kind of fringe country. And this integration, I believe, will probably not be carried out in our lifetime.

3. The *Kojiki* (Record of Ancient Matters), completed in 712, is Japan's oldest historical record.

体験

# 13

## MARION JANSEN
Dutch
Teacher

She studied Japanese language and culture at the Sorbonne, Paris, for four years before going to Japan for the first time in 1969. In her late twenties, she has lived and worked in Tokyo for four years.

RB: Not a few Western visitors have felt a certain enchantment with Japan that has faded as their familiarity increased. Because you are one of these people, I'd like you to describe your relationship with Japan and the Japanese.

MJ: I studied Japanese and Japanese culture in the university in Holland and Paris. I studied art, history, religion, and I saw in the books I read pictures of beautiful Japanese houses, gardens and temples and art works. Naturally, I wanted to go to Japan, and I thought, I will go there and I will really mix with the people, not be a part of the foreign community, but live with the Japanese and make lots of friends among them. That was my dream.

When I arrived in Japan I traveled to Tokyo by the monorail and I got my first shock—it is so ugly! I thought then, Well, the harbor areas in Holland are not nice either and probably this area is an exception. At first I lived on the outskirts of Tokyo in a small, old room. It was too crowded. Once, late at night, I found two little kittens near this dormitory. I tried to take them into our rooms and some of the Japanese girls said, Oh no, it's against the rules. When I asked them what we should do, they said I should leave the kittens outside. When I insisted and brought the kittens inside the girls got angry. That night I learned my first real lesson about the Japanese, that rules are more important than feelings, animals' or humans'.

While in Paris I had been interested in Shinto, and soon after I arrived in Japan I tried to enter one of the universities at which it was taught. The school authorities simply could not understand why a foreign woman wanted to study Shinto. And my Japanese acquaintances—when I told them, they were surprised that I wanted to study Shinto. They'd say things like, Why Shinto? Shinto, what's that? They had no interest in it and could not understand why a foreigner would have any. Most of them did not know the first thing about it.

The image we have in Europe—the mystical and beautiful Orient—should really be changed. And, you know, the Japanese embassies and Japan Air Lines, they do a lot to continue this image, they advertise it everywhere. I never saw a book in Europe that showed the four-and-a-half-mat rooms, and the "beautiful" slums the Japanese live in. When I saw Japanese living conditions, I was shocked. It was like falling out of a blue sky into a dirty slummy world.

My biggest disappointment was the people. I was interested in them but their interest in me was only on the surface, just politeness. They speak to foreigners to practice their English. A lot only practice superficial friendliness and superficial politeness. But of course I have good Japanese friends, too. When a Japanese boyfriend and I went looking for a house, suddenly they were no longer available, suddenly the vacant rooms and houses were already rented when they saw my face. When I met Japanese students in Holland or Paris, I invited them to my home because I thought they must be lonely. I brought them home for the holidays and my family welcomed them and tried to make them comfortable. But I will never forget my first New Year's in Japan. No one invited me to their home, none of my superficial friends thought that I might want to see how the Japanese celebrate their holidays at home. It was a very lonely time for me.

RB: Of course, the Japanese don't ordinarily invite people to their homes.

MJ: Yes, I know that now. But although I read hundreds of books about Japan in Holland and Paris, not one of them said anything about that. Besides, they shouldn't be so narrow-minded about inviting people into their homes.

RB: What do you think about male-female relationships in Japan?

MJ: In Holland and Paris four or five Japanese women who were married to Dutchmen said to me, Never, never marry a Japanese man! You'll be very unhappy! I thought they were exaggerating. In Japan, however, I found that men find it perfectly natural for a girl to do everything for them. For instance, when my boyfriend's friends came to visit us and I asked them if they want coffee or tea, they would answer, Uhh! So I'd say, That means yes, please? You know, I'd make them feel they should be a little polite. They're just not polite to women at all. They treat them like housemaids.

Male-female relations in Japan are something like the master and the maid. The Japanese make girls think they should be stupid and sweet and innocent and have no opinions at all. Economically, the women are in a very bad position. They are often dismissed from their jobs when they become about twenty-five. And then later they may be hired back as part-time workers at a lower wage. Many girls are frightened, and they try to get married before they turn twenty-five. And how do you get married in Japan? By being very sweet and gentle towards a man. Otherwise you won't get a husband. By law they are not allowed to make the kinds of sex discrimination that they do, but this is part of their social system. I know of a few girls who were dismissed and so took their case to court. They won and they were rehired and went back to work. But at the company, people turned their backs on them and would not talk to them—even the other girls! If you fought for your rights in Holland, people would respect you, even if they didn't agree with you on the matter. But in Japan, you've broken the rules of society, so they turn their backs on you. You see, it's necessary for Japanese girls to marry, though things are changing gradually for the better.

I remember a young woman I was teaching English. She said she was getting married soon, and I said to her, You must be very happy. She answered only, Hmm. So I asked her if she didn't love him, and she said, He's fat and he's boring. When I asked her why she was marrying him she said, *Shiyo ga nai,* it can't be helped. Today I talked to one of her friends and asked how the married woman was getting along. She said, All right. She's a good housewife and so is happy. I said, No, not that, is she really happy? She said, Oh, that. I don't know. Probably she is, because she's a good housewife.

Another thing is that in some cases even if a woman is twenty-nine or thirty and she applies for a job she probably won't get it if she doesn't tell them she lives with her family or relations. If she lives alone, you know, they're afraid she might have male visitors. Isn't that a crazy system!

RB: An acquaintance of mine recently remarked that modern technological societies tend to produce people who are "like fat sexless laboratory rats," and that, of all the places he'd visited in recent years, Tokyo displayed this tendency to the highest degree. He attributed this condition to the "general widespread docility of the Japanese before authority, their materialism, their easy acceptance of over-crowded and terribly inadequate living facilities, and their low-keyed lifestyles." Does this view of Tokyo and Tokyoites correspond in any way to your own?

MJ: Very much. And the educational system is mainly to blame. They are taught from the time they are little children that they must blindly follow all the rules, that they must study very hard so they can go to Tokyo University so that they can get into the big companies and have a chance to become a top executive, the top position in the social system. They are not allowed to develop their own ideas about their own lives—not much, anyway. They are taught to accept the system, to *gaman suru*, endure, and not complain. They should change the system, but because they are trained from an early age they don't know how to change it. But now it does seem to be changing, for a lot of university graduates stay workless, as they don't want to get incorporated into the big companies.

It's easy to communicate with the Japanese who have lived abroad. And it's interesting that so many of them have difficulty adjusting to Japanese society—not the company people but the young ones who went abroad for school or travel. Many of those whom I have known don't work for large organizations; they free-lance or start their own small business. They are also less afraid of the system, more independent.

It's not the fault of the Japanese people that they don't change their society, that they're weak. It's because they are educated that way, they don't know any better. I'm sure the people who run the society wouldn't want to change it greatly. If the Japanese had the kind of socialist government we have in Holland, the bosses wouldn't ride around in chauffeur-driven cars, wouldn't spend thousands and thousands of dollars in cabarets for "business," and wouldn't have huge bankrolls, because a lot of their money would be taken for taxes to help the poor people and provide welfare services. The bosses of Japanese government and business want a docile people, so any good changes must come from the people. But I can't see any such changes coming. The Communist Party gained some seats in the last elections, though, so perhaps some people are not happy about the social system. But I'm afraid changes will come very slowly.

RB: What do you like most and least about Japan?

MJ: I do like the temples of Kyoto, especially the ones on Mount Hiei, but the great number of tourists spoil them. I also like the fact that there are so many public telephones and a lot of taxis, unlike Europe, where you can never find a telephone or a taxi. Also that the shops are open till very late— it's very convenient! I like the Japanese countryside as long as there are no villages or towns around because they are a mess. The books tell us the Japanese are close to nature, but that is nonsense. They have very ugly towns and cities and they can spoil natural beauty so completely. Even where they have plenty of space, they build slums, shacks crowded up against each other.

What I like least about Japan is the narrow-mindedness of the people, this feeling of being a unique race. And a lot of them are inconsiderate and rude to foreigners and will not treat them with the politeness they use for their own people. Not all the people are that way, of course. As I said, some of the people who have been abroad are not so narrow-minded. The people of Tokyo are the worst: cold, stupid, insensitive. The people in the small towns are better because at least they talk to you. But they too immediately ask rude questions about your personal life, questions they would never dare ask a newly met Japanese. And they stare at you endlessly, though that might be true in many countries where there are only a few foreigners.

RB: In one of the English-language newspapers recently there was a headline that said, "Foreigners Still a Curiosity in Canton." When I read it I thought, Well, they are still curiosities in many parts of Tokyo!

MJ: Yes, the staring doesn't stop in Tokyo, especially if you are a foreign woman walking with a Japanese man.

One thing that bothers me greatly about the Japanese is their apathetic attitude toward pollution. The way they treat the victims of the Minamata pollution disease as though *they*, not the polluters, were pariahs. And the apathetic attitude toward big business. The newspapers and the people only speak about the victims but say nothing against the polluters. Though it is interesting to note that a lot of young people who came to work in Tokyo have gone back to their villages fed up with pollution, high prices, small rooms. They want to be happy again in their villages. The first thing they should do is make them stop polluting! But the Japanese don't yet look at it that way! The government could stop it because they have so much money—look at the huge trade surpluses—but they do nothing but talk and spend money on committees that just talk. What is incredible is that the people who are ruining the country don't seem to realize that they are ruining it for themselves, too. How can they be so stupid! Perhaps they don't care because they can fly to Hawaii and Guam and other places for their vacations while the workers vacation at polluted seashore and mountain resorts.

A lot of people laugh at me when I tell them that I eat very little fish because of all the poisonous chemicals they carry nowadays. To me the reports about the very high rate of pollutants in the hair of fishermen and fish restaurant operators is frightening. But a lot of people laugh when I warn them that their bones too may deteriorate and their limbs shrivel up in ten years or so. They seem to realize that their country is being destroyed but they want to ignore it, perhaps because they don't want to accept the responsibility for having to do something about it. It seems they don't want to believe it, except for a minority who are doing something about it. I suppose they are waiting for the government to do something. But because the government and big business are so close, nothing will be done in time.

Social welfare in this country is terrible. One of my friends' grandmother gets three thousand yen [about $11.50] a month. Can you imagine! His mother, who is a widow and had to raise him, never got a penny from the government. There are many cripples and blind people in this country, and the help they get from the government is unbelievably small. And some Japanese have the nerve to boast that their country is equal to Holland because their salaries are as high, and higher than those in England. Of course, they have no sense of social justice, so they are blind to the important problems. Recently a young cripple traveled around the country in a wheelchair. He used public transportation and at train stations he got no help unless he asked for it. He was told more than once that he was a nuisance and should stay home. That's typical. The Japanese are said to be very polite, but they're not at all kind to the people who need it most. Most of them think the blind and the crippled should be hidden away.

If they think you are weaker than they, they won't like you. It's because they are forced from childhood on to work hard to get to the top, to the top school and to the top company. They admire only the ones at the top. And so they drive the young people to study. No wonder so many students commit suicide. It is a cruel system! I would be frightened to be poor or seriously ill or crippled in Japan. The people just don't seem to think that they too may be sick or crippled someday.

RB: Do you think that there are any aspects of Japanese culture that could and should be exported to the West?

MJ: I like the way they arrange flowers. Ikebana is being taught in the West, and that is good. And I like the tea ceremony because it creates quietness and peacefulness. The Japanese have forgotten so much of what they knew about the value of peace and quiet. Instead of stressing economic development, they should study the valuable parts of their culture.

RB: In that respect, do you think the term "economic animal" is fitting?

MJ: Oh yes! Because they are trained to be number one. And they've been taught to work for Japan or for the company. I ask them, What is the company? Isn't it the people who work for it? Aren't they the most important part of the company? They don't think yet that the ordinary workers should have a decent share of the tremendous profits even though they work bloody hard. In Europe it was the same before the war, and then slowly they got self-conscious, a thing I see happening now among young workers. The workers have few recreation facilities, they live in tiny gloomy rooms and ride to work on dangerously crowded trains. And everything is outrageously expensive.

A cup of coffee is between 150 and 220 yen [about 55¢ and 85¢]. Why do they accept such conditions? They are fools to sacrifice themselves for the company or so that Japan can be number one.

The Japanese are covering up all the greenery, and are covering up the rivers with concrete roads. The government is especially to blame; they are destroying their country, and all the people can say is, It can't be helped. The prime minister has a plan to remodel the country. What does it mean? The bulldozers have gone to all the undeveloped areas, especially the northeast, and they are destroying the beautiful country by building petroleum *Kombinats*. So that Japan can be number one. Number one what? I ask them. But they only smile, because a lot don't know themselves, either.

RB: Which of your Japanese contemporaries do you respect the most?

MJ: Jun Ui from Tokyo University. He teaches about air pollution and is trying to make the Japanese conscious about what they are doing to themselves. He teaches anybody who will listen—students or nonstudents. He teaches in a simple way so that his message can reach everyone. He wants them to know what the big companies are doing. Naturally he's unpopular with the government.

I also admire the man who was the head of the government's environment agency for a while, Bunshichi Oishi. Even though he was a Liberal-Democrat politician, he took his job seriously. A lot of government people didn't like his policy. They get their money from the big businessmen who are responsible for the pollution, so the politicians don't like any member of their party to cause trouble with business. When Oishi was in charge there was some hope that the country would be saved. But not now. The government is too corrupt. I'm afraid that Jun Ui will not be able to do much either because the government controls Tokyo University and they hate his guts.

I don't like any Japanese groups. They have too much of the sheep mentality. There are probably some groups that are doing good things—the Red Cross, perhaps. And there is that women's consumer group, Shufuren: those women are trying to open the eyes of the consumers to what business is doing to them. And they have organized retail businesses that sell things at wholesale prices. I respect them. And there are probably more such groups.

I've met a few of the women activists, but they were like the American women's libbers. I don't believe in that kind of militancy. Japanese men are arrogant enough, and when you use women's lib methods on them they become even worse. Also most women don't like Japanese women's libbers. The activists do things like marching down the street shouting, *Onna! Onna! Onna!* [Women! Women! Women!] Nobody in Japan likes that behavior. I do sympathize with women's lib and am actively involved in it myself, but I practice patience. I don't believe in militancy.

RB: That's a primary characteristic of Japanese militant groups, to go from one extreme to the other, in this case from docility to arrogance.

MJ: That's right. The radical students are a good example. Even though they fight the corrupt government they make themselves look like little children. In the demonstrations they are led by one man with a stick who holds them back while they snake dance around the street. They look like sheep. Who could take such people seriously! What is worse is that they spend more time fighting each other than they do fighting the government. Lately some groups have even been murdering each other, even their own group members, though of course this is a minority radical group. Who would be crazy enough to support them!

The young women are among the least conscious people. They are always giggling. When you ask one a question she lets her boyfriend answer, I get mad then and say, Don't you have an opinion of your own? Don't you have a mind of your own? But she doesn't answer—though I have also met some girls with opinions.

The girls giggle a lot, but that's from nervousness or shyness. There is little humor in Japan. The Japanese seem to think it's bad manners to laugh aloud. You're not supposed to show feeling. I visited Korea recently and there the people really laugh. Not the Japanese—except when they're drunk. Always these dull, gloomy faces!

RB: I don't think the Japanese are really humorless, although I do believe that they have a far narrower range of humor than we in the West do. For instance, black and macabre humor don't draw many laughs here. Nor is there much appreciation of ironic humor. The Japanese poke fun at others far more gently and less often than we do. When you have to be so careful of other people's feelings—as you must by their social codes—you can't really poke fun at others, can you? And then there's the fact that they like and even cultivate melancholy feelings. Somber, elegiac, melancholy matters are felt to be somehow elegant, aesthetically correct, while humorous incidents are simply vulgar, not important. From my point of view it's a lopsided development. There's not much that is as pathetic as a sweet, lively young girl who is deliberately taught to hide her feelings so that she will become that sad creature the *o-jo-sama,* a "young lady," with all the artificiality and somberness that that term conveys.

MJ: They are such a passive people. They seem to like to endure a lot, really like it. It's a virtue. Work hard, endure bad conditions, don't let your private life interfere with your business, and don't display any strong emotions; at least they've always been taught to be like that.

RB: It would be hard to deny that there is a strong masochistic strain.

MJ: I'm afraid they'll endure and endure and find that they have ruined their country and their lives. It's sometimes a virtue to endure hard conditions, but they make a vice of it, they endure things that they don't have to endure, situations that could easily be corrected if they were not so weak-willed and didn't always say *shiyo ga nai,* "it can't be helped."

RB: One acquaintance of mine made the remark that Tokyo seems to be slowly becoming the lure to expatriates that Paris was in the twenties and thirties. Do you see this happening?

MJ: Of course I've noticed that the number of foreign tourists in Japan is increasing greatly. I meet a great number of foreigners, most of them Europeans, and I would say that ninety percent of them come here with the kind of image of Japan that I had. They've been brainwashed by the books and magazines and travel posters. They have thought they were coming to beautiful Japan and the mystical Orient. They do not stay long. Many of the young Europeans I meet have traveled a bit, they've seen India and Thailand, they've stopped in Nepal, Bali, Singapore, and Hongkong. Ninety-nine percent of them say, The people are terrible here. They pretend to be polite, but they don't really care about you. Nothing comes from their heart. Not all, of course; there are good ones, too.

The Americans seem to like the Japanese. It seems that American cities are as bad as or worse than Japan's and so the Americans don't feel it like I do. Maybe the Americans are used to alienation at home so they don't mind that almost all the Japanese are indifferent to them or just want to practice English on them. The Germans, Dutch, French—many feel nonaccepted here. Many of them say that they feel the Japanese sometimes are making fun of them. People look at foreigners and talk about them, and because the foreigners can't understand what is being said, they feel uncomfortable. Also, they come here with the idea that living in Japan is very cheap and they are shocked because everything is so expensive. They are also shocked to find that there is so little of the traditional culture left. The Japanese have given up their culture so they can concentrate on making money. But most of all, the Europeans hate the superficial friendliness and politeness of the majority of the Japanese.

Most Europeans leave Japan within one year. Those that

stay do so because they can make more money here, teaching English, working as movie extras or models, and the women can make a lot of money working as bar hostesses. Many of them say they save their money and take trips to India or Thailand or Korea, where the people are poor but nice.

I think the Japanese should stop believing they are unique. They should come back to the world and think not only of Japan. Even now where they are in large numbers they are called the "ugly Japanese," "economic animals," and "economic slaves." The Japanese should study becoming international. They are always so narrow-minded: I hate the phrase *ware ware Nihonjin,* we Japanese. I think the idea that Tokyo could become an international city is ridiculous. Rich Americans might like it, but young Europeans find it gloomy, polluted, expensive. You can't have much fun here unless you have a lot of money. They wouldn't like the night life, either. There are disco bars here but they are not cozy or much fun, and if you talk to a Japanese you have never met, they think you are a *hen na gaijin,* an odd foreigner. Even when you talk to them in Japanese, they think it's odd—a foreigner talking Japanese? Oh my!

The Japanese think Holland and Britain are second-class countries because the economy is not as good as Japan's, but Amsterdam and London are far more international than Tokyo, and that is why so many young people visit them. Even the young Japanese who are not tied to their mamas or to a company are going in great numbers to Europeans cities and they are staying, even when they have to wash dishes in Stockholm or Copenhagen or become beggars in Paris.

Tokyo is not becoming more popular; more people come here because more people travel, but young people won't stay here. What can they do here? Paint the slums and plant trees? That would be a good thing.

体験
# 14

## BARRIE MUSGRAVE
### British
### Potter

He lived and worked in Japan for four years during the period 1968–73, beginning his potting apprenticeship at Kasama in Ibaraki Prefecture and continuing it at Mashiko and Motegi in Tochigi Prefecture. At present, thirty years old, he plans to spend a half-year or so studying yoga at an Indian ashram before returning to England, where he will build a kiln and try his hand at making ceramics in the English tradition.

RB: How has living in Japan affected your outlook on life, your personality, your way of dealing with people?

BM: Although I lived in Tokyo at first, I've spent most of my time in Japan in the countryside. I'm from London, and in the Japanese countryside I came awake to flowers. I now know the names of more flowers in Japanese than I do in English, and I can identify more Japanese flowers.

I've also become interested in food, especially from the angle of nutrition. Macrobiotics interests me. I studied under George Ohsawa, the macrobiotics master, for a short while. When I came to Japan I weighed about eighty-five kilos and now I'm down to about seventy. I was too heavy. Now I have a physique that is like the Japanese physique, a slender physique, although I'm much taller than the average Japanese man. As a result I feel better, healthier.

Some of the foreigners in Japan get around and meet a lot of people. I haven't. It seems to me that the British are like the Japanese in that they don't find it easy to meet strangers. We need a third person to introduce us and, sometimes, to get the relationship going. The young Americans of today whom you meet all over the world don't have this trouble. They can go up to anybody and begin talking to them. They don't have this shyness. And, well, living among the Japanese hasn't made me any less shy with strangers.

I came to Japan to learn Japanese potting techniques. Japanese techniques are very basic in that they are closely related to what people use in their daily lives. I like this functionalism. And I hoped by learning Japanese techniques that I could learn to do something similar in Britain, I mean make things that the British people could use in their daily lives. Of course, we eat different foods and serve them in different ways, so our pottery shapes are different from the Japanese, but the basic techniques of working with clay and a wheel are the same.

RB: Of all the kinds of ceramics in the world, why did you choose to concentrate your study on Japanese techniques?

BM: When I first came to Japan I didn't know much about Japanese ceramics. In fact, I came here because a man I met in Australia told me Japan was one of the few countries in the Orient where you could find work that would pay enough—you know, teaching English and things like that—to let you travel around and see the country. Well, after I arrived I didn't travel much. I lived and worked in Tokyo. I did see some ceramics and I liked the traditional stuff that I saw. I got interested in doing rubbings, Buddhist statues mostly, and when I returned to England after two years I thought about the medieval brass plaques that are found set into the floor of old English churches. For a while my wife and I drove around England making rubbings. They were very nice—you know, knights and their ladies, anywhere from a foot and a half to five or six feet. I got the idea that the Japanese would appreciate these rubbings and I sent a number to Japan and tried to arrange a showing and a sale. Then I got the idea of returning to Japan and learning to pot there. I knew I'd have to learn basic Japanese to speak to the potters, but I didn't think that would be too big a problem.

So I went back and soon found an apartment in Kasama. I found a family of potters who were willing to take me on. In the morning I worked for them, although I wasn't much use at first since it was hard for me to make two sakè cups of exactly the same size and shape. The old potters—who can make any shape if you'll just tell them what you want—would sit at a wheel and turn out hundreds of cups exactly alike. When I wasn't making sakè cups, I taught English conversation or practiced making other pots on the wheel. I was able to arrange an exhibition and sale of the medieval rubbings, but when they were being trucked into Tokyo they caught fire and almost all of them burned up. The gallery—the Fran-Nell Gallery—held a sympathy sale in which the gallery artists donated works that were sold on the day the exhibition was to have opened, and the proceeds were given to me. It was a very nice thing for them to do.

Later I lived and potted for a while in Mashiko and then moved to nearby Motegi, where I built my own kiln and have been potting and studying yoga and Oriental ideas about nutrition.

When I returned to England a few years ago, I studied ceramics for a while at an art school and I visited a few potteries. I decided that the techniques I'd seen weren't very good. For instance, the teacher I had couldn't make a set of coffee cups all of the same size. In Japan I'd visited Mashiko twice and I'd seen that even young boys were turning out hundreds of identical items by hand. I'm not much interested in becoming an artist-potter but a craftsman and I decided—probably prematurely, because I hadn't traveled around much—that I couldn't learn to become a craftsman in England. I've since seen magazine articles that show that good ceramics are being made in England. It was in Japan, I believed, that I could learn the fundamentals of becoming a ceramics craftsman. And that's what I've been doing.

Japanese ceramics are honest, I feel; the glazes and textures fit the pots, they are effective. I saw quite a bit of low-fired ware in southern Europe, pieces with bright colors and pleasing decorations, the kind that northern Europeans like for the happy feeling they give. But I really like the quiet look of Japanese ceramics. Also, the fact that they are high-fired means that they are more functional, less easy to break.

Something I like, and one of the first things I noticed when I was invited out to Japanese restaurants or homes, is the great numbers of small dishes and bowls that are used at the table. In England, you know, there are a few serving dishes, and each person gets one large dish on which everything is just sort of slopped together. The Japanese way is really more pleasing. Also, because you can pick a little bit from a dozen or more serving dishes, people don't tend to overeat as they do in Europe.

RB: What do you think of the lifestyle of the average Japanese potter?

BM: In Japan at this time there is a kind of potting fad. At one of the large potteries in Mashiko, for example, there are about twenty or thirty young people studying. During the day they work for the potting company, and in the evening they are allowed to throw whatever pots they please, make glaze tests, and so on. They are allowed to, but most of them don't use their evenings that way. They're only in pottery because it's the thing to do, it's *kakko ii*, smart. They really don't seem to be interested in learning what you really must know to become a good craftsman-potter. Just as in Europe, there is an overflow of people in the arts; it's the fashionable thing to do.

Not so long ago the young Japanese potter studied with a master for about four years. Now most of them can't wait that long; two or three years are enough. And as I said, they don't work very long at it. When they think they are ready to start out on their own, they get the master to introduce them to a few shops to which they can sell, and he usually helps them to have an exhibition or two. In Mashiko now, everybody and his dog is a potter. Farmers give up farming and become potters, whether they have any talent or not. As a result the ceramics that are being turned out are unbelievably bad.

About fifty years or more ago a movement to further folk art, or *mingei,* began in Japan. The men who got it going were disgusted with what was happening to the traditions of craftsmanship. Their biggest interest was that the products of the folk arts should be functional, and they really helped to save the old traditions. But nowadays with magazines and television pushing the folk arts, the movement has become distorted. Folk pottery is supposed to be cheap so that ordinary people can use it in their everyday life. But *mingei* pottery is so expensive now that the ordinary people can't buy it; in other words, it's not really *mingei,* not folk pottery. What's wrong is that most potters want to become art-potters. Let me give you an example. Shoji Hamada was one of the leaders of the *mingei* movement. He's a man that I admire very much. He works in Mashiko, and he's so good that what is called Mashiko ware ought really to be called Hamada ware; people copy what he's done. He can sell anything he makes. As soon as he makes something, somebody will buy it. And they will pay a very high price for a genuine Hamada piece, no matter if it's a good piece or not. The prices for his work are so high that a buyer can't afford to use a Hamada piece in his house. So what does the buyer do? He puts it in a special box and only brings it out to impress his friends and acquaintances. The things Hamada is making are of no real use. He insists he is a real *mingei* artist, and he dresses like an old peasant, but he's just kidding himself.

This is what is happening to good potters all over Japan—and not only to good potters. And what the ordinary people can afford are the mass-produced porcelains you see in the department stores, machine-made stuff. This is the real *mingei* today.

Actually, and it hurts me to say it, the designs of a lot of this mass-produced stuff are quite good. It hurts because it means the end of the traditional handmade stuff. People have more money now and they want more refined ceramics and these can be produced in molds quickly and cheaply. I like the simpler handmade products better than the mass-produced ones, but I don't blame people who live in Western-style apartments for buying factory-made ceramics. They feel that the traditional wares don't fit the new styles of living. And they are right.

RB: Do you think that you could find satisfaction living and working as Japanese potters do today?

BM: Even if I wanted to, I don't think I could be integrated in a Japanese community. Some of my friends who are potters and who have Japanese wives are partly integrated, but I don't think they'll ever be fully integrated. They are conscious of the fact that they are foreigners. I live alone and I'm known as "the foreigner on the hill." I have to admit I haven't made much of an effort to integrate myself. The one person in the town I can talk with is the *tofu* [bean-curd cake] maker, and he's Korean, so he's an outsider, too. Among my friends, the foreign potter who is the most integrated into the Japanese community is still judged as a foreigner. If he makes good pots it's because he's a foreigner, and if he makes bad pots, it's because he's a foreigner. Judgments always include the fact that he's a foreigner.

I've said I haven't tried hard to integrate, and one reason is the shyness I mentioned. The other is that I want to return to Europe and make European-style pottery. I like large teapots and coffee jugs and cups with handles. I want to integrate myself in the English tradition of ceramics. I wasn't born into the Japanese tradition—for instance, I can't use a brush as well as so very many Japanese can. They learn to use a brush as small children; we don't. This—and a feeling for design, traditional design—is ingrained in them. They've soaked it in while growing up, and I missed out on it. I've learned almost all my techniques in Japan, but still my work has a foreign feeling about it. The Japanese recognize this difference, and I think they buy my pots because they are close to the genuine thing but have a certain foreign flavor to them.

RB: Is the way of Japanese craftsmen too humble, too lacking in opportunity for individual expression, to suit Westerners?

BM: It was humble and it was a good way and potters made very good pots. It's not now. It seems that if you have a full stomach and warm clothing there's not much need to work at making good pots. The potter nowadays picks up the telephone and says, I've had a firing, come and pick up the pots. The dealer comes and takes the stuff and pays him off. It's very easy to get by.

Where people still work hard as craftsmen I've found them very much aware of the way, of the correct way of doing things. And these people are humble. The older potters at Kasama that I mentioned earlier, they are of that type. They live like they have always lived, except that perhaps they make a little more money now. They can make anything you ask them to. I don't think they can come up with anything original, but if they've seen it they can duplicate it. They are real craftsmen, and I'm afraid that in twenty years there won't be any of the old true craftsmen left. One old potter that I worked closely with had made the same kinds of pots for twenty years, the large water crocks and pots to hold growing plants. Nowadays nobody uses these kinds of large pots, except maybe to stand umbrellas in.

RB: And you admire these old men?

BM: Yes, and they're the kind of humble men that you could pass right by without noticing. They have an inner shine that is very strong. It comes from a life that is very simple. Of course it isn't just potters who are like this; they could as well have been farmers or blacksmiths or carpenters. I think what they have comes from a settled occupation. They are not bright modern people who live by whim. The young people should spend some time with these simple old men and they would learn something of value about living. But of course they want nothing to do with them.

RB: What do you think of the present-day potter's relation to his community?

BM: The Japanese are buying a great deal of pottery these days, and as long as this keeps up their potters are going to be well off, at least materially. The community demands certain kinds of wares and the potter answers the demand. It has a very direct relation to what he makes. In Europe it's different, I believe; there the potter makes what he wants to make and tries to sell it. The European potter has more freedom of expression than the Japanese potter, who, like any businessman, is tied to the demands of the marketplace.

RB: So you think the European way is superior?

BM: I do, I'm for free expression. Of course, free expression sometimes goes too far to suit my taste. When potters get away from functional ceramics, they leave me behind. The funk style or movement or whatever it is in the United States is an example. Some of the techniques the American funk potters have come up with are superior to anything I've seen anywhere. They've come up with techniques for making textures and colors I've never seen in Japan or Europe. At a recent exhibition I saw what looked like a pair of boots until I got right up on top of it and discovered that they were ceramic boots. They looked just like leather boots. It was incredible! But it wasn't craftsmanship. I don't close my eyes to it, but that kind of art doesn't interest me much, except perhaps as I can use the techniques for functional wares. I'm interested in continuing traditions.

RB: Have you met any other people, foreigners or Japanese, who are interested in continuing traditions?

BM: The young potters I've met aren't interested in continuing traditions. Most of them would like to express themselves freely. They'd like to do as the European potters do, but they have to keep making the traditional shapes, this for the tea ceremony, that for flower arranging, and that for tableware. The Japanese potters can open up a little bit but not much. They have to make the old forms even though the old samurai way, the austere way of the warriors, is dying. The young potters are really just interested in making a good living, not maintaining traditions. I get the feeling that they could just as well have picked another occupation and that maybe they chose pottery because they can wear long hair and a beret and people will think they're artists.

RB: Does the future look to you like more of the same?

BM: I'm afraid the Japanese potters in the near future are going to flood the market with absolute trash.

RB: Do you think Japanese potting methods and pottery could be successfully transplanted in the West?

BM: You can't use a Japanese teacup in an English house. And we've got no tradition of brush calligraphy. When a Westerner takes up the brush he should take it up in a Western attitude, not in a Japanese attitude. Then he can apply the brush to his pot, which in my case will be an English pot, made of English clay in an English form. I noticed at an exhibition that Bernard Leach had tried to glaze some of his pots like those done in Mashiko, using English materials. It just didn't come off. If he'd used his local materials in England, I believe he'd have been better off. It also seems to me that when the Japanese make a coffee cup, they have taken a *yunomi,* a handleless Japanese teacup, and added a handle. The handle doesn't seem natural, and it isn't. It doesn't enhance the cup but takes something away from it. Japanese potters are highly adaptable, but I still have my doubts that their wares could find a place in Europe.

# 体験
# 15

## ANONYMOUS
### Homosexual

RB:  Will you describe the current "gay scene" in Japan?

AN:  The scene is much like it is anywhere in the world except that here in Japan it is more relaxed, the people are more easygoing. Also the relations are more subtle and intricate than in other places I've visited. There are many married men in it and they seem to be in it with the knowledge of their wives. They are rather open about it. Also, in Japan you have a rather closed homosexual circle, one with the hierarchies of a subculture.

RB:  What are the general attitudes of the Japanese toward homosexuals?

AN:  The attitude of most of the people I've met toward the gay world is a relaxed one. They accept it. After all, there is a long tradition of homosexuality in Japan. It's rooted in the culture. It's traditional; but the attitude of people toward it is changing, probably because of influences from the West. The changes are not for the good, I think.

RB:  Where and how do homosexuals meet in Japan?

AN:  Oh, many places, in bars, parks, public toilets, on street corners, hotel lobbies, train stations, department stores—almost anywhere. You can meet just by eye contact—the way someone looks at you, the expression on his face—or someone

*213*

may touch you, tentatively, on trains or in movie theaters, places like that. There are also special clubs and bars. And you meet by being introduced; for instance, you and a friend find that you are not compatible lovers, so he will introduce you to someone he thinks you have something in common with.

RB:   How do the Japanese authorities treat homosexuals?

AN:   As far as the authorities go, there is no trouble. There're no laws against homosexuality in Japan. That is, the police won't bother you unless you become a public nuisance.

RB:   What do you mean by a "public nuisance"?

AN:   Well, if someone goes around overexposing themselves, going too far in public so that the police are forced to look into the matter. But that situation is rare. The police have occasionally made roundups, I've heard, but in cases like these they have been looking for hustlers, men who prey on homosexuals, not for homosexuals.

RB:   A Japanese writer recently implied that Japan is a paradise for foreign homosexuals because they can indulge themselves here with impunity. Is this a kind of backhanded boasting or is there really a swinging gay scene here?

AN:   A paradise? No, though I will say that some of the foreign homosexuals who have settled here have taken the easy way out. There's none of the harassment here that they have to endure in some other countries. They can be more free in public here. But I think that many of them have settled here just because they like Japan, not because it's a good homosexual scene. You know, some people just prefer yellow, just as some prefer brown. Of course, some just like the atmosphere here.

But yes, there is a swinging gay scene here, very swinging. It's particularly good for older foreign men. Many young Japanese men are attracted to mature, experienced foreign men. I think this is because the young men don't have good relations with their fathers; they don't feel free to talk over their problems with them. It's what you could call a father complex. They want friendship and guidance as much as, if not more than, they want sex. Some of them probably do not even want sex, but for the sake of friendship they will make love to the older man.

Actually, I think there is a stronger lesbian scene here than a male homosexual one. Particularly in the art business world. But let me qualify that by saying that it's not a purely sexual lesbianism; it's more psychologically sexual than physically sexual. These are women who are trying to escape from manipulation by males. They form close relations to further business and career links.

RB: I've read that in America relations between male homosexuals are often characterized by jockeying for power positions, that the sex act is used to upgrade the self while degrading the partner. In your experience in America, did you find this to be true?

AN: Yes, I'm afraid it is all too common there.

RB: Does this sort of thing characterize homosexual relations in Japan?

AN: No, it doesn't. At least it doesn't in relations between foreigners and Japanese.

RB: Would you contrast the homosexual scene in Japan with that of some other country?

AN: In Japan there is the illusion that love is just around the corner—although you may never find it. And here when a relation is over, it is *definitely* over.

RB: What do you mean, "definitely over"?

AN: The love is not rekindled, or at least only very rarely. In Italy I found the men to be more flirtatious, there is a great deal more show, more bombast, and the depth of the relations does not seem to be very great. In Sweden, in spite of their reputation, the emphasis is on verbal sex, not on psychological sex. I thought they were very uptight. Everyone says homosexuality is okay, but people talk behind each other's backs. There's a lot of backbiting in Sweden. In Japan the men are characterized by melancholy, melancholy and ennui. Whereas in Italy it's all fire, all pomp and circumstance. Really overdramatic! In Sweden there is a lot of cold calculated reserve. But I must admit that the Swedes are good lovers. At least those that I knew were.

RB: What occupations do Japanese homosexuals work at?

AN: All occupations: jockeys, store clerks, truck and taxi drivers, waiters, students, artists, musicians; they are men in business, law, design, and music.

RB: Would you say they predominate in the arts?

AN: Perhaps, but if so, they are not predominant by a very large number. In America I found many in law, banking, and medicine. And there is a large number in the arts there. These others are the queer ones.

RB: What do you mean, the "queer ones"?

AN: Well, they haven't integrated their sexuality into their lives is what I mean. They haven't accepted that part of their nature. Perhaps one could say they are schizophrenic in this sense. They try to keep their sexuality and the other aspects of their personalities separate. Now, the artist-homosexuals I've known haven't been troubled by this two-facedness. The relations between these people—the artists—are more enduring and are deeper. They are not troubled by any double standard.

RB: Do you mean that those who try to hide their homosexuality cannot become involved in any but promiscuous relations?

AN: Yes, because they are afraid of being found out.

RB: And you think that in Japan, because of less social censure, there is less of this "sexual schizophrenia"?

AN: Yes, I'd say so.

RB: Foreign males, especially Americans and Englishmen, often say that Japanese men are effeminate. Do you agree?

AN: I disagree. Japanese men are not effeminate. In fact, they are most masculine—and yet many are homosexual. Being tender and openly emotional does not mean that a man is effeminate. Real effeminacy is usually deep—deeply hidden. You take a man who looks real butch. There is a good chance that he is effeminate and his butchness is just a façade, a defense mechanism.

RB: In its report on homosexuality in the U.S., *Life* magazine several years ago said that married men with children who indulged in weekend homosexual activities were sometimes picked up by the police. Have you ever come across any of these "part-time homosexuals" in Japan?

AN: Yes, I've known homosexual married men who have had children, and I've had them for lovers. But I don't like the term "part-time homosexuals." You can't be a homosexual sometimes and at other times not.

RB: What I mean here is not that, but that they only indulged on weekend nights or times like that.

AN: Or like salesmen when they are out of town. But here in Japan you find less of that than you do in other places. If a Japanese man is hiding his homosexual activities, it is to protect his love mate, not himself.

RB: Protect him from what?

AN: From social conflicts. Say that he's married: well, then he doesn't want to cause any tensions with his wife or family.

RB: You said earlier that many wives don't mind.

AN: Yes, but of course some do. In any case it is a good idea not to create tension-making situations. I know, for instance, that some wives accept a homosexual lover for their husbands more easily than they do a relationship with a bar hostess. Because there is little chance of losing her position, of having her home broken up. I have heard of one case where a man left his wife for his male lover—he divorced her. They had no children. But that is a very rare case.

RB: Does John Rechy's book *City of Night* accurately portray the homosexual scene in America as you know it? There is an astonishing variety of homosexual types in America, according to that book. Is there as broad a range of types among the Japanese?

AN: Rechy's book is very interesting. Much can be learned from it. But it doesn't do complete justice to the gay world there. In fact, there is a broader range of types, although I don't like to use that term, in the U.S. Also more in Japan.

RB: They were such a wayout bunch that I wondered if Rechy wasn't caricaturizing them.

AN: Yes, I thought so too. I think they were a bit stereotyped.

RB: Have you ever had any experiences with male prostitutes in America or Japan?

AN: Yes, in both countries. But in America it was unknowingly.

RB: How could that happen?

AN: What I mean is that a young friend of mine and some of his friends were hustling. I didn't know it for a long time, perhaps a year.

RB: That's not what I mean. Have you ever paid a man to get him to let you make love to him?

AN: No, I never have. But I have been paid. I've slept with older Japanese men and sometimes in the morning they would hand me some money and say, Here is taxi money, even though the sum might be twenty times what a taxi would cost me. And sometimes I'd take it and sometimes I'd turn it down. Just depended on how I felt.

RB: Did you ever have any relations with the men who work as gay boys in the bars?

AN: No, never. I don't see why men are attracted to other men who pretend to be women. If they want a woman, why don't they get a real woman?

RB: Have you ever been the target of violence simply because you are a homosexual? Have you any knowledge of violence against homosexuals in Japan?

AN: No, no to both questions.

RB: Have you ever come across a policeman pretending to be a homosexual pickup?

AN: No, never. I have met policemen who were real homosexuals, though.

RB: Have the Japanese police ever bothered you?

AN: No, but I did have an interesting affair with a Japanese policeman. It was amusing and pleasant. He thought that he was going to seduce me and it turned out the other way round.

RB: Does the butch or the drag type of lover appeal most to you?

AN: Type has nothing at all to do with it. It depends on the individual.

RB: Have you ever thought of wearing drag?

AN: Some of the things I wear every day some people would call drag. At least they are semidrag. The way one dresses, I'd say, is often camouflage to create an image. Sometimes an image of what you'd like to be and sometimes an image that is exactly the opposite of what you are. I have found that unusual clothing is effective in shocking away superficial interest in me.

RB: Have you found many butch homosexuals in Japan?

AN: Yes, there are many butch homosexuals in Japan. They are not like the Hell's Angels sado-masochistic type that you find in the U.S., though. Here you have the tough young men who hang out in pachinko parlors, the swaggering *yakuza* gangsters, or the tough-looking student who wears only wooden *geta* [high clogs] on his feet on cold winter days. I've had some very interesting relations with *yakuza*.

RB: Really? Of all the Japanese people it is the *yakuza* that I've found to be the coldest, to show the least amiability toward foreigners.

AN: That hasn't been my experience. They are just as curious about foreigners as any other Japanese, and when you get past that tough-guy barrier they can be quite interesting. Usually we've met on the street, in Shinjuku or somewhere, and when they saw that I wanted to talk to them as well, they would invite me to a bar or a restaurant and we'd talk. Naturally, they could see that I am homosexual, and there was never any trouble about that. Really, they were nice to me, and interesting. What I said about butch camouflage before, with some of the *yakuza* it was true, they were tough-looking and they swaggered, but as lovers they could be effeminate, and usually quite tender. I don't mean they were all effeminate, or even that most of them were. But enough were. It's very interesting to get behind a person's social disguises this way.

There is, by the way, a large sado-masochist scene here, both heterosexual and homosexual. The homosexual SM world is closed up tight, though. It's very hard to penetrate.

RB: What do you think of Japan's two most famous "gay-boy" entertainers—Akihiro Maruyama and Peter?

AN: Maruyama is a great artist. He is much more than an entertainer. Within his field he is a superb actor. He has a good voice and a very commanding female presence. Peter is very young, of course. He is a rather bad takeoff on Maruyama. He's not nearly as intelligent, I think, as Maruyama. He is not a good singer—at least, I don't enjoy his singing.

RB: Have the men who have been your lovers been purely homosexual or have they been bisexual?

AN: I've had all kinds. My best lovers have not been homosexual, but have been men having their first homosexual relation. I don't live in a closed homosexual society. And I don't have any strong preferences. I just like men—I just like sex is what I really mean. When I say I don't have strong preferences, I mean I take my lovers as individuals; it doesn't matter what kind of homosexuals they are.

RB: In America there has been a swing away from considering the homosexual as a villain. There are even homosexual heroes of a sort—Ginsberg, Genet, Burroughs. What do you think of this trend?

AN: I haven't thought much about it. There is a lot of talk about permissiveness these days, but I would say that people are becoming more realistic rather than permissive. They are destroying the Victorian restraints—and this is a good thing. I hope it will mushroom. I hope, for instance, that America will really become a land of the free and the equal. It is one of the least free nations that I know of.

RB: I've read that in ancient times in Japan homosexual couples consisted of an older man and a man many years his junior, the older man being sort of a patron of the younger. The source also said that when the younger man reached middle age, he in turn might establish himself as the patron of a young man. Is this a characteristic pattern of present-day relationships?

AN: Yes, I think it is a common pattern. But rarely does an older Japanese man act as the patron of a young foreign male. This sort of relationship, by the way, can grow to be a very beautiful one. It can be a long-lasting relationship. Often, too, the patron will be helping the young man for personal reasons: because he admires him, and not largely for sexual reasons. I think the reason why a Japanese will rarely become the patron of a foreigner is less a matter of sex than a matter of clannishness. In this tightly knit society a Japanese is always going to look out for his fellow Japanese first.

# 16

## JESSE KUHAULUA
### American
### Sumo Wrestler

He stands six foot three, weighs about 365 pounds, and has wrestled his way to the top ranks of sumo, the first non-Oriental to do so. More interestingly perhaps, in becoming a *sumotori* with the professional name Takamiyama in 1964, he entered an arcane world whose traditions and rituals are considered esoteric by many a modern-day Japanese. Of Polynesian descent, Jesse was born in Wailuku, Maui, Hawaii, in 1944.

RB: Sumo is noted for its rigid traditionalism, and as such it has very little appeal nowadays for young Japanese men. It is surprising then that you got into and stayed in sumo, nine years now. Why did you get into it and why did you stick it out?

JK: It started back in my freshman year in high school. I went out for the football team and made the squad. Because my leg was bad the football coach encouraged me to take up weightlifting and sumo to make it stronger. That was my introduction to amateur sumo—there's a lot in Hawaii.

Then in 1964 a group of sumo wrestlers, professionals, came over from Japan to Hawaii on a good-will tour. I saw them fight and my interest in sumo grew stronger. My former stable boss, who died a year ago, saw me practicing sumo and invited me to Japan to try out for professional sumo. I thought that I had a challenging chance, so I took him up on the offer.

RB: Did you realize it was such a tough world you were getting into—one that would be extra tough for you as the only foreigner in it?

JK: No, I was just eager to get away from Hawaii, to see someplace else, something different. And wrestling with the amateur group in Hawaii got me interested. I liked sumo, so I went to Japan and joined the Takasago Stable.

RB: If you knew then what you know now about sumo, would you still have become a sumo wrestler?

JK: Yes, I would have. I like sumo.

RB: What has it been like to be the only foreigner in sumo?

JK: At first I had a hard time getting along with the other young wrestlers because I couldn't talk to them—I didn't know any Japanese at all. It was a completely different world.

RB: How did the fans react to your entry into sumo?

JK: I didn't have much contact with them. Although people came to the stable to see me, I didn't have much contact with them. My boss was very strict; for the first year he kept me in the stable and wouldn't let me go out drinking with the fans or anything like that.

People were curious about me, so they came to see me, but I didn't get to mix with them. At that time, too, some of the sports writers were writing that I wouldn't last long because of the hard training, the tough discipline, and the strict regulations.

RB: How did your experiences as an apprentice *sumotori* differ from the average beginner's?

JK: It was exactly the same except for the first two months, when I was allowed to eat first—with the senior wrestlers—and bathe first, but after that I was treated exactly the same. Once I got a little used to it, I didn't get any special treatment.

RB: You had to do all the things the other apprentices do, like scrubbing a senior wrestler's back, combing his hair, preparing and serving his food?

JK: Yes, the same as the other guys.

RB: There must have been times when the training got to you and made you angry. Why did you stick it out?

JK: Because a lot of people encouraged me. During my first year I wrote to Hawaii telling some people there that I wanted to go back to Hawaii. A lot of people wrote back encouraging me to stick it out. And people here in Japan said they were proud of me and made me feel that I really had to try harder.

RB: What are your relations with the Japanese sports writers and fans?

JK: I get along good with the Japanese press, but we have our ups and downs, you know. When I'm winning I get a lot of write-ups, but when I'm not doing so well they don't have much to say about me.

The Japanese fans treat me like a regular *sumotori*. Everywhere I go, not only in Tokyo but all over Japan, they know me and they come up and say to each other, Oh, that's Jesse. He's the wrestler from Hawaii, and they ask me for my autograph. And almost everybody knows me.

I've got a lot of Hawaiian fans. I'm really surprised at the popularity of sumo in Hawaii now. Sumo fans in Hawaii used to be just the Japanese-Americans, but nowadays there are a lot of other people following the sport. The TV films are sent from Japan to Hawaii and the fans there get to see the matches a couple of days after they are fought. That's helped me with the fans there. And we make a trip to Hawaii once every two years to put on exhibition bouts. I've got about ten fan clubs in Hawaii and six major ones in Japan, although I don't have any idea how many members they've got in them.

RB: What do the fans do for you? What's your relation to them?

JK: Well, they take me out drinking a lot. And they help to support me, buy me things like my ceremonial aprons, which cost a lot of money. They give me spending money, too— the pay a sumo wrestler gets is pretty low, you know, so we need outside help.

RB: Have you ever felt any resistance against your presence in the sumo world—from, say, ultranationalists?

JK: Not that kind. The only thing was that when I began to wrestle here there was some feeling—ah, Japanese don't want to lose to a foreigner, you know. It's natural. This is their national sport. So I felt then that all the young wrestlers were against me. I didn't mind too much—I just wanted to make good.

RB: What do you like best about sumo?

JK: The history and the rituals—the tradition. When I was in school my favorite subject was history and even today I like to hear people talk about history. And sumo does have a long history—it's hundreds of years old. It really interests me.

RB: What changes could you suggest for improving sumo?

JK: I wouldn't want to change it, except for the salaries, which are too low. I like sumo like it is.

RB: The training system is satisfactory?

JK: Nowadays you have to encourage the recruits, not beat them up like in the old days. But other than that it hasn't been changed, and it shouldn't be changed. If you start to change small things you're going to change the whole system, and then it won't be sumo anymore. Better not to change anything. Changing salaries won't hurt, though, especially since everything in Japan costs so much these days. Prices are way up.

RB: Do you think the relationship between the older wrestlers and the younger ones is a good relationship?

JK: I don't think anything ought to be changed. If we change the relationships, too much else will change. Then sumo will become a show. And you know sumo is miles and miles away from pro wrestling. There is no comparison.

RB: What happens to most old *sumotori?* Do they haunt the training areas as old boxers do fighter's gyms?

JK: Some stay in sumo as coaches and such and others get out completely, go into business for themselves or go to work for somebody else. To become a coach you have to buy stock from the Sumo Association and there are only a certain number of shares. If none are available, you have to wait until someone retires or dies.

Sumo people don't last too long, you know, not if they stay in sumo. There's a lot of diabetes and bad hearts. And if you stay in you do a lot of drinking; wrestlers drink a lot. That will do you in pretty quick. It's better to get out, I think, because it's really hard on you if you keep up that life.

RB: Do you think it would be to sumo's benefit to recruit a large number of foreigners—if that were possible?

JK: For the foreigner who enters sumo it's like being reborn. You have to learn a whole new life, start all over again. It's like going backward and starting all over again. That's a tough way. It's hard on a foreigner to adjust to things like eating Japanese food—especially the regular sumo food—sleeping and sitting Japanese style, learning to wear traditional sumo clothes, and learning all the Japanese courtesies and the language. The language is really hard. And all those traditions! The young wrestlers have to take care of the older ones, dress their hair in the traditional style, prepare and wash their clothes, serve their food, run errands for them, take care of their things for them, and even scrub their backs in the bath—so in the beginning you're not just looking out for yourself. And the training is very hard, especially the exercises for your legs.

I think the hardships are too much for almost all foreigners. Another thing is money. Young guys now say right away, How much will you pay me? How much can I get a month? It's the first thing they think of. And in sumo you don't get much in the beginning. You get an allowance from the Sumo Association—like a kid gets from his father—six times a year. And it ain't much, not much at all.

So you really have to have real determination to make it as a sumo wrestler.

RB: Do you ever receive letters from foreigners wanting to get into sumo?

JK: Yes, but nothing comes of it. Recently a real big kid— about six-four and over three hundred pounds—from Hawaii decided he'd like to try it. But then he asked about money and when I told him the truth he dropped the idea like a hot potato. I guess he thought he could be some kind of bonus baby and get rich right away.

Sumo is a complete turning away from your ordinary life. And when you're a wrestler you can't do what you like to do. You do what the stable boss tells you to do, and if he's not around the older wrestlers boss you around. You can't just decide you want to go spend a couple of days at the beach in the summer or take a Christmas vacation; you got to train or fight instead.

RB: You can't even move freely about in Tokyo, can you?

JK: Not in the beginning. Later, when you win bouts and get promoted, you get more freedom. But even then you have a full schedule of six fifteen-day tournaments, plus exhibition tours and special bouts, and there's always training, lots of it. You don't win unless you train hard.

RB: It doesn't look anything like an easy life. The stable, for example—that's a good word for it—it's like a combination gym and dormitory, maybe part of a special correction institute for young guys whose crime is being overweight.

Nobody can say it's a swinging place or it's got any glamor.

RB: The sumo life has its good points. I like it; otherwise I wouldn't have stuck it out.

RB: Why do you think very large numbers of foreigners have taken up Japanese martial arts like karate, judo, and aikido though few have shown any interest in learning sumo?

JK: There's a lot of reasons, I guess, but one is the exercise we do to strengthen our legs and hips—the *shiko*—not many foreigners can do it, and until you get used to it, it hurts like hell. You spread your legs wide, then lift one leg up and out to the side as high as you can and then bring it down as hard as you can on the dirt floor. It doesn't look too hard 'cause it's not complicated, but it's a tough exercise. The Japanese can do it because of the way they are raised, the way their legs are trained by the traditional way of sitting and being carried on their mother's back. But even for them it's hard, especially for kids who aren't trained in the old ways. Lots of young Japanese kids nowadays can't sit for long in the traditional way. It hurts their legs.

Another thing is the way we dress—wear kimono and wooden clogs, the topknot hairstyle; and the loincloth we fight in is a little like a jockstrap and leaves you almost bareassed.

Except for the people in Hawaii, most people don't get a chance to see sumo. And when they do, it's so different from most sports they watch, they don't know what to make of it. It's the tradition—the Japanese understand it and like it because they're used to it. Even the emperor comes to watch sumo once a year.

RB: The sports I mentioned and such diverse things as Zen, flower arranging, sukiyaki, and sakè have been exported to foreign lands with at least some success, but you don't think sumo ought to be made attractive to foreigners, to make it an international sport, do you?

JK: Not if it changes sumo. I'm talking about professional sumo, of course. Amateur sumo is something different. That could be started in boys' clubs, school gym classes, YMCAs.

RB: To create enough interest for that, I think people would have to see a lot more of the real thing or movies or TV films, don't you?

JK: Yeah. In Hawaii, on each island there's a sumo club, and each year the wrestlers from these clubs fight in two large tournaments. A lot of people come out to see them. The Japanese community in Hawaii is a big one and many of the sumo fans are of Japanese descent. But nowadays more and more Hawaiians who aren't Japanese are getting interested in sumo. It's a big thing there.

RB: Here in Japan it's a compulsory sport in public schools, isn't it?

JK: Yes, because it's a national sport. It's a popular amateur sport in Japan nowadays, too, but there aren't many recruits for professional sumo. You know, jobs are easy to get these days.

体験
# 17

## EUGENE LEE
American
Scholar

He first went to Japan in 1968 as a Fulbright scholar in commercial law at Tokyo University. At present he is a professor of international business and law at Tokyo's Sophia University and is a partner in Woodhouse, Lee, and Davis, an international law firm. He is a coauthor (with Robert Ballon) of *Foreign Investment and Japan,* editor of *Law in Japan,* a scholarly journal, and the author of numerous articles and translations.

RB: During most of its history Japan has been relatively isolated from the rest of the world and in many ways this has resulted in unique social and political institutions. What sort of legal institutions has this brought into being?

EL: For the proper perspective we have to go back at least to the pre-Meiji period, that is, before 1868. Japan was ruled then by the Tokugawa shogunate, a military dictatorship that was organized centrally, but for many purposes government was highly decentralized. It worked this way: from time to time the shogun would issue decrees that affected the country as a whole, but political and legal power rested chiefly in the hands of the local *daimyos* [feudal lords] and a class of warrior-bureaucrats. These people had the power to make laws, interpret laws, and enforce laws.

With all the power concentrated in the hands of the warrior-bureaucrats there was no separation of powers, nor was any assumed to be necessary. The first thing a system like this suggests to a Westerner is the possibility of abuses of power. These of course did occur, but there was a built-in means of limiting abuses through paternalistic, orthodox Confucianism with its emphasis on the five human relationships and their attendant obligations, that is, the relationships between ruler and subject, father and son, husband and wife, older and younger brother, and between friends. In these relationships the superior had a certain amount of power over the subordinate, but he also had the responsibility to take into consideration the other person's situation. If he didn't, if he abused his power, he was in a sense morally at fault. The person in the inferior position had a duty to obey his superior as best he could. What is important here is that nowhere is there any mention of rights.

The long shadow of the warrior-bureaucrat has cast itself all the way down to the present. Modern legal institutions still reflect considerable Confucian-style hierarchical thinking and "rights consciousness" is relatively undeveloped.

RB: Where does the attorney come into the picture?

EL: As late as the late eighteen hundreds there were no lawyers in Japan. The closest thing to a lawyer was the innkeeper. An out-of-town litigant usually asked his innkeeper how to make contact with the local magistrate. The innkeeper, who acted as an intermediary, would offer his services for a fee, promising to make introductions, and even plead the case. Obviously, such innkeeper-lawyers had a vested interest in prolonging litigation.

RB: How much of the custom of prolonging litigation survives today?

EL: Litigation in Japan is a slow process, but the reason it is is usually the heavy case load judges carry, as well as a tendency to promote out-of-court settlements, rather than overt acts on the part of lawyers.

RB: And these lawyer-innkeepers, is there anything of their character in Japanese law today?

EL: Yes. You'll remember that in traditional Japanese society the warrior class was at the top and the merchant class at the bottom. Perhaps lawyers have had some difficulty in moving away from their merchant-class origins. In any case, the legal profession in Japan is not as prestigious, for example, as it is in the United States.

RB: How did the traditional system fare under the impact of Western institutions and customs?

EL: When the Japanese decided to end their long isolation because of pressures from the West, they soon found that they would have to alter key institutions, as well. In law, the major pressures for change came as a result of the Western powers' insistence on extraterritoriality. The Westerners did not believe their citizens would get fair treatment under Japanese law, so they insisted that until Japan brought her legal system into closer conformity with the West's, they could not let their citizens be subjected to Japanese law.

Leading Japanese scholars were sent abroad to study the legal systems of, primarily, France, Germany, England, and to a lesser extent the United States. These study missions made some very sound proposals. In 1880, Japan enacted the Criminal Code, based on the French system, and in 1882, the Code of Criminal Procedure, also based on the French system. Later, in 1890, they adopted the German Code of Procedure, and 1896, the German Civil Code.

What is interesting about this is that these were nearly word-for-word translations. There was no effort to adapt Western law to Japanese institutions. One problem faced by the translators was that there was no Japanese word for "rights," a concept central to Western law.

The third important stage in the development of Japanese law began with the post–World War II Allied Occupation, when there was a massive infusion of American law. The leading contribution was the new constitution, which was American-inspired certainly, and largely written by Americans. An anecdote—perhaps apocryphal—that is of long standing among Japanese lawyers says that at the very time MacArthur was having the draft of the new constitution delivered to the prime minister he had an impressive flight of warplanes fly over his house.

Another important law pushed by the Americans was the antimonopoly law. Before this time the Japanese had not seen any reason for an antimonopolistic law, and because of this tradition in economic philosophy, the Fair Trade Commission, which enforces the antimonopoly law, is viewed with disfavor by many Japanese.

Securities and corporation law are also indebted to American influence. Not long ago I met a man who had worked with the Allied Powers during the Occupation. He had just got out of law school in Illinois, and not long after his arrival in Japan, he was put to work writing a corporation law for Japanese use. Since the only corporation law he knew was the state of Illinois', he used it for his model. His draft was accepted and is now Japan's corporation law.

RB: Have these laws undergone much change since the end of the Occupation?

EL: In some instances, like the corporation law and the securities law, there have been periodic revisions, but to a large extent they reflect revisions made in the country of origin as much as a Japanization of foreign law.

RB: How were the Japanese able to apply foreign law to their institutions?

EL: There's the rub. How these laws are applied and how they work with Japanese institutions are often very different from applications in the West.

RB: Twenty-five years ago it was reported that most civil cases in Japan were settled by arbitration or through the offices of go-betweens and that the courts figured very little in disputes between individuals or groups. Has this feature of Japanese law changed at all?

EL: Litigation is still a relatively little-used technique for resolving disputes. In Japan, a nation of over one hundred million people, there are only nine thousand lawyers. That's about the same number that you have in the states of Washington and Oregon, which have a combined population of about five million people.

A Japanese normally would not hire a lawyer unless he were absolutely forced to go to court. What people normally do is this: take a situation in which a man has been involved in an automobile accident and had a claim against the other party. This man would find some other person to be an intermediary. Usually the third party would be older than either of the others and someone both would respect.

One of the important things the claimant would want would be an apology. This, very likely, would be more important than any money he hoped to get. The private conciliation might take a year or two years to complete and would be done quietly with a minimum of friction between the parties, thanks to the "buffer" role played by the intermediary. After a settlement has been reached, the intermediary will be paid an honorarium by the parties.

There is an element of disgrace, it seems, in going to court.

In a sense it's like hanging your dirty linens out in public. When a case does go to court, the judge normally doesn't interpret the law in a Western sense, as we might expect. Rather, he tries to guide the parties toward conciliation by hearing the case through a series of special hearings. At each hearing he may inquire whether the parties held private settlement discussions and perhaps will encourage them to do so. It wouldn't be unusual to find in a Japanese court that six months after hearings have started absolutely no progress, by Western standards, has been made by the judge. From a Western viewpoint, we would conclude that the judge's energy has been expended toward conciliation rather than toward judgment of the particulars of the case.

RB: It seems that he's less interested in determining who's right and who's wrong than in getting the disputants to come to an agreement.

EL: Or perhaps he's interested in creating "harmony." Another interesting feature is that Japanese district courts have a special branch known as the conciliation branch. Once a suit is filed with the district court, the litigants have the choice of having it heard by the conciliation branch rather than a formal court proceeding. There a panel consisting of a professional judge and two laymen hears the case, generally unencumbered by rules of evidence or other formalities.

This panel runs things rather loosely. You don't even require a lawyer if you don't want one. There are no rules of evidence: you can say what you like and the panel can ask what questions it likes. None of this Perry Mason type of courtroom regimentation. When the proceedings are completed, the panel will issue a verdict, but this verdict isn't binding. The disputing parties can accept it or reject it. Once it's accepted, however, it's as binding as a court judgment. If either party rejects the verdict, the case can go back to the regular court, where a formal hearing is held and a binding verdict issued. This is an institutional way of helping people to conciliate their disputes, rather than relying on strict black-and-white verdicts based on public hearings in which someone is going to be forced to lose face.

RB: Whether stated baldly or not by the Japanese, the object of the conciliation method appears to be to save face and to dampen potentially explosive situations.

EL: Yes. Some years ago I made an interesting study. I went through the American legal digest systems that listed all the cases that were decided in the United States between 1955 and 1965, looking for all reported court cases that involved Japanese litigants. During this ten-year period I found fewer than twenty-five commercial cases. Most of these were cases in which Japanese were unavoidably forced into court. In light of the tremendous amount of commerce going on between the U.S. and Japan during that period, these statistics are truly revealing. However, I suspect that a subsequent study of the following ten-year period will show some changes.

RB: Richard Halloran, author of *Japan: Images and Realities,* maintains that the changes observed in postwar Japanese society are primarily superficial, and that the culture remains fundamentally unchanged. In your opinion, does this hold true for the legal system or have significant changes in jurisprudence occurred?

EL: The infusion of American law, particularly the constitution, has brought about significant changes. The constitution injected some very fundamental human-rights-oriented principles that didn't exist in Japanese law before. Also the antimonopoly law injects very new elements into the legal system.

Nevertheless, I tend to agree in principle with Halloran's contention in that Japanese law as it is practiced, in comparison to its written codes, reflects the social background. The way people use lawyers and the courts seems not to have changed fundamentally since the Occupation.

RB: Numerous Japanese students have said to me that theirs is the freest society in the world, in the sense of the absence of repressive laws. Older Japanese can often be heard remarking that the laws are too few and too weakly enforced, while policemen are reported to be complaining that their hands are too often tied by the the present legal setup. From the legal standpoint, how would you evaluate freedom and its absence in Japan?

EL:   In terms of legal guarantees, Japan is a very free society. Such guarantees always make things complicated for law-enforcement officers. For example, they must have a warrant, give the defendant the right to counsel, et cetera. At the same time, sociologically speaking, Japanese don't have some of the very basic human rights that, say, Americans have. Freedom of expression and freedom of privacy are good examples of what I mean. There are scores of weekly and monthly magazines in Japan, many of them no more than scandal sheets given over to publishing all kinds of gossip, often unverified. Except for hit-or-miss censorship of pornography, these magazines are free to print whatever they want, even libelous gossip. The public figure in Japan has less recourse in these situations than his Western counterpart. Japanese legal writers have sometimes reflected that there is no recourse for a slandered person but to go home and cry himself to sleep.

RB:   If you were accused of a crime in Japan, would you feel that the legal guarantees given you by Japanese law would be adequate? Would you get a fair trial?

EL:   I think I would. The basic guarantees are there. In addition to these, there is a very deep sense of humanitarianism in Japanese law, in the way people are treated. If you are a wrongdoer, and if you have some good human excuse for being a wrongdoer, it's likely you'll be treated with sympathy; extenuating circumstances may be more important here than in the U.S.

Take, for example, tax liability. The United States takes a very strict approach, and officials and judges tend to consider the letter of the law. Not so in Japan: the law is one thing and the attitude of the tax official is often something else. The tax official may be more understanding of the reasons for the ir-regularities and less dogmatic in sticking to the letter of the law. He often works toward bringing about a compromise. This is a humanistic rather than a legalistic approach.

RB: I've heard it said that in Japanese law, it's often very important whether a convicted person shows repentance or not. If he sincerely regrets what he's done and convinces the judge of this, he's liable to get a lower sentence than someone who remains antisocial.

EL: This is often so. Japanese are most shocked by the person who commits a serious crime and then refuses to say he's sorry. They have very little sympathy for him.

RB: This bears on what I would judge to be the stiff sentences the radical students have received in recent years. In some cases, the sentences are stiffer than what many murderers have gotten.

EL: Because the students are not repentant?

RB: Yes, many of them are defiantly against the political system and the law that represents that system. They reject the courts.

EL: On the other hand, some of the sentences given to students a decade or so ago were quite lenient. At that time I think Japanese society as a whole was rather impressed by the "noble purposes" of the students. Incidentally, a "noble purpose" is another factor often taken into consideration by Japanese courts in sentencing. Now, in regard to the students, this image has changed to that of hard-core radicals.

RB: It seems to me that if one is charged with a crime by the government and is tried, judged, and sentenced by a government-appointed judge, without a hearing by a jury, that one has not received a fair trial. What is your opinion about this matter?

EL: The assumption behind your statement is that the Anglo-American system of justice is best. The Japanese system is based on that of continental Europe, which does not provide for trial by jury, either.

Actually, there are many advantages to trial by judge rather than jury. In Japan it is not a government-appointed judge that hears your case, it's a man who has been specially trained to be a judge. In Japan, a judge receives special training, usually finished when he is about twenty-five; after that he is a judge for life. The younger judges often work with older experienced judges and usually only handle minor cases alone. Japanese judges are career judges, they are fair-minded, they are proud that they are judges, and they are proud of their reputation. Such a man may be better equipped to hear cases, to weed out what is not important, and to make the proper application of law to the facts than a jury of laymen.

The basic idea of trial by jury was that a man should be judged by a jury of his peers. At the time when this system originated, one's peers in a rural society knew the accused and the circumstances surrounding his alleged crime. At a time when social strata were rigid there was fundamental justice in "judgment by peers" rather than judgment by an aristocratic judge.

The Japanese judge, unlike his American counterpart, takes a very active part in a case. His mission is to search for the truth; he doesn't simply referee opposing attorneys. He often interviews witnesses himself, and if a lawyer doesn't ask the questions he should ask, the judge probably will ask them himself. And if a lawyer is obviously not doing his job, the judge often will in effect take over for him in the sense of bringing out necessary information. The judge may even look for better witnesses who have not been called to court and have them brought in.

Here, there is some advantage in not having a jury. In the United States our rules of evidence are designed to keep the jury from hearing information they might not be capable of sifting for the truth. Thus, hearsay evidence, evidence to which they should not pay any attention, is not admitted. A trained judge, of course, can hear everything and sift it for himself. He can decide what has value and what hasn't.

RB: I can understand the advantages of professionalism, but I still feel there is great danger in a system where the judge is so much a part of the Establishment. It doesn't seem to me that a person who opposes the system, who wants to change it, is going to make much headway against this setup.

EL: On the other hand, Japanese judges are proud of their professionalism as career judges and generally try to further this reputation. This type of person is in quite a different position from judges who are political appointees or who have to stand for election by a largely Establishment-oriented public.

RB: I think that no observant person will disagree that women do not enjoy equal standing with men in many areas of Japanese society. How do they stand legally compared to men?

EL: Legally speaking, the rights of women have been very carefully guaranteed in at least two places in the constitution. Because of these guarantees, in all subsequent laws women have virtual equality with men. In practice, we are seeing more and more women assuming positions traditionally held by men. In law, we are seeing more and more women lawyers. At least one of these that I know personally is considered a colleague by male lawyers and is treated with respect by them. Another woman has been appointed as the head of one of the major district courts in Japan. And one of the members of the very prestigious Federal Trade Commission is a woman. I think that this shows that there are career opportunities for women in Japan, although probably fewer than in the U.S.

Chie Nakane, a professor of Tokyo University—and a woman—contends that Japan practices discrimination according to status rather than sex. It so happens that in Japan most positions of high status are filled by and have been filled by men. She contends that once a woman has status, she is treated as a colleague in a very profound sense.

Another feature of Japanese male-female relationships which is often overlooked is that Japanese women have great power in the home. For instance, Japanese women frequently have complete control of family finances. When the family is seen outside the home, the woman invariably defers to the man: she is quite clever at making him look and feel important. When they return home, however, the roles may be quite different.

RB: I think that there are a lot of social barriers that stand in the way of women getting ahead, getting into the right lower schools and universities, getting their parents to agree to their striving for nontraditional jobs. There are great social pressures against them for doing "unwomanly" things, and they are ridiculed for even wanting to do things normally reserved for men. Women who are trying to break out of the present system are really having a hard time.

EL: I would agree that women are encouraged to make certain types of decisions concerning their future. They are still encouraged to think of marriage as the major goal. Girls are sometimes afraid to go to the most prestigious universities because it would rank them too far above many men and reduce their chances of finding a husband.

The women who were my classmates at Tokyo University, however, were respected by their classmates, were included in class functions, and when they graduated they were aided by the professors in finding jobs suitable to their education. Some of them found positions that were far more prestigious than those found by most of their male classmates.

RB: More than once you have referred to the power the bureaucracy holds in Japan, and what bothers me is that abuses can occur and of course have occurred under this system because of the lack of controls on these men.

EL: Yours is a common reaction. The foreigner, when he looks at the Japanese system, sees the unfettered authority of the bureaucrat and is dismayed by the lack of safeguards built into the system. But it does not necessarily follow that if there is an opportunity for abuse there will be abuse. I think the bureaucrat's real sense of duty and his genuine pride at being a bureaucrat work together to keep abuses of power to a low minimum. With all the safeguards in their systems, the countries of the West experience as many abuses if not more than the Japanese. Tradition plays an important role here. If the bureaucrat acts improperly, he goes against centuries-old traditions and the values he has grown up with. This is a genuine deterrent to abuse.

Abuses have occurred, of course, but I don't think Western-type safeguards would have had much effect against them.

RB: Is the trend in post-Occupation Japanese law toward greater or less restrictiveness?

EL: Society in Japan is becoming less restrictive, and in many ways this means that law is becoming less restrictive, as well. Certainly young people feel free to do things that other young people didn't do ten years ago. And under the law they are free to do these things.

However, in certain areas the law has become more restrictive. Immediately after the war there was a rather widespread feeling that there was something fundamentally wrong with the country, that what had just occurred was caused by a sick society or a bankrupt system. It was felt that a lot of changes were necessary. This meant, in legal terms, that different philosophies were investigated, more emphasis was placed on human rights, and new freedoms were introduced. Now, after a period of testing the new freedoms, it seems as though the pendulum is swinging back toward greater respect for the old traditions, and the war period and the decade or so before it are presently being looked at as not the product of a bankrupt system but the result of particular circumstances, of too much power in the hands of a military clique.

The Japanese authorities are carefully watching the social disruption in the West, the climbing crime rates, and the problem of drug addiction. They want very much to avoid these problems and no doubt will react vigorously to control the rise of these problems in Japan.

The "weathermark" identifies this book as having been planned, designed, and produced at the Tokyo offices of John Weatherhill, Inc., 7–6–13 Roppongi, Minato-ku, Tokyo 106. Book design and typography by Ronald Bell. Composition, printing, and binding by Samhwa Printing Co., Seoul. The text is set in 11-point Monotype Baskerville with hand-set Baskerville for display.